a handbook for student writers

John R. Willingham / Donald F. Warders

University of Kansas

a handbook for student writers

HARCOURT BRACE JOVANOVICH, INC.

New York   San Diego   Chicago   San Francisco   Atlanta

Library of Congress Catalog Card Number: 77-80348
ISBN: 0-15-530810-6

Printed in the United States of America

For permission to use the selections reprinted in this book, the authors are grateful to the following publishers and copyright holders:

HARCOURT BRACE JOVANOVICH, INC. For the excerpt from *A. Philip Randolph: A Biographical Portrait,* copyright © 1972, 1973 by Jervis B. Anderson, as first published in *The New Yorker* in a slightly different version; and for "anyone lived in a pretty how town" from *Complete Poems* 1913–1962 by E. E. Cummings. Copyright, 1940, by E. E. Cummings; copyright, 1968, by Marion Morehouse Cummings. Both are reprinted by permission of Harcourt Brace Jovanovich, Inc.

HARPER & ROW, PUBLISHERS, INC. For excerpts from pp. 123, 206–207, 317–318 and 326–327 in *Only Yesterday* by Frederick Lewis Allen. Copyright 1931 by Frederick Lewis Allen; renewed 1959 by Agnes Rogers Allen. Reprinted by permission of Harper & Row, Publishers, Inc.

HOLT, RINEHART AND WINSTON For the excerpts from "Birches" from *The Poetry of Robert Frost* edited by Edward Connery Lathem. Copyright 1916, © 1969 by Holt, Rinehart and Winston. Copyright 1944 by Robert Frost. Reprinted by permission of Holt, Rinehart and Winston, Publishers.

NEW DIRECTIONS PUBLISHING CORPORATION For "The Heavy Bear Who Goes With Me" from Delmore Schwartz, *Selected Poems: Summer Knowledge.* Copyright 1938 by New Directions Publishing Corporation. © 1966 by Delmore Schwartz; and for "The Red Wheelbarrow" from William Carlos Williams, *Collected Earlier Poems.* Copyright 1938 by New Directions Publishing Corporation. Both are reprinted by permission of New Directions Publishing Corporation.

CAROL SALVO For "The Cycle of Life" by Carol Salvo. Reprinted by permission.

H. W. WILSON COMPANY For the entries from *Readers' Guide to Periodical Literature.* Copyright © 1972, 1973. Material reproduced by permission of the H. W. Wilson Company.

A Handbook for Student Writers grew out of a search for one useful, basic text for composition courses. Our aim was neither to overwhelm busy students and instructors with an all-inclusive, endless rhetoric-handbook nor to add to the growing collection of terse pamphlets filled with impenetrable technical jargon. Rather, we have combined an undidactic, brisk review of English grammar — including recent changes that have become accepted usage — with a systematic introduction to basic expository writing.

We have concentrated on what a student ought to be able to do, such as analyze and explicate a poem and write a research paper. To this end, three sample writing assignments are provided — a brief essay, a critical essay, and a documented research paper — from students we have had the pleasure to instruct. From our own experience of teaching composition, we compiled a list of frequently confused and misused words, which are included as a glossary; we have provided cross-references and examples in sentences.

The division of the book into two parts, a rhetoric and a grammar handbook, together with the keying in the end-papers of the subdivisions of every topic treated in the text, forms an anatomy of the book and makes it possible for it to be used in various sequences of instruction.

We have been able to test most portions of the book in our own courses. Our colleagues and former students will recognize many traces of ideas, suggestions, and questions they have shared with us. We gratefully acknowledge all their good counsel. Gordon Fairburn, Betty Gerstein, Cecilia Gardner, and John Holland steered us expertly toward this completed book.

J. R. W.
D. F. W.

one rhetoric

words, phrases, clauses, and sentences

1

The four main units of discourse—the word, the phrase, the clause, and the sentence—simply represent levels of size, complexity, and internal structure. Because they are the basic units of communication in English, their successful use in writing requires only a grasp of their functions and experience in their use.

1a the word

To quote St. John in the New Testament as a statement of our purpose, "In the beginning was the Word." Thus does a language develop both for nations and for individuals— with the word. Our first experiments with language usually involve a single word, for infants name their parents and things before they begin to make statements about them. And writers must be in control of their words before they can give significant attention to clusters of words— that is, to phrases, clauses, or sentences. Obviously, a rich vocabulary acquired from reading and experience offers the writer a significant advantage; but it is never too late to begin a critical examination of the words at our disposal or to form good habits in using words. In the following paragraphs some of the basic considerations to be applied in the successful use of words will be explored.

1a1 exactness and precision

People usually mean what they say, but careless use of words may very well defeat the purpose of communicating meaning. Therefore, to be a successful writer or speaker, you must exercise such control over the individual words in your discourse that you project exactly the meaning you intend. As Mark Twain reminds us, in his witty criticism of

James Fenimore Cooper's *The Deerslayer,* the successful writer must "use the right word, not its second cousin." And, fortunately, there is a readily available resource for the writer who desires control over and precision for her or his words.

1a2 use of the dictionary

Most of the time, one of the several good "collegiate" dictionaries will offer you all the information you need about a given word: its correct spelling for American usage; the part or parts of speech in which it is classed (sometimes a word — for example, **drive** — may be used as either noun or verb); its meaning in some kind of historical order or within special contexts; and information about its origin from other languages. Some of the more familiar "collegiate" dictionaries are *Funk & Wagnalls Standard College Dictionary* (New York: Funk & Wagnalls, 1974); *The American College Dictionary* (New York: Random House, 1966); *Webster's New Collegiate Dictionary*, 8th ed. (Springfield, Mass.: G. & C. Merriam, 1973); *Webster's New World Dictionary of the American Language*, 2nd college edition (Cleveland: World Co., 1972); and *The Random House Dictionary of the English Language*, college edition (New York: Random House, 1968).

Although the order of arrangement of information under an entry may differ somewhat, all these "desk-size" dictionaries present substantially the same kind and degree of support to the writer. A somewhat larger book is *The American Heritage Dictionary of the English Language* (Boston: Houghton Mifflin Co., 1969). When more detailed historical information about a word or finer etymological tracings are needed, you may wish occasionally to consult one of the large, unabridged dictionaries which usually grace the reading rooms of libraries; such dictionaries are *Webster's Third New International Dictionary* (Spring-field, Mass.: G. & C. Merriam, 1961); *New Standard Dictionary of the English Language,* unabridged edition (New York: Funk & Wagnalls, 1963); *The Random House Dictionary of the English Language,* unabridged edition (New York: Random House, 1966); or, for very specialized information about changing meanings of words, *The Oxford English Dictionary* (often referred to as the *OED*), revised edition; 13 volumes (New York: Oxford University Press, 1933). With such a wealth of dictionaries readily available, as a careful writer you will consult one or more whenever you are uncertain about a word's exact meaning, correct spelling, or proper division into syllables.

1a3 synonym and antonym

Frequently the writer must make a hard choice between words that seem to mean almost the same thing but have different implications. Such words that have exactly or almost the same meanings are called *synonyms,* and often dictionaries will offer advice about the kinds of discriminations that should be made among a group of such words; for example, under the entry for **contrary** as adjective, one collegiate dictionary offers a synonym note for related words like **perverse, restive, balky, forward,** and **wayward** in which their slight differences of implication are considered. In making such a precise choice of exactly the right word instead of its "second cousin," the writer is able to control choices based on *denotation* — the exact dictionary meaning — or *connotation* — the emotional or suggestive value of a word. The words **lady** and **woman** have much the same denotation but diverge spaciously in connotation; likewise, **pinhead** and **fool.** A word that casts a favorable light on its subject is said to be an *ameliorative* term; one that casts an unfavorable light — for example, **pig** for **policeman** — is called a *pejorative* term.

1a4 jargon, pretentiousness, and slang

Any intrusion of jargon, pretentiousness, or slang may jeopardize your relationship with your readers and compromise your claim to control of language. The presence of such language also suggests bad taste and perhaps uncertainty about your writing.

a. Jargon   Highly technical language or language that tends to be the special property of one activity or a specialized group is called *jargon*. Such language has almost no place in most college writing. Terms that would be useful, perhaps necessary, in writing for professional engineers, physicians, accountants, educators, or automobile mechanics, might be totally meaningless or, at best, puzzling to outsiders. Therefore, you should use words that have a good chance of appealing to—and being understood by—an educated audience with general interests. **Peer group** may sound more profound and authoritative than **equals** or **schoolmates,** but it should remain in the reports of sociologists or educational research writers.

b. Pretentiousness   Closely related to jargon is *pretentiousness*—the kind of language some people use because they suppose it is more elegant than simple words or because they suppose it will mask the inadequacy of their ideas. Some of these artificial substitutions are listed below with their much more specific equivalents:

in the matter of	
(or **with respect to**)	**about**
a long period of time	**a long time**
in the capacity of	**as**
reach a decision	**decide**
at that point in time	**then** (or **in April 1976**)
make an attempt	**try**

You can extend the list indefinitely, of course, for we have all been the victims of such pretentiousness — and wordiness, too. Evasive writers will also sprinkle their prose with such meaningless words as **elements** and **factors** when they are not really sure of what they mean. (See the Glossary of Usage on page 271.)

c. Slang   All places, eras, and generations have their special words and phrases that have caught on, that sometimes are indeed very colorful, but that carry a decided risk in serious writing. The 1920's celebrated the **flapper,** the **vamp,** and the **jelly-bean,** and the terms therefore are valid in the fiction of F. Scott Fitzgerald; but they are not likely to be familiar terms to most college students today. The period of Watergate — the last two years of the Nixon administration — unleashed such terms as **the limited hangout route** and **stonewalling;** but general understanding of those terms probably will not survive the mid-1970's. For informal writing, slang is a rich resource but should not be overused.

1a5 variety

The last three paragraphs have emphasized kinds of words you should generally avoid. But every reader knows that monotony in language is quite as deadly as the inappropriate use of jargon, pretentious or "highfalutin'" language, and slang. Some sound ways to achieve variety in using words are the following:

1. the use of adequate and clear pronouns to avoid needless repetition of nouns
2. the use of concrete words in preference to abstract words
3. the use of synonyms
4. caution in frequent repetition of any word
5. a determination never to use a cliché — a word or

phrase that has lost its once fresh and arresting metaphorical value—for example, **a bed of roses, my better half, Joe College, doughboy, the primrose path,** or **the break of dawn**

1a6 parallelism

In all the following sections about larger verbal units—the phrase, the clause, and the sentence—there will be emphasis on *parallelism*. Let's begin to emphasize that very important principle of arrangement before we leave this section on the word. Even with single words in a series, we encounter parallelism: **oranges, apples, and bananas; green, tasteless, and wormy apples; a strange, unsettling, and sickly green;** and so on. The point we are emphasizing is that once such a grammatical structure is established, it must be preserved:

Next weekend Jim will mow the lawn, Ellen will wash the windows, and Ted paints the porch. (not parallel)

Next weekend Jim will mow the lawn, Ellen will wash the windows, and Ted will paint the porch. (parallel)

By the same token, words should not be mixed with phrases or clauses:

This summer I learned swimming and how to dive. (word plus phrase—not parallel)

This summer I learned swimming and diving. (word plus word—parallel)

1b the phrase

Phrases are *groups of words* that form a unit and can be considered according to either (1) their *grammatical formations* or (2) their *functions* within a sentence.

1b1 grammatical types of phrases

Even when they are isolated from the rest of a sentence, we can identify phrases by their grammatical components.

1. *Prepositional phrases* are composed of a preposition (for example, **to, with, after, under, over, beneath, of, by, toward, before, because of, in, into, beside**) *plus* a substantive — noun or pronoun: **with malice toward none, with charity for all; beside a stream; for want of a horse.**

2. *Verbal phrases* are groups of words formed from parts of verbs but functioning as something other than verbs:

    a. *Participles,* like verbs, have present, past, and perfect forms but function as adjectives — for example:

The policeman, ***foaming at the mouth,*** bit a dog. (present participle)

The policeman, ***having foamed at the mouth,*** pursued the dog. (past perfect participle)

The ***suspected*** dog chased the policeman. (past participle)

    b. *Infinitives,* also like verbs, have present and past perfect forms but always contain or imply the preposition **to** as part of the unit.

To be or not ***to be.*** (present infinitive)

To have tried redeems failure. (past perfect infinitive)

Infinitives are used as nouns, adjectives, or adverbs.

To write a novel was Tom's plan for the summer. (noun)

The plan ***to write a novel*** seemed realistic. (adjective)

Tom sent Chuck ***to rope a new calf.*** (adverb)

c. *Gerunds*—verbs plus **–ing**—have present and past perfect forms, and always act as nouns.

My favorite recreation is *jogging.* (present gerund)

Having read the epic was enough reward. (past perfect gerund)

1b2 functional roles of phrases

More important than their basic grammatical classification and constituents, however, are the various functions of phrases within sentences.

1. *Noun phrases.* Phrases may be used in a sentence wherever a simple noun or pronoun might be used.

a. *As subject.*

To read a newspaper required some concentration.

Reading a newspaper was an effort.

b. *As object.*

He enjoyed *walking home.*

She offered *to drive the car.*

c. *As object of a preposition.*

For *running the mile* George prefers old sneakers.

After *sailing his boat,* Jim felt restless.

2. *Adjective phrases.* Participle or infinitive phrases may be used wherever a simple adjective might appear in a sentence.

Sailing his boat, Jim felt glorious.

Having sailed his boat, Jim felt tired.

His desire **to secure power** ultimately caused the President's failure.

3. *Verb phrases.* Often, more than one word is required to form the complete verb in a sentence.

At Christmas Tom **will have read** Scott's novels.
I **have neglected** my piano practice.
When **will** that bore **leave** the party?
The cashier **counted out** the exact change.
He **gave up** an exceptional opportunity.

4. *Adverbial phrases.* Sometimes more than one word is required to perform the function of an adverb.

George exercised **to lose weight.**
She drove **with real assurance/after some instruction.**
Larry took Spanish because **of his interest in Mexico.**
He skyrocketed **into the air.**

1c the clause

Clauses, like phrases, contain more than one word; the difference is that a clause contains at least one subject and at least one predicate. Some clauses may even stand alone, because they make complete and satisfactory statements and do not depend grammatically upon another clause:

The first celebration of the Bicentennial in our state took us by surprise, but *we were ready for the next one.*
Most early American churches represented English Gothic, for *the early settlers had no other forms to imitate.*

Such clauses, therefore, are called *independent clauses* and are really sentences.

I worked in the mornings, and I played in the afternoons.

Here are two independent clauses, either of which makes a complete statement and is grammatically independent. The conjunction **and** emphasizes their equality as grammatical units and complete statements in their own right. Such independent clauses are joined either by a coordinating conjunction — **and, but, or, for,** or **nor** — or by a conjunctive adverb — **however, therefore, consequently,** or **moreover.** They may also be joined directly by a semicolon between the two independent clauses:

I worked in the mornings; I played in the afternoons.

Or, of course, they may be separated into two equal sentences with a period at the end of each clause:

I worked in the mornings. I played in the afternoons.

Other clauses, however, are *dependent clauses* — dependent either as grammatical units or as units of thought. They depend for their significance on a clause that is independent (a *main clause,* as it is sometimes called). The dependent nature of *subordinate clauses* (as they are sometimes called) is usually signaled by the kind of conjunction (subordinating conjunction) or pronoun (relative pronoun) that introduces them.

She sang **while she worked.** (dependent clause introduced by the subordinating conjunction **while**)

She worked **as she sang.** (dependent clause introduced by the subordinating conjunction **as**)

He knew **that she was singing.** (dependent clause introduced by the subordinating conjunction *that,* here a "function word" to introduce a *noun clause* — see below)

The singer, *who had often performed before the king of Sweden,* was a favorite with American college students. (dependent clause introduced by the relative pronoun *who* and functioning as an *adjective clause* — see below)

The question of *which was the culprit* preoccupied us most of the hour. (dependent clause introduced by the relative pronoun *which* and functioning as the object of the preposition *of* and thus part of a prepositional phrase)

I could see *that was wrong.* (dependent clause introduced by the demonstrative pronoun *that* and functioning as the object of the verb phrase *could see*)

Moreover, in noun clauses **that** is often used as a subordinating conjunction and is frequently omitted in speech or writing because it is understood quite clearly.

She advised us *that we could not move during the semester.* (The noun clause is the direct object of the verb *advised; that* is not a relative pronoun here, but a subordinating conjunction because it links dependent clause to independent clause but does not have any other function within the clause it introduces.)

She advised us *we could not move during the semester.* (Same sentence, really, with *that* omitted but clearly understood and usually preferable except in highly formal writing or in possibly ambiguous sentences such as *He felt [that] her heart belonged to Daddy.*)

1C1 testing clauses for independence or dependence

A simple test can be made to determine whether a clause is dependent or independent: Does it make sense alone and fulfill our expectations of a statement? Obviously, **while she worked, as she sang, that she was singing,** and

who had often performed before the king of Sweden will not fulfill our expectations of complete assertions in English. Because such clauses cannot stand alone, they are dependent and must be placed (as they are in the sentences above) within a context that can contain them and stand alone.

1C2 grammatical types of clauses

Like a phrase, a dependent clause must have a function within the sentence of which it is a part. That function may be one of three: as a noun, as an adjective, or as an adverb. To designate those functions properly, we speak of *noun clause* (a clause that functions as a noun), *adjective clause* (a clause that functions exactly as a single adjective would — to modify a noun or pronoun), and *adverbial clause* (a clause that functions as a single adverb would — to modify a verb, an adjective, or another adverb).

a. Noun Clauses   A clause functioning as a noun takes the place of a noun within a sentence — that is, as subject or object of the predicate or as object of a preposition. Noun clauses are nearly always introduced by a relative pronoun — **who, whose, whom, which,** or **that.**

She asked **who would make the sign.** (object of **asked**)

The poet asked **whose woods these are.** (object of **asked**)

Atkins discovered **whom I was seeing every weekend.** (object of **discovered**)

That Tom should drive was the unanimous decision. (subject of the sentence)

The question of **which was the culprit** preoccupied the board members all afternoon. (object of the preposition **of** and therefore part of a prepositional phrase)

Remember, **that** introducing a noun clause is not always a relative pronoun; sometimes it is a subordinating conjunction because it merely connects the dependent clause to an independent clause and has no grammatical function (as subject or object) within the clause it introduces. Often **that** used as a conjunction is omitted in speech or writing even though it is clearly understood. Do both of the sentences below make good sense?

Our English instructor suggested **that we proofread our themes several times.** (The dependent clause introduced by **that** is the direct object of **suggested.** In this sentence **that** serves merely as a connective for the two clauses; it has no other grammatical function.)

Our English instructor suggested **we proofread our themes several times.** (same sentence with **that** omitted but clearly understood)

    b. Adjective Clauses   Clauses function as adjectives when they modify nouns or pronouns. Such clauses are introduced by the relative pronouns **who, whom, which,** or **that,** although quite often the relative pronoun is not stated but understood.

The counselor **that I remembered** smoked a fat cigar. (Here the adjective clause modifies **counselor.**)

The counselor **I remembered** practiced belly dancing between appointments. (The adjective clause still modifies **counselor,** though a relative pronoun—**whom** or **that**—is not stated but simply understood.)

A counselor, **whose name I can't remember,** read all of the college regulations aloud to me. (Again, the clause modifies **counselor,** the subject of the sentence, and is introduced by the relative pronoun **whose.**)

    Adjective clauses are either *restrictive* (essential to the meaning of the noun or pronoun modified) or *nonrestric-*

tive (not essential to the identity of the noun or pronoun modified). The first two of the adjective clauses above are *restrictive clauses,* essential for the identification of **counselor.** But in the third sentence the adjective clause is *nonrestrictive* because it is not absolutely essential to the identification of the noun; the added information, though it modifies **counselor,** is simply additional detail. In the sentences below, the clauses are *nonrestrictive* because they are not absolutely essential to the identification of the nouns they modify:

The counselor, **whose name I can never forget,** was Gertrude Steinsong. (The adjective clause beginning with **whose** is not essential to the identification of **counselor;** and its nonrestrictive nature is indicated by the commas that set it apart from the noun it modifies.)

"Pokerface," **who expertly dominated the last auction,** is really a professor of French. (The clause that follows **"Pokerface"** supplies interesting but apparently unnecessary information about him; it is therefore a nonrestrictive clause and should be set off by commas.)

 c. Adverbial Clauses Clauses may also function as adverbs—that is, they may modify verbs, verbals (participles, gerunds, and infinitives), adjectives, other adverbs, and even other clauses. They are introduced by *subordinating conjunctions* of time, place, comparison, or logic, such as **when, as, until, before, after, where, than, if, since, although, because.**

Darkness came **before we reached the campus.** (adverbial clause of time modifying the verb **came**)

Arriving **after the football crowd had gone,** we found the dormitory quiet and peaceful. (adverbial clause of time modifying the participle **arriving**)

The dormitory parlor was bigger **than we had expected.** (adverbial clause of comparison modifying the adjective **bigger**)

Shouts and laughter came sooner **than we had expected.** (adverbial clause of comparison modifying the adverb **sooner**)

As all of us knew, the weekend would probably be unforgettable. (Here the introductory adverbial clause seems to modify the entire main clause, **the weekend would probably be unforgettable,** although many conservative grammarians would prefer to say that the adverbial clause modifies only the verb **would be.** Our feeling, however, is that the whole idea **the weekend would probably be unforgettable** rather than merely **would be** is what "all of us" **knew.** Ultimately, we do not see any real problem in calling the adverbial clause either a modifier of the verb or a modifier of the entire independent clause.)

Additional material on clauses, from a somewhat different perspective, appears in the following section and in Chapter 6, "Grammar."

1d the sentence

1d1 from phrase to clause to sentence

Writing well entails putting words together in effective ways—combining words to make phrases; combining subjects, verbs, and their modifiers to make clauses and sentences. We recognize the difficulty of defining a sentence, for as we all know, even a grunt or similar human expression is an assertion. **Not bloody likely!** or **Anchors aweigh, my boys!** is for all practical purposes a sentence. However, in written English, when a clause expresses a complete thought (even though information from adjacent sentences may be essential to complete understanding) and can stand alone, grammatically independent of any other group of words, it is normally designated a sentence. The sentence is the basic unit of composition and is the unit that most significantly determines the effectiveness with which the writer uses language.

The art of writing is a matter of mastering the sentence—that is, of making precise, informative, forceful assertions or predications—and learning to play the almost infinite variations on its basic structure. Take the following sentence: **The woman from the village fell in love with the man who had rescued her. From the village, in love,** and **with the man** are all phrases, groups of words which do not contain a subject–verb pair but which modify **woman, fell,** and **love,** respectively. **Who had rescued her** is a clause because it does contain both a subject and a verb **(who** and **had rescued),** but it clearly does not stand alone in the sentence; rather, it modifies or identifies **man.** However, all of these groups of words—the phrases and the clause—serve to amplify, qualify, and refine the fundamental assertion or bare predication wanted by the writer—namely, **The woman fell.** Having **the woman** as a subject, the writer states *something about her.* This affirming, declaring, proclaiming, even questioning, when it exists independently, is the main clause or core of the sentence, the primary communication by its writer. No matter how complex or lengthy a statement may be, it contains a core, or *kernel,* that says or asks something about the subject, as in the following examples, in which the subject is underlined once and the verb that asserts something about the subject is underlined twice:

a. In the beginning ***God*** ***created*** the heaven and the earth.

Holy Bible

b. While the people retain their virtue and vigilance, no ***administration,*** by any extreme of wickedness or folly, ***can*** very seriously ***injure*** the government in the short space of four years.

Abraham Lincoln

c. ***Reading*** ***maketh*** a full man, ***conference*** a ready man, and ***writing*** an exact man. (twice-implied verb: ***maketh***)

Francis Bacon

d. Whenever a man's friends begin to compliment him about looking young, ***he may be*** sure that they think he is growing old.

Washington Irving

e. ***Two may talk*** and ***one may hear,*** but ***three cannot take*** part in a conversation of the most sincere and searching sort.

Ralph Waldo Emerson

f. Shortly before the meeting ended, ***Chairman Thomas,*** angry at and disappointed with the scant progress they had made on this crucial matter, ***assigned*** each member of the board a task, to be carried out immediately.

g. Given the renewed interest in science, the ***university should determine*** the size of faculty necessary to teach the larger number of students wishing to study chemistry, physics, and related disciplines.

h. Professional ***football,*** for many years a shoestring enterprise carried on in relative obscurity, ***has*** suddenly ***surpassed*** professional baseball as America's favorite spectator sport, though there are thousands of fans who would disagree.

i. The ***house*** where I was born ***reminds*** me of Hawthorne's house of seven gables, and just as the fictional house shaped the lives of those who lived within it, so our family ***home left*** its imprint, both for good and ill, on me.

j. Perhaps the most pressing ***need*** of individuals today ***is*** some moral and spiritual framework which will permit them to make decisions and commitments confidently and hopefully.

k. ***Take*** the Lewis and Clark Turnpike to Ransom; ***turn*** north on Highway 50 and ***proceed*** 35 miles to Kingdom City, the seat of Ardmore County. (subject implied for each verb: ***you***)

l. ***Does it*** always ***snow*** this much in Wisconsin?

m. The ***jury found*** him innocent of the charge, despite damaging testimony by the two men who had allegedly helped him in planning the robbery.

In each of these sentences above, regardless of the order of the words or of the degree of amplification, the writer has predicated *something* about a subject, via the verb and its possible completing words (to be discussed later), and it is this core that might be called the "freight" of the statement. If all else were stripped away, generally the statement could still deliver the writer's meaning, though not so fully and precisely as she or he might wish. *Qualification* (restriction) and *amplification* (extension) are the possibilities open to the writer for modification — for making the assertion as exact as possible.

1d2 kernels

The basic core, or kernel, of the sentence is the subject–verb pattern. However, as may be seen above, a slightly fuller description of the assertion or predication is possible and may be of much use to the writer in building his or her own sentences or in analyzing those already written. Looking at the examples above, we might label the kernels of independent clauses not only in terms of their subjects and verbs but also in terms of *objects* and *complements*. A *direct object* receives the action of the verb; an *indirect object* is the noun or pronoun to or for which the action is done. In the sentence **Tom read me the story,** the direct object is **story** and the indirect object is **me.** A *subjective complement* modifies or renames the subject when it has a *copulative* or *linking verb,* as in this sentence:

```
     S   V   SC
The army is obsolete.
```

An *objective complement* modifies or renames the object when the modification or renaming is necessary to complete the action of the verb:

```
  S    V      DO   OC
She drove her father insane.
```

It is possible to identify the main kernels of the majority of English sentences by one of the following five patterns:

S–V	(Subject–Transitive or Intransitive Verb)
S–V–DO	(Subject–Transitive Verb–Direct Object)
S–V–IO–DO	(Subject–Transitive Verb–Indirect Object–Direct Object)
S–V–SC	(Subject–Copulative Verb–Subjective Complement)
S–V–DO–OC	(Subject–Transitive Verb–Direct Object–Objective Complement)

(Remember that only *transitive* verbs are followed by objects; intransitive verbs do not take objects to complete their meaning. A more extensive discussion of verbs appears in Chapter 6, pages 203–9.) The kernels of the thirteen illustrative sentences above are, then, the following:

a. God–created–heaven and earth   (S–V–DO)

b. administration–can injure–government   (S–V–DO)

c. reading–maketh–man   (S–V–DO)
conference–(maketh)–man   (S–V–DO)
writing–(maketh)–man   (S–V–DO)

d. he–may be–sure   (S–V–SC)

e. two–may talk   (S–V)
one–may hear   (S–V)
three–can take–part   (S–V–DO)

f. Chairman Thomas–assigned–member–task
(S–V–IO–DO)

g. university–should determine–size   (S–V–DO)

h. football–has surpassed–baseball   (S–V–DO)

i. house–reminds–me   (S–V–DO)
home–left–imprint   (S–V–DO)

j. need–is–framework   (S–V–SC)

k. (you)–take–turnpike   (S–V–DO)
   (you)–turn   (S–V)
   (you)–proceed   (S–V)

l. it–does snow   (S–V)

m. jury–found–him–innocent   (S–V–DO–OC)

Identifying or labeling is most useful only for the main clauses of the sentence, because only they usually determine the essential character of the sentence. The dependent clauses, as we said, modify, amplify, and refine, but seldom alter the fundamental assertion.

One further kernel we will identify, though because it is relatively weak and tends to be overused by some writers, it is not as important as the five patterns already described. It is the kernel formed by an expletive plus a form of **to be** plus the real subject: **There**–V–S or **It**–V–S, of which examples are numerous:

                Expl V   S   S
To everything *there is* a *season,* and a *time* to every purpose under the heaven.
Holy Bible

Expl   V   V   S
There may never *be* a more masterfully played chess *match,* no matter how skilled and dedicated the opponents or how high the stakes.

                  Expl V   S
After the election, *it will be* our *duty* to compare passionate campaign promises with actual official performance.

Since the **There / It**–V–S construction contains unnecessary words, this kernel should be used sparingly.

The concept of sentence kernels is of real help in two fundamental ways: (1) in analyzing the kinds of sentences you are actually writing, thereby enabling you to ensure variety in your structures, and (2) in generating complex yet exact assertions through expansion of kernels. Perhaps the most used and strongest of the five kernels is S–V–DO with variations. Indeed, writing that features a high percentage of sentences of this pattern, in which the subject acts on an object, usually cannot help being vigorous, muscular prose. Conversely, prose that employs a high percentage of sentences of some form of the S–V–C pattern, in which the verb is copulative (linking subject and complement or merely showing a state of being), is usually static, lifeless, colorless.

For the very same reason, you should avoid overusing the *passive voice* in S–V kernels. In the *active voice* the subject acts; in the *passive voice* the subject is acted upon: **Mary hailed a cab** (active voice); **A cab was hailed by Mary** (passive voice). Not only is the first statement stronger, more vigorous, but it is also more concise. The passive voice should be employed when it is logically called for (as in this sentence or as in the following example: **The experiment was conducted at 2 atmospheres pressure and 30 degrees Centigrade**). *Appropriateness, variety,* and *forcefulness* are always the goal. Either as you compose or as you revise, therefore, you will want to look closely at the kernels of the main clauses of your sentences in order to ensure these three properties.

In the following paragraph, for example, the writer demonstrates a command of the three characteristics of good prose:

The biographer who works from life, as Boswell did, has an extraordinary advantage over the biographer who works from the document, whether he plays scene shifter or not. He has seen his man in the flesh, he has been aware of a three-dimensional being, drawing breath and sitting in the midst of an age they both share. In his mind he retains a sharp image of his subject. He has heard the voice and seen the gesture (and even in our age no recording, no cinema picture can provide a substitute for that). The latecoming biographer hears only the rustle of the pages amid the silence of the tomb. This is explanation enough for the fact the greatest biographies in our literature have been those which were written by men who knew their subjects and who painted them as the painter paints his picture—within a room, a street, a landscape, with a background and a context rich with its million points of contemporaneous attachment. Boswell, Froude, Lockhart, Forster, repose upon our shelves with vividness and mass and authority which later biographers cannot possess. Leon Edel, *Literary Biography*

This paragraph features essentially S–V–DO kernels, but employs others as well. The result, as we see, is a passage full of vitality. Test your understanding of sentence kernels by trying to identify the kernels of the main clauses of each of these sentences.

You may use the kernels not only in the process of revision, as is most common, but also in the process of composition itself, as a way to generate sentences. The method might never be as simple as our following explanation would suggest; nevertheless, effective prose can be composed by expanding kernels in even rather deliberate ways. Let us take, for example, the sentence kernel **Students write papers** (S–V–DO), and expand it into a more exact and inclusive structure. For convenience, we might diagram it as follows, using numbers to show the positions at which various modifiers may be added to flesh out and develop the sentence.

	S		V		DO	
1	STUDENTS	2	WRITE	3	PAPERS	4

Then we could simply fill the successive slots:

Most STUDENTS WRITE PAPERS.

Most STUDENTS enrolled in English 1 WRITE PAPERS.

Most STUDENTS enrolled in English 1 WRITE eight 500-word PAPERS.

Most STUDENTS enrolled in English 1 WRITE eight 500-word PAPERS during the term.

With very little effort we have succeeded in expanding this three-word kernel into a fourteen-word sentence. Let us expand it even further, filling all four of the positions with additional modifiers.

According to the report from the Chairman of the English Department, most STUDENTS enrolled in English 1, the basic composition course at Jackson University, WRITE, sometimes at home and sometimes in class, eight 500-word PAPERS during the term, even though they may have had a good college-preparatory English course in high school.

The three-word kernel has now become a fifty-four-word sentence, long enough and specific enough for any occasion. One more example, in two stages, should suffice:

S	V	C
CARS	ARE	OBSOLETE.

Large luxury CARS produced by Detroit manufacturers ARE, we have come to conclude, OBSOLETE, especially in urban areas.

At a time when American technology has reached its peak, large luxury CARS produced by Detroit manufacturers in ever greater quantities and models ARE, we have come to conclude in the midst of our bewilderment, OBSOLETE, especially in urban areas where traffic, pollution, and energy problems are most severe.

The unit, once a kernel of three words and then a sentence of eighteen words, is now a highly informative statement of forty-nine words. Even so, the two expansions above are perhaps overloaded beyond usual sentence requirements. And while no one would suggest that the composition process be conducted quite so methodically (or mechanically), essentially the writer does, in some implicit way, work through these steps, carrying out the expansion and filling the several slots of possible modification to the limits of his or her creativity. If you have experienced difficulty in generating assertions with desirable qualifications and variety, this technique of sentence expansion may be of great help. Think of the kernels as tools for composing, analyzing, and revising your sentences.

1d3 fragments

Sentence fragments are phrases and dependent clauses offered as complete sentences. Trying to construct kernels for a given string of words will usually reveal whether the string is a complete sentence or merely a fragment. For example, **swimming in the ocean** is either a noun (gerund) phrase or a modifier (participial phrase); there is no verb, no statement is made, so we do not have a sentence. Most often the passing off of fragments for sentences is unintentional, the writer simply failing to perceive that he or she has not made a grammatically independent assertion:

Seeing her again in the fall.
John, who found the wagon hidden behind the rocks.
The impact of the story on the girls as they listened to the old man.

In the first example, **seeing** either modifies a missing subject or is itself the subject of a missing verb. In the second example, the subject **John** has no verb; **who found** is a subject–verb unit, but it modifies **John** and therefore cannot stand alone. In the third example, the subject **impact** has no verb; **they listened** is a subject–verb pair but it modifies the missing predicate of **impact** and therefore cannot stand alone. These units do not and cannot stand alone: in every case some essential part of a proper sentence is missing. Often the fragment is nothing more than a kind of appositive to what has gone before, as in the following examples:

[Euclid alone has looked on beauty bare.] Real beauty!

[Our trip ended at New Orleans.] The best part of the trip!

Generally, you should avoid fragments for the obvious reason that they are incomplete and often quite ambiguous in meaning or totally meaningless.

On the other hand, when there is no possibility of confusion and it seems appropriate to use a fragment to achieve a special effect, to emphasize a point, or to avoid tiresome repetition, the calculated use of the fragment may actually enhance your writing. But the right occasions are few; and if you tend too easily to write fragments, you should try to avoid them altogether. The fragments below are justifiable:

The season's record for the Mustangs was a poor 3–8. Unless one counts the preseason games, in which case the record was 5–10.

For a good many readers, the most striking characteristic of William Bradford's writing is his deep compassion for the sufferings of the Pilgrims at Plymouth Plantation. Their continual struggle against harsh climate, disease, hunger, and hostile Indians.

The road led northward toward the Benson Ranch. Just ahead, perhaps over the next hill, the home of Gene Benson!

The most legitimate use of the fragment is in narrative, when the particular effect of natural speech is desired:

"Once we're married, you'll give up your career, won't you?" Gordon asked. "Not on your life!" Lynn replied promptly.

Seldom in formal expository prose is the sentence fragment an effective strategy; however, when you are in command of your thought and of the possible structures for conveying it, you may choose to employ the fragment occasionally.

1d4 grammatical sentence forms

The sentence kernels presented on pages 21–27 *describe* sentence structures; together they make up what may be called a simplified descriptive system for analyzing sentences. But now we proceed to another system, in which sentences are identified *prescriptively,* or in terms of their traditional grammatical features. In the prescriptive system, all sentences are of four fundamental types (in addition to the fragment):

> *Simple sentence:* Contains one independent clause and no dependent clauses.
> *Complex sentence:* Contains one independent clause and one or more dependent clauses.
> *Compound sentence:* Contains two or more independent clauses and no dependent clauses.
> *Compound-complex sentence:* Contains two or more independent clauses and one or more dependent clauses.

As we have said before, independent clauses are groups of words containing a subject–verb pair that stands alone (that is, does not modify anything in the sentence), and dependent clauses are those which function as some kind of modifier within the sentence. All of the illustrative sentences thus far in this section on sentences can be identified according to their prescriptive grammatical types. And the following sentences (with the subject–verb pairs of independent clauses underlined once and those of dependent clauses underlined twice) offer additional examples of the prescriptive grammatical forms:

a. Simple Sentence

      S   V

All ***progress*** ***is based*** upon a universal innate desire on the part of every organism to live beyond its income.

Samuel Butler

On the breast of her gown, in red cloth, surrounded with an elaborate embroidery and fantastic flourishes of gold-

         V   S

thread, ***appeared*** the ***letter A.***

Nathaniel Hawthorne

Of all the studies of America and Americans, the most per-

               S V

ceptive and useful ***work*** ***is*** *Democracy in America* (1835) by Alexis de Tocqueville, a French nobleman with firsthand experience of this country during its formative years.

             S

Daily ***newspapers,*** particularly *The New York Times* and

               V

the *Washington Post,* ***have been*** the most searching and effective critics of the federal government's failure to respond to the needs and wishes of the people.

                  S

Reversing a trend of the past few years, ***most*** of the lists

                  V

naming the year's ten best movies ***contain*** at least six films made in the United States.

b. Complex Sentence

 S   S   V

Man, biologically considered, and whatever else ***he*** ***may be***

            V

in the bargain, ***is*** simply the most formidable of all the

                     S   V

beasts of prey, and, indeed, the only one ***that*** ***preys*** systematically on its own species.

William James

                  V

When in the course of human events, it ***becomes*** necessary

                    S   S

for one people to dissolve the political bands which

   V

have connected them with another, and to assume among the powers of the earth, the separate and equal station to

             S   V

which the *laws* of nature and of nature's God *entitle* them,

         S   V

a decent *respect* to the opinions of mankind *requires* that

  S   V   S   V

they should declare the causes *which impel* them to the separation.

                           Declaration of Independence

       V   S

If it *is* not possible *for you to come* to the office downtown,

            S   V   S   V

where the *records are kept, you may request* that a

     S   V

representative of our firm *visit* you in your home.

  S   V

Critics have recently *discovered* that T. S. Eliot's **The**

      S   V

Waste Land *has* vital connections with the problems of the poet's own life, particularly the mental breakdown which

      S   V

his first *wife experienced* and his own psychological disintegration and increasingly acute alienation from society.

        S

The *conception* of the university as a place where young

    S   V

people come to prepare themselves for a profession and a

                       V

role in the community *is* swiftly *being replaced* by the idea

         S   V   S   V

that the *university is* an institution *which reaches* out into

                 V

the environment and *instructs* people of all ages in whatever

        S   V

interests *they may have.*

c. Compound Sentence

          S   V   S

The morning ***stars*** ***sang*** together, and all the ***sons*** of God

  V

shouted for joy.

> Holy Bible

         S   V   S   V

An ***American*** ***cannot converse,*** but ***he*** ***can discuss,*** and his

  S   V

talk ***falls*** into a dissertation.

> Alexis de Tocqueville

                    S   V

The first federal ***judge*** appointed in the Fourth District ***was***

                                     S   V

a woman named Marilyn Carson, and ***she*** ***served*** in that position with distinction for five years, resigning her judgeship to run for the state House of Representatives.

                S   V

College ***teachers*** often ***find*** their best students to be female,

                      S   V

and yet these same ***women*** seldom ***succeed*** in the professional and business worlds to the same degree as men, a disparity increasingly shocking to thinking persons of both sexes.

                                 S   V

For highway travel, automobile ***manufacturers*** ***recommend***

                                 S   V

the heavy, roomy models; for city driving, ***they*** ***suggest*** the light, compact models.

d. Compound-Complex Sentence

          V   S   S V

There ***are*** only two or three human ***stories,*** and ***they*** ***go*** on

                                     S   V

repeating themselves as fiercely as if ***they*** ***had*** never ***happened*** before.

> Willa Cather

$$\overset{S}{A} \ \overset{}{woman} \ \overset{V}{can \ forgive} \ a \ man \ for \ the \ harm \ \overset{S}{he} \ \overset{V}{does} \ her \ but$$

   S   V   S   V

A ***woman*** ***can forgive*** a man for the harm ***he*** ***does*** her but

 S   V   S   V

she ***can*** never ***forgive*** him for the sacrifices ***he*** ***makes*** on her account.

W. Somerset Maugham

         S   S   V

When ***I*** and my ***friends*** ***were*** teenagers back in the late fif-

                     S   V

ties, nearly every free ***evening*** ***was spent*** driving battered automobiles up and down the main streets of our town,

            S   V   S   V   S

and when ***midnight*** ***came*** ***we*** all ***wondered*** how ***we*** ***had***

 V

been able to do so little with so much time.

         S   V   S   V

Some ***citizens*** ***turn out*** to vote only when ***they*** ***feel*** particu-

                                     S

larly keen about some issue; but in fact, ***being*** a good citi-

 V

zen ***means,*** among other things, responsibly voicing one's opinions on as many issues as possible.

                                  S   S

Even at the sandlot level, where ***uniforms,*** ***officials,*** and

 S   V   S   V

coaches ***are*** seldom ***seen,*** team ***sports*** ***can be*** fun and

                      S   S

healthy; the ***enthusiasm*** and ***effort*** of the participants

                                  V

rather than the trappings largely ***determine*** their worth.

e. Fragment

Illustrated in section 1d3, this structure (or incomplete structure) should be reserved for very special uses and must never be used inadvisedly, as we have explained above.

The conscientious writer will find the prescriptive system for sentence analysis a very practical check on variety or its absence. A series of short, simple sentences quickly becomes monotonous and deadening to the reader. Analyze your rough drafts carefully, rewriting in order to gain a large proportion of complex sentences and a reasonable variety of the other three types. Effective prose makes basic statements qualified by suitable nuance and condition. Thus the prescriptive system will tell you whether your sentences deliver to the reader not only basic assertions but also any desirable modifications and qualifications, and will establish the proper, logical, and precise relationships within and between sentences. A mass of short, jerky, generally simple sentences is the inevitable trademark of an uncritical writer like the author of this paragraph:

> Emerson returned from Europe in 1832. It was his first trip abroad. While there he met Carlyle, Coleridge, Wordsworth, and Landor. He also met a number of other famous men. He decided that he could no longer continue with the vocation of minister. It was basically a matter of conscience with him. He had slipped into this vocation easily as a young man without questioning it. Therefore, he resigned his pulpit at the Second Congregational Church of Boston. He had served it faithfully for four years.

The effect of this unrelieved succession of short, staccato sentences is the worst sort of monotony. Even worse, the important relationships of ideas — some coordinate, others subordinate — are simply not expressed. Our writer has thrust upon the reader the responsibility for establishing the real relationships. This tissue of mainly simple sentences is poverty-stricken prose which basically coordinates them all — that is, gives them all equal weight and structure. The experienced writer will take these seemingly coordinate ideas and blend them into a comprehensive statement that brings together the ideas in a structure that clearly shows which ideas are major and which are minor; which have independent status and which have dependent status; which of the ideas belong in independent clauses and which in dependent clauses. Such a revision (with its independent clauses underlined once and its dependent clauses underlined twice) might look like this:

> When ***Emerson returned*** in 1832 from his first trip to Europe, where ***he met*** with Carlyle, Coleridge, Wordsworth, and Landor, as well as other great sages of the day, ***he decided*** that ***he could*** no longer in good conscience ***continue*** with the vocation of minister ***he had slipped*** into so easily as a young man. Consequently, ***he resigned*** his pulpit at the Second Congregational Church of Boston, which ***he had served*** faithfully for four years.

As you can see, we now have two readable and informative complex sentences, tied together in style and continuity of thought (from cause to effect). The first sentence emphasizes **he decided that . . .;** the second emphasizes **he resigned his pulpit.** The remaining words in the two sentences — clauses and phrases — are structures of modification, effectively qualifying and refining the two assertions. If you can grasp these concepts of *subordination* and *coordination* and put them to work, generally your writing will improve strikingly and rapidly.

Thus, as you have already inferred, the fundamental structure of the compound sentence is coordination; the fundamental structure of the complex sentence is subordination. A succession of simple sentences is, in effect, coordination; a combination of coordination and subordination, of course, produces the compound-complex sentence. To ensure that these concepts of subordination and coordination are absolutely clear, we present several more examples (with connectors between the clauses set in bold italic type):

	Proper structure
Idea	*Subordination*
We do not know what education could do for us. We have never tried it.	We do not know what education could do for us, **because** we have never tried it.
	Robert Hutchins
	Coordination
Unto every one that hath shall be given, and he shall have abundance. From him that hath not shall be taken away even that which he hath.	Unto every one that hath shall be given, and he shall have abundance; **but** from him that hath not shall be taken away even that which he hath.
	Matthew 25:29
Defense is an important element of football. Developing good defensive units has made Coach Wallace the most successful coach in the NFL.	Defense is an important element of football, **and** developing good defensive units has made Coach Wallace the most successful coach in the NFL.
	Subordination
Mary loved her dog. Her dog could do no tricks.	**Even though** her dog could do no tricks, Mary loved it.
James Fenimore Cooper finished *The Prairie* in Paris. He was far away from the primeval American wilderness that had stirred his imagination deeply.	**Although** he was far away from the primeval American wilderness that had stirred his imagination deeply, James Fenimore Cooper finished *The Prairie* in Paris.
	Coordination
A bad book is as much of a labour to write as a good one. It comes as sincerely from the author's soul.	A bad book is as much of a labour to write as a good one; it comes as sincerely from the author's soul.
	Aldous Huxley

The connectors above — **because, but, and, even though, although,** and **;** — are (except for the semicolon) called *conjunctions* and show the precise relationship of the clauses — which are independent and which are dependent. Those which coordinate (like **but** and **and**) are, obviously, *coordi-*

nating conjunctions; those which subordinate (like **because, even though, although**) are *subordinating conjunctions.* You will be able to think of other examples of each type — for example, the following:

Coordinating conjunctions	*Subordinating conjunctions*
or	if
nor	whereas
for	while
either . . . or	despite
neither . . . nor	since
not only . . . but also	

As in the Huxley example, a semicolon may serve for a comma plus **and,** or it may provide a closer connection than would result from using a period and making the following independent clause a sentence. In this sense, then, the semicolon functions as a coordinate conjunction. Generally, your proficiency as a writer is directly related to your skill in handling subordination in sentences and signaling it clearly by conjunctions, such as those above. You thereby achieve not only predication with appropriate qualification and preciseness but also conciseness and, in the context of other sentences, variety. Exactness of predication, conciseness, and variety virtually determine the effectiveness of writing at the level of the sentence.

1d5 rhetorical sentence forms

A third and last system for generating and analyzing sentences makes use of the effect which certain structures produce in the reader — the system of rhetorical forms. Some of these structures, quite pronounced in their effects and familiar to writers in all times and places, can be readily identified and recommended to the beginning writer as yet other ways to achieve variety and, in some cases, conciseness in sentence structure. Even more important here, these forms may be used to stimulate interest and attention in readers by satisfying their expectations, sometimes withholding temporarily that satisfaction, or sometimes pleasing their sense of rhythm and relationships by repeating structures. The most important rhetorical forms for our purposes are the following:

> *Loose sentence:* A sentence in which the main kernel or independent clause is essentially stated at or near the beginning, with the remainder of the sentence being structures of modification.
> *Periodic sentence:* A sentence in which the main kernel or independent clause or some important element of it is withheld from the reader, being preceded by structures of modification, and is revealed at the end of the sentence, to coincide with the period (or other end punctuation).
> *Balanced sentence:* A sentence that contains and is primarily distinguished by at least two coordinate or parallel clauses, either counterparts or opposites. (Parallel elements, it will be remembered, are simply similar thoughts put in similar grammatical structures. Parallelism at the level of the clause is termed *balance*.)
> *Mixed sentence:* A sentence that has neither a clearly loose structure nor a clearly periodic structure, but elements of both so that its effect is not pronounced.

The addition of parallelism to either the loose or periodic sentence produces two sentence types in addition to these pure forms:

> *Loose sentence in combination with parallelism*
> *Periodic sentence in combination with parallelism*

a. Loose Sentence   The loose sentence is the most common and natural of these rhetorical forms. It begins by stating the main idea and then concludes with whatever modification and qualification are appropriate, as in the following instances (in which the kernel of the main clause is underlined):

He was deficient, however, in energy, and consequently, in that spirit of enterprise which is here so absolutely requisite.

Edgar Allan Poe, *The Narrative of Arthur Gordon Pym*

The **_investigation_** of the politician's finances **_lasted_** well over a year, primarily because he refused to cooperate with the committee by turning over personal records which, he maintained, could not legally be used as evidence against him.

Fraternal **_organizations_** on college campuses **_are making_** a **_comeback_** now that students have largely abandoned the social activism so popular in the late '60s, a time when institutions of all kinds came under fire.

The **_meeting lasted_** for well over two hours, despite Mr. Allen's efforts to keep discussion of the research department's new products as brief as possible.

Pedestrians usually **_panic_** when they find themselves in the middle of the street during rush hours in New York City, particularly if they are out-of-towners who have perhaps never seen anything quite like this near-chaos.

In every case the basic meaning of each of these sentences is clear once the kernel is completed, but notice how much richer and more precise the statement becomes as a result of the qualifying detail which the writer adds. The effect of the loose sentence is satisfying to readers, as they receive a basic message almost immediately, and with that message clearly in mind they can then more readily digest and appreciate the nuances of modification in the remainder of the sentence. It also satisfyingly reveals the writer's very evident control over the material.

b. Periodic Sentence   Whereas the effect of the loose sentence is casual and relaxed, the effect of the periodic sentence is anticipatory and even suspenseful. The writer deliberately refuses to convey the complete kernel — that is, withholds some crucial part of it — until the reader's interest in it has been aroused. The writer then completes the kernel as he or she ends the sentence (with a period or other mark of end punctuation). The effect is somewhat like that of the punch line of a joke. The periodic sentence — more calculated, perhaps even more artful, than the loose sentence — delivers a message to the reader, but delivers it on its own terms, only after it has stimulated the reader's interest, engagement, and expectation.

Here are some examples of periodic sentences with their kernels underlined:

When people get it into their heads that they are being specially favoured by the Almighty, ***they had better*** as a general rule ***mind*** their ***p's and q's.***

> Samuel Butler, *Way of All Flesh*

At the present time young ***people,*** especially those of the upper middle class at universities, where experimentation with social modes generally precedes change in the larger society, ***are trying out alternatives*** to marriage.

No matter how much I protest about my lack of voice in family matters, my ***wife,*** sensitive person though she is, particularly to our children, ***makes*** all ***decisions*** concerning summer vacations.

Ray Thomas, who prides himself on his command of his team during games, in a display of temper seldom witnessed by Garden fans, even the most veteran of them, ***blew up.***

According to Oscar Wilde, whose outrageous opinions continue to startle us long after his death in 1900, ***art,*** which most people find instructive and delightful, ***is,*** without qualification, ***useless.***

The periodic sentence is most effective when used consciously but moderately. A succession of periodic sentences would quickly eliminate the element of suspense, and suggest to most readers that the writer cares only about the effects of the writing and not its truth. In short, overuse of the periodic sentence neutralizes its intended effect and at least arouses the suspicion of the reader that the writer is unreliable. However, when used strategically—for generating anticipation and suspense, marking climax, creating a sense of finality, driving home a point—the periodic sentence can add variety, interest, and emphasis to prose.

c. Balanced Sentence   This rhetorical type carries the concept of parallelism into the clause structure of the sentence. As described earlier, words and phrases performing the same functions in a sentence are given the same grammatical structure, thereby displaying both clear relationship of parts and economy of diction. The same advantages can be obtained at the level of the clause, though parallelism is used less often in the larger scope of the clause because the effect is rather ornate. The degree of calculation involved in the balanced sentence often exceeds even that of the periodic sentence. Therefore, you should use it, too, primarily when the thought itself calls for it, when greater economy would be achieved, or when a particularly pointed expression is needed:

Understanding the French is difficult, but understanding the Russians is impossible.

I realized my mistake, and I corrected it immediately.

I came, I saw, I conquered.

Indeed, the balanced sentence often has the character of a proverb or maxim. Excessive use of this rhetorical form will alienate even the most sympathetic reader rather quickly; who, after all, wants to be preached to continuously?

In the balanced sentence, the parallel clauses may be counterparts or opposites:

Counterparts

Wisdom crieth without; she uttereth her voice in the streets.
> Proverbs 1:20

Bullfighting is the only art in which the artist is in danger of death and in which the degree of brilliance in the performance is left to the fighter's honor.
> Ernest Hemingway, *Death in the Afternoon*

As no man is born an artist, so no man is born an angler.
> Izaak Walton, *The Compleat Angler*

For want of a nail the shoe is lost, for want of a shoe the horse is lost, for want of a horse the rider is lost.
> George Herbert, *Jacula Prudentum*

Persons attempting to find a motive in this narrative will be prosecuted; persons attempting to find a moral in it will be banished; persons attempting to find a plot in it will be shot.
> Mark Twain, Epigraph, *Huckleberry Finn*

Opposites

Hatred stirreth up strifes; but love covereth all sins.
> Proverbs 10:12

Man proposes, but God disposes.
> Thomas à Kempis, *Imitation of Christ*

For every thing you have missed, you have gained something else; and for every thing you gain, you lose something.
> Ralph Waldo Emerson, *Compensation*

It matters not how a man dies, but how he lives.
> James Boswell, *Life of Johnson*

His words leap across rivers and mountains, but his thoughts are still only six inches long.
> E. B. White, *World Government and Peace*

The possibilities, of course, are many; here we offer some examples of balanced sentences that are plainer in style.

The evergreen tree grew in the front yard, and the rosebush bloomed beside the garage.

Papers from graduate students must be turned in no later than December 1, but papers from undergraduates may be turned in as late as December 15.

What a man does with his life is seldom under his control; what he does with the given moment is very often his own decision.

Before you leave the house, please be sure that the dog has her bone, the cat has his ball, and the neighbor has our telephone number.

When our marriage began, Mary and I had a number of illusions about each other, but when it ended, we had nothing much of anything.

The patterning of major elements such as clauses requires considerable care by the writer; and when it is done particularly well, the effect is indeed pleasing. Although you should not strain after this effect, when your thoughts can be balanced structurally so as to enhance variety, economy, and emphasis, you should seize the opportunity to employ this artful rhetorical mode.

d. Mixed Sentence   Probably, most sentences fall into this category. The mixed sentence is distinguished neither by looseness or periodicity nor by balance or parallel elements. Thus, it cannot have the effects of casualness, suspense, or symmetry. But, as we have suggested several times, effects such as these are best used sparingly, are best reserved for just the right occasions. Most of the time the writer is simply concerned with making precise, vigorous assertions, letting the thought itself discover and direct which structures shall be used. Special effects should be just that—special. Here are some mixed sentences, whose primary purpose is to convey the thought clearly and succinctly without attempting to control the reaction of the reader to it.

Whosoever looketh on a woman to lust after her hath committed adultery already in his heart.

Matthew 5:28

Every man feels instinctively that all the beautiful senti-
ments in the world weigh less than a single lovely action.

James Russell Lowell, *Rousseau and Sentimentalists*

Despite the precautions which the police officers took,
several persons were injured as the rescue operation pro-
ceeded.

The game of Monopoly, which has been around nearly
forever, it seems, continues to sell very well in all parts of
the United States.

Even though they are exercises in rationality, scientific discoveries often owe a great deal to the hunches of the ex-
perimenters involved in them.

If it had not been for the reality of Stalinism in the 1930's,
the Communist Party would have gained a much stronger
hold on America, which, because of the Depression, was
particularly vulnerable to Marxism.

You will often find that your rough draft consists almost
entirely of these mixed sentences and that in revision many
of them will rather naturally lend themselves to conversion
into one of the other rhetorical forms. This is sound writing
procedure: you concentrate first on getting your thoughts
down on paper and then polishing their expression by
choosing rhetorical modes and effects. But interestingly
enough, it is almost impossible to keep some parallelism or
some degree of looseness or periodicity out of any structure unless it is very short and unnatural. Almost always
the mixed sentence leans toward one of the other types,
simply because those types are so natural to the art of
both thinking and writing.

    e. *Combinations of Types*   Mentioned above in pass-
ing were two additional rhetorical types: the loose sentence
with parallel elements and the periodic sentence with parallel elements. All we need to do with them here is to
illustrate them briefly, since their construction is quite
obvious.

Loose sentence with parallel elements:

She paid over $500 for the dress, an original creation by Pierre of New York, which she had seen at a fashion show last winter and had been unable to get out of her mind.

Enrollment at many large universities is often a nightmare, lasting as it does for several days, held usually in some cavernous building, and subjecting students to the most mechanical procedures imaginable.

Reading newspapers can be a pleasure when a person has ample time, when the paper provides a variety of topics, and when the writing itself is professional.

Periodic sentence with parallel elements:

Unless you pay this bill before April 1, when the new rates go into effect, your water will be turned off and you will be billed a $5.00 service charge.

Because militant feminists like Gloria Steinem, Germaine Greer, and Billie Jean King have demonstrated that women can be self-reliant and successful in their careers, American women are changing their ideas about themselves.

New York, that impossible but real city, where the very best and the very worst of life may be found, ever mystifies me.

Combinations of the primary rhetorical types such as these are as numerous as your mind is fertile; and whether or not you work consciously with these forms in the original expression of your thought, to help you in generating it, you can surely profit from knowledge of and practice with them in the task of rewriting.

1d6 sentence variety

Throughout the discussion of sentences, three qualities have been stressed: economy, emphasis, and variety. Individual statements should, as a matter of course, be concise and pointed; statements in succession should, in addition, be various. We discussed exactness and precision in the section on "The Word"; we have recommended emphasis in this section on the sentence, in the attention paid to the choice of kernel and verb form, both of which determine the nature of the assertion.

The principle of variety, however, even though involved to some extent in this section on the sentence, must receive additional consideration because of the difficulty many inexperienced writers have in mastering it. Actually, imparting variety to sentences is not at all difficult if you have a grasp of the three systems of analyzing sentences described above: sentence kernels, grammatical forms, and rhetorical forms. These obviously offer you a stock of devices for ensuring the desired changes of pace. If you wish, you may check your sentences for economy, emphasis, and variety, using first one and then another of the systems. Consider the sentences on the opposite page, which make up a paragraph.

Such analysis helps you to see what kind of control you have over your prose — whether you stress actions and decisive ideas or allow acts and ideas to assume a basically passive role and thus be *acted upon*. The analysis demonstrates one kind of self-test you can apply to the sentences in your paragraphs and whole essays. If you tend to overuse passive voice and linking verbs, the analysis will tell you so. In that case, you will want to make some revisions to strengthen your sentences, changing excessive passive voice and linking verbs to strong, decisive active voice and transitive verbs. You can tell by the analysis whether you've achieved sentence variety, as well as precision. And you'll probably discover through this analysis whether you're adequately relating sentences to each other and using passive voice and linking verbs *only* when the context justifies such use.

Perrine's version of the Old Testament narrative about Susanna and the Elders pinpoints crucial *acts* as its heart — the unsuspecting woman **aroused** the old men's lust as

	Analysis		
	By kernels	*By grammatical forms*	*By rhetorical forms*
1. The story of Susanna and the Elders is told in the Apocrypha and in the Douay Bible, Daniel 13.	S–V	Simple	Mixed, with parallel elements
2. The beauty of Susanna, wife of a rich man in Babylon, aroused the lust of two elders who had recently been appointed judges.	S–V–Do	Complex	Mixed
3. Concealing themselves in her garden, they watched her bathe, then threatened her with blackmail unless she lay with them.	S–V–DO	Complex	Mixed, with parallel elements
4. When she refused, they raised an outcry which summoned her maids, and accused her of unchastity with a young man.	S–V–DO	Complex	Mixed, with parallel elements
5. Because of their position as judges they were believed and Susanna was condemned to death.	S–V	Compound	Balanced
6. The prophet Daniel, however, trapped the elders in conflicting testimony, convicted them of false witness, and had them put to death instead.	S–V–DO	Simple	Periodic, with parallel elements

Laurence Perrine, *100 American Poems*

they **watched, threatened, raised an outcry,** and **accused her.** Thus the *acts* of the innocent woman are contrasted with the unworthy *acts* of the elders. On each end, the brief narrative is enclosed by passive constructions, which place and evaluate conduct, before Daniel comes along to set things right by way of action told with active verbs.

Two other characteristics of the sentence are extremely important in determining the readability of a succession of statements: sentence length and sentence beginnings. One of the most effective means of changing the pace for the reader, of keeping prose from becoming monotonous and dull, is simply to produce sentences of varying lengths. An occasional long sentence and an occasional short sentence will prevent sentences from falling into a predictable rhythm or beat. This danger is particularly great in the case of shorter sentences, which in succession set up a staccato effect. A series of short, choppy sentences is called, appropriately, "primer style": **See Jane. See Jane run. . . .** But in the main, when a writer is turning out substantial sentences of approximately twenty words or more, then it is simply a matter of varying the rhythm now and then with a sentence significantly longer or shorter than the typical sentence in the series. In the paragraph above, the breakdown by number of words is as follows: (1) 19, (2) 23, (3) 19, (4) 20, (5) 15, (6) 22. There is, clearly, some variety of lengths, made even more effective by the variety of structures; with that point we come to the concept of sentence beginnings.

Even though the range of words per sentence in the paragraph on p. 47 is only 15 to 23 words, with no very short or very long sentence, the reader never finds the prose monotonously repetitive. The varied sentence structure (analyzed above) is largely responsible for such a pleasing effect, and particularly the different ways in which the writer begins his sentences. As was mentioned earlier, the most common technique in the English sentence is to begin with the subject, followed by the verb and whatever qualification and modification are required. Therefore, variety may be achieved by altering this basic strategy from time to time. Returning to the idea of sentence kernels and "slots" (those positions preceding and following basic parts of kernels) to be filled with structures of modification, we can analyze the sentences in the narrative above (X shows that the slot for modification is filled):

Positions of Modifiers Within Sentences

Sentence number	A. Modifier before subject	Subject	B. Modifier between subject and verb	Verb	C. Modifier between verb and direct object	Direct object	D. Modifier after direct object
1.		story	X	is told	X		
2.		beauty	X	aroused		lust	X
3.	X	they		watched		her	
						bathe	
				threatened		her	X
4.	X	they		raised		outcry	X
				accused		her	X
5.	X	they		were			
				believed			
		Susanna		was			
				condemned	X		
6.		prophet	X	trapped		elders	X
				convicted		them	X
				had		them	
						put	X

Thus, we can see that in sentences 3, 4, and 5 the writer has begun with a participial phrase, an adverbial clause, and a prepositional phrase, respectively, and this filling of the "A-slot" with *different* structures of modification contributes significantly to the suitable variety found in the paragraph.

To understand more fully the many ways in which sentences may be begun, let us expand the following kernel using only this initial position:

Beginning		S	V	DO
		Hearings	outrage	people.
word (adjective)	Closed	hearings	outrage	people.
phrase (adverbial modifier)	In most cases	hearings	outrage	people.
clause (sentence modifier)	Whether Congress realizes it or not	hearings	outrage	people.
combination	Whether Congress realizes it or not, in most cases closed hearings outrage people.			

This exercise, which could of course be greatly expanded, should convince even inexperienced writers of the possibilities for variety in ordering their thoughts. If you will be sensitive to sentence length and sentence structure (particularly sentence beginnings) in the process of revision, then your readers will find your writing fresh and lively, and will remain closely engaged with your explanation or argument.

1d7 common sentence problems

Following is a list of mistakes often made by the inexperienced or careless writer. Some of them have been defined and explained in previous sections, but deserve reiteration and reemphasis in this list of problems, which may serve as a brief summary of the section on the sentence.

a. Sentence Fragment   A group of words without an independent subject–verb pair is a sentence fragment:

Serving his country with distinction when others clearly failed to do their duty.

The girl whose name I could not remember, even though we were graduated from the same high school only two years ago.

When the train had left the station to make the run to Denver.

The first two strings of words fail to provide verbs for their subjects; they can be made into statements. The third string of words is a dependent construction, needing something to modify.

Serving his country with distinction when others clearly failed to do their duty won Jim the gratitude of his countrymen. (Add the verb **won** for the subject **serving**.)

The girl whose name I could not remember, even though we were graduated from the same high school only two years ago, married Tom Jones last Saturday. (Add the verb **married** for the subject **girl**.)

When the train had left the station to make the run to Denver, I drove Mother home. (Add the independent clause **I *drove* mother home.**)

Often, simply checking to see whether or not a group of words makes a clear assertion (or reading aloud, for some writers) will reveal sentence fragments. But you should always make sure that your statement contains an independent subject–verb pair.

b. Comma Splice A comma splice is the serious error of trying to yoke independent clauses with a mere comma when a stronger break is needed in order to show the precise relationships of the clauses. Two independent clauses joined only by a comma need the stronger and more explicit coupling of either (1) a comma and coordinating conjunction or (2) a semicolon with or without a conjunctive adverb like **however** or **therefore.** If they are not in fact closely related, they may also be connected by (3) making each an individual sentence, in which case an end mark of punctuation replaces the comma and capitalization begins the second sentence. Following are examples of the comma splice and necessary corrections:

After the flood the Johnsons moved to Phoenix, many of the other villagers moved back to their homes. (comma splice)

After the flood the Johnsons moved to Phoenix, *but* many of the other villagers moved back to their homes. (Add the coordinating conjunction ***but.***)

He could not bring himself to abandon the dog, he had cared for it so long. (comma splice)

He could not bring himself to abandon the dog; he had cared for it so long. (Replace the comma with a semicolon.)

The Giants must win their game on Thursday, if they lose they will finish in second place.

The Giants must win their game on Thursday. *I*f they lose they will finish in second place. (Make the two clauses into separate sentences by replacing the comma with a period and using capitalization.)

I passed all my examinations, I could go on the class picnic with a clear conscience. (comma splice)

I passed all my examinations; ***therefore,*** I could go on the class picnic with a clear conscience. (Add a semicolon and a conjunctive adverb.)

Short independent clauses with parallel structure may be joined simply by a comma:

He came, he saw, he conquered.
The temperature decreased, the danger increased.

But, in general, main clauses not closely related require stronger connection than a comma.

c. Fused Sentence Two independent clauses simply run or fused together constitute exactly the same error as the comma splice, but this mistake is even more serious because it creates more difficulty for the reader. In the fused sentence both structure and meaning are needlessly vague. The proper punctuation will clarify the relations of the independent clauses to each other and thus will clarify the meaning of the sentence.

Movies are entertaining a person can often throw off the cares of the day by watching one. (fused sentence)

Movies are entertaining**, and** a person can often throw off the cares of the day by watching one. (Add a comma and the coordinating conjunction ***and.***)

He found the situation confusing her car, at least, should have been there. (fused sentence)

He found the situation confusing**;** her car, at least, should have been there. (Add a semicolon.)

He finished the novel and went off to Paris for the summer in New York the publishers waited impatiently for some word from him. (fused sentence)

He finished the novel and went off to Paris for the summer**.** *I*n New York the publishers waited impatiently for some word from him. (Make the two clauses into separate sentences by adding a period and using capitalization.)

Fused sentences inevitably suggest the writer's lack of "sentence sense" and indifference to the conventions of punctuation.

d. Faulty Agreement: Subject–Verb and Pronoun–Antecedent Verbs must match their subjects in person and number, and pronouns must match their antecedents in number. Errors of this kind most often occur simply because the writer has not carefully proofread her or his work.

A chart of the groups within the larger organization **help** acquaint the new employees with the company. (The singular noun **chart** requires the singular verb **helps.**)

The coach and his staff **lacks** experience but **makes** up for it in enthusiasm and desire. (The plural compound subject **coach and his staff** requires the plural verbs **lack** and **make.**)

Everyone who has tried the candy claims it makes **them** sick. (The singular antecedent **everyone** requires the singular pronoun **him**—or **him or her.**)

Women who have careers outside the home often find **her** family life improving. (The plural noun **women** requires the plural pronoun **their.**)

Correctness in agreement always helps to promote clarity of expression.

e. Vague or Absent Antecedent   Sometimes, especially in the heat of composing swiftly, most of us use the demonstrative pronouns **this** and **that** and the personal pronoun **it** to stand for or refer to some noun-idea that exists in our minds instead of on our pages. We often encounter the problem especially when we think of the meaning of a preceding verb, a whole clause, or even an entire sentence as somehow being the equivalent of **this, that,** or **it.** The following passage from an essay answer on an examination illustrates the vague or absent antecedent:

(1) Poe linked sadness and beauty. (2) **This** is exemplified by his idea that the death of a beautiful young woman is the most poetic topic we can imagine.

It is not clear whether **this** refers to **sadness and beauty** or to Poe's linking of sadness and beauty. The pronoun obviously cannot refer to the entire sentence; therefore, we must correct the problem in one of these ways:

1. Change sentence 1 into the subject of sentence 2 and remove the unattached **this:**

Poe's linkage of sadness and beauty is exemplified in his idea that the death of a beautiful young woman is the most poetic topic we can imagine.

2. Turn **this** into a noun phrase:

Poe linked sadness and beauty. **This relationship** is exemplified in his idea that the death of a beautiful young woman is the most poetic topic we can imagine.

f. Dangling Modifiers or Misplaced Parts (Improper Modification)   One of the most common errors in writing is faulty modification, which occurs when a group of words, because of its position in the sentence, improperly relates to or qualifies a part of the sentence other than the part intended by the writer or a part totally missing from the sentence. Consider, for example, these statements:

The next morning he was found lying on the floor by a cleaning woman.

The next morning a cleaning woman found him lying on the floor. (sentence changed from passive to active and restructured to eliminate unintentional humor by placing **lying on the floor** next to **him,** thus getting the cleaning woman out of an otherwise compromising situation)

Weeping and pleading for mercy, the sentence was pronounced by an unmoved judge.

Weeping and pleading for mercy, the old drunkard received his sentence from an unmoved judge. (sentence restructured to supply a missing subject, **drunkard,** which the otherwise dangling **weeping and pleading for mercy** can now properly modify)

To pass Calculus I, there must be an average of 70 or above on all tests.

To pass Calculus I, a student must make an average of 70 or above on all tests. (sentence restructured to supply the missing subject, **student,** which the otherwise dangling **to pass Calculus I** can properly modify)

Getting into the car, the gunshot wounded him fatally.

Getting into the car, he was wounded fatally by the gunshot. (sentence restructured to eliminate unlikely modification of **gunshot** by participial phrase, **getting into the car**)

I subscribed to three magazines through my book club that featured excellent photography and incisive articles.

Through my book club, I subscribed to three magazines that featured excellent photography and incisive articles. (sentence restructured to put **magazines** and the modifying adjectival **that** clause next to each other)

The losing pitcher threw his glove into the crowd with a curse.

With a curse the losing pitcher threw his glove into the crowd. (sentence restructured to place prepositional phrase, **with a curse,** in a position to modify **threw** rather than **crowd**)

g. Excessive Coordination   Immature writing is quite often characterized by a failure to show the proper relationship of ideas through the use of subordination. The writer will simply link one idea to another indiscriminately, using either a coordinating conjunction or a conjunctive adverb to connect the ideas in one sentence, or a period and capitalization to connect the ideas in a series of short, choppy sentences.

Whitman published *Leaves of Grass* in 1855, and it received a warm welcome from Emerson, but it puzzled most of its readers.

Whitman's *Leaves of Grass,* published in 1855, though it received a warm welcome from Emerson, puzzled most of its readers. (Other emphases through subordination are possible. Essentially, the first two clauses are subordinated to the third clause.)

She lived on the north side of town, and she ran a fruit stand in front of her house; consequently, people thought she was poor.

Because she lived on the north side of town and ran a fruit stand in front of her house, people thought she was poor. (The first two clauses are subordinated to the third clause.)

Thomas Jefferson wrote the Declaration of Independence. He wrote it in 1776 at the request of the Second Continental Congress. At the time he was a representative of Virginia.

Thomas Jefferson, a representative of Virginia, wrote the Declaration of Independence in 1776 at the request of the Second Continental Congress. (The second and third clauses are subordinated to the first clause.)

The ball was hit sharply. The left fielder was playing deep. He still managed to catch the ball.

Although the ball was hit sharply, the left fielder, who was playing deep, still managed to catch it. (The first two clauses are subordinated to the third clause.)

The revised sentences, in addition to being more compact than the original versions, express their thoughts more accurately.

h. Faulty Subordination   Sometimes a writer will overload a sentence by subordination or will place main ideas in subordinate clauses or phrases and subordinate ideas in main clauses or phrases. The former practice creates an unwieldy and confusing sentence; the latter, an unemphatic, even ludicrous, sentence.

The freshman, who may have had little or no practice in writing when he comes to the university, often finds his theme assignments, sometimes covering topics about which he knows very little, extremely difficult, even when the instructor, who is thoroughly trained in the teaching of composition, carefully prepares the students for writing, as the English Department requires.

The freshman often finds his theme assignments extremely difficult, even when the instructor carefully prepares the students for writing. (Deleted clauses and phrases add inessential or questionably essential material.)

Bret Harte, whose stories about the Old West almost everyone has read and who befriended Mark Twain when the Missourian was a struggling young writer, lived out the latter part of his life in England, where he cultivated a sophisticated and somewhat effete life-style, never fulfilling the promise he had shown early in his career as the author of tales filled with local color and regional elements.

Bret Harte, whose stories about the Old West almost everyone has read, lived out the latter part of his life in England, never fulfilling the promise he had shown early in his career. (Deleted clauses and phrases add inessential or questionably essential material.)

Even though the car crossed the finish line, both rear tires blew out.

The car crossed the finish line, even though both rear tires blew out. (Despite one thing, the other thing happened, as may now be clearly seen.)

Winter approached bringing with it thoughts of aging and dying, as the woman simply gave up.

As winter approached bringing with it thoughts of aging and dying, the woman simply gave up. (The time sequence is now made clear.)

A reasonable amount of care will nearly always eliminate the error of "upside-down subordination"; however, good judgment and experience are the only defenses against excessive subordination.

i. Absent or Inexact Parallelism   The principle of giving similar ideas similar grammatical and rhetorical forms to ensure exactness and economy of expression is stressed throughout this book. It applies whether we are dealing with the word, the phrase, or the clause, and the following examples and their revisions illustrate this fact.

The ship in the distance looked gray and had a sinister appearance.

The ship in the distance looked gray and sinister. (**Gray** and **sinister** are parallel adjectives.)

The dog charged at the trespasser, knocking him to the ground, and he forced him to drop the bundle.

The dog charged at the trespasser, knocking him to the ground and forcing him to drop the bundle. (**Knocking him to the ground** and **forcing him to drop the bundle** are parallel participial phrases.)

That was the game which Thomas won for the Red Sox and Herbert was the loser for the Mustangs.

That was the game which Thomas won for the Red Sox and Herbert lost for the Mustangs. (**Which Thomas won . . .** and **[which] Herbert lost . . .** are parallel dependent clauses.)

Corporal Shaw returned home to banners waving and people cheering; Corporal Miller found only silence as his greeting.

Corporal Shaw returned home to banners waving and people cheering; Corporal Miller, to silence. (The two clauses are parallel independent clauses.)

In each case the revision has eliminated deadwood — words that contribute no meaning — and has improved the emphasis of the sentence.

j. Lack of Variety   The concept and importance of sentence variety are discussed at some length on pages

45–50. Briefly, as explained there, you should make it a point to vary both the length and the structure of your sentences. By so doing, you will avoid a "primer-style" succession of short, choppy sentences (habitually beginning with the subject of the sentence) and an overuse of sentence patterns employing relatively weak copulative or passive verbs. The following short paragraph and a revised version of it illustrate the principle quite well:

The Gilded Age, bad book that it is, prepared the way for Mark Twain's greatness. Beyond presenting the Colonel, it pictures for the first time the towns and villages of back-country America, and if it does so with a grim realism, that very realism (which was to reappear in later works) was also the matrix for Twain's ideal vision of that world. For one thing, in *The Gilded Age* he explored the world of luxury, self-deception, hypocrisy, and greed, the contempt for which was to force him back to his dream of the morning world of Hannibal. What the bliss of marriage and financial ease had done to turn his thoughts back to boyhood was now compounded by disgust at the ways of the world of success into which he had penetrated.
Cleanth Brooks, R. W. B. Lewis, and Robert Penn Warren,
American Literature, Vol. II

The Gilded Age is a bad book, but it prepared the way for Mark Twain's greatness. It presents the Colonel and in addition pictures for the first time the towns and villages of back-country America. It does this with a grim realism, and that very realism (which was to reappear in later works) was also the matrix for Twain's ideal vision of that world. Then, too, he explored the world of luxury, self-deception, hypocrisy, and greed. The contempt he had for these was to force him back to his dream of the morning world of Hannibal. The bliss of marriage and financial ease had turned his thoughts back to boyhood. These were now compounded by disgust at the ways of the world of success into which he had penetrated.

Subordination, the key to variety in the first paragraph, is all but lost in the second. The original version is richer and more attractive; its varying sentence lengths, sentence beginnings, and transitive verb patterns all contribute to making the paragraph livelier and more effective.

k. Vague Predication We began this chapter by describing the sentence as an assertion or predication, and we end it by stressing the need to make these assertions and predications just as sharp and emphatic as possible. Indeed, at its core, good writing is little more than a logical sequence of carefully shaped statements, and bad writing is often little more than a succession of vague or obscure statements. You must therefore strive to define the topic of each sentence and then to make your assertion about it as precise as you can. Precision and concreteness in identifying the subject and exactness in the choice of verb are the keys, as may be seen in the following examples:

The reason for the engine's failure is because a piston rod broke.

The engine failed because a piston rod broke. (Eliminate deadwood; supply concrete and exact diction.)

Two prestigious pundits of the mass media delivered themselves of comments about the president's aired views.

Two prominent news commentators evaluated the president's televised speech. (Supply concrete and exact diction.)

Students must remember that Physics II is one of the requirements for a diploma.

Physics II is a requirement for the Bachelor of Science degree. (Eliminate deadwood; supply concrete and exact diction.)

The couple walked in a leisurely manner to the building where students hang out.

The couple strolled to the Student Union. (Supply concrete and exact diction.)

The man in charge adjusted an instrument for measuring heat before initiating the activity.

The technician calibrated the thermometer before beginning the experiment. (Supply concrete and exact diction.)

The employment opportunity was rendered inoperative because he procrastinated concerning the submission of his credentials.

He didn't get the job because he failed to submit his credentials in time. (Supply concrete and exact diction.)

For each sentence the revision produces not only a more precise statement but a more emphatic one as well. Clear meaning, stated emphatically, is the goal of all writing; and by understanding the common sentence problems identified in this section and some methods for dealing with them, you can write more effectively.

paragraphs

2

As far as visual signals in written language are concerned, the paragraph is a fairly recent device, recognized and used in the Renaissance but analyzed and studied only late in the last century. Well into the nineteenth century, strict principles governing shifts from one paragraph to another were lacking, as the prose of Ralph Waldo Emerson, Matthew Arnold, or Thomas Carlyle amply shows. Even in our own day, paragraphing practice varies: for example, Ernest Hemingway's prose typically avoids long paragraphs (as it typically avoids long sentences), whereas William Faulkner's paragraphs are spacious and complex (again, mirroring his sentence structures). Obviously, modern journalism has affected our notions of what paragraphs may and should be like; and that effect has been toward brevity.

2a four major paragraphing techniques

In any case, most careful writers today consciously build their units of thought by their arrangements of paragraphs, and they signal, through *indentation,* new developments or new levels of presentation within a composition, an essay, or a chapter. At each indentation (usually five to seven spaces on typewritten copy) readers expect to find some meaningful clue to the function of this new paragraph and its relationship to what has gone before. Moreover, they expect a stated or implied justification for the existence of any given paragraph.

Thus, among the standard practices of writing prose, we can quickly identify four major techniques of paragraphing:

1. *Indentation.* The beginning of the first sentence of a new paragraph will be indented several spaces from the left margin of the page.

2. *Topic sentence.* Somewhere within the paragraph

will be found a stated or implied generalization about the total meaning or purpose of the paragraph.

3. *Transition.* Verbal signals—either word, phrase, or clause—carry the reader from one sentence to the next. The following paragraph illustrates some of the devices of transition:

2

The summer heat shimmered everywhere upon the prairies in 1934. *It* assaulted the harvesting crews and tormented cattle and poultry. *It* invaded the kitchens where wives and daughters of the crews labored frantically to cook the stacks of steak, mountains of mashed potatoes, gallons of gravy, and platters of biscuits. Not a leaf stirred on the parched trees; the dogs and cats lay panting in the shade under the houses. Even at night the heat persisted until very early morning, when it was time to rise for another struggle with sun and drought.

Pronoun *it* twice refers to *heat*
Parallel verbs *—shimmered, assaulted, tormented, invaded*

Entire sentence *Not . . . houses* as reinforcement for *heat . . . shimmered everywhere*

Prepositional phrase *with sun and drought* restates by synonym *heat* and its domination of the prairies

Entire sentence *Even . . . drought* restates idea stated in first sentence

4. *Details.* Details within a paragraph—illustrations, reasons, steps in a process, parts of a scene or event— serve (1) to expand the topic sentence adequately and (2) to justify the existence of the paragraph as a separate unit of discourse within the composition.

2b paragraphs in context

The following three paragraphs, which begin a bio-graphical article about A. Philip Randolph, the famous black leader of the 1920's and 1930's, illustrate these four techniques and the three essential qualities of effective paragraphs, to be discussed below:

Indentation

Tentative topic sentence

Blacks had been coming to New York long before the Great Depression. One was A. Philip Randolph, who lived in Harlem through most of its history as a black community, having arrived from Jacksonville, Florida, **in 1911,** at the end of the first modern wave of black migration to the North. **During the First World War,** there was an even greater flow —the one that furnished the Northern reservoir for Marcus Garvey's great black-nationalist movement. And then there was the swell **after the Depression.** The migrants, especially the ones **before the Depression,** did not come only from the South: thousands came from the West Indies. Nor were all the Southerners from the cotton fields: some were **businessmen** or **aspiring politicians,** and some, like the young Randolph, were budding intellectuals, filled with **hope for careers** in art, education, or mass culture, or in the arenas of political protest and radicalism. And to all of

Details of time sequence

Time pattern and motives for migration merged

2

them New York City—Harlem—was ***the promised land.***

Complementary topic sentence

Indentation

Of course, things did not turn out ***that way. A few people found what had chiefly drawn them there.*** Aspiring black Republican politicians—men like Charles W. Anderson and Edward Johnson—achieved great power in Harlem during the first two and a half decades of the century. Real-estate men and speculators did so well for themselves that they are to be credited with having opened up Harlem as a black residential community. And those who came in search of nothing more than "houses with bathrooms, electricity, running water, and indoor toilets" cannot have been disappointed. But the essence of what New York City, or Harlem, promised was freedom from the "color problem"—an equal opportunity for the pursuit of racial and political happiness—and that kind of freedom ***has proved elusive*** to this day.

Transition

Topic sentence

Analysis of motives (details) begins

Details to support idea of apparent success

Assertion of lack of genuine satisfaction

Enlarged and more emphatic restatement of topic sentence

Indentation

Yet the early experience in Harlem was not a total loss. The migrants—***especially those who came during and after the First World War***—established the most important black cultural and political community in America. By the mid-nineteen-twenties, the relatively young community had generated one of the most

Transition

Topic sentence

Qualification by time

Details providing reasons why "not a total loss"

spectacular bursts of black cultural activity—the Harlem, or Negro, Renaissance—the country has ever witnessed. Politically, Harlem was also, for all its limits and for all the aspirations it imprisoned, a somewhat freer place in which to operate, to articulate the demand for black freedom, than any other oppressed black community or any colonized black country in the world. Because of this, Harlem became, even before its Renaissance, the international center of black-nationalists and black-radical agitation—giving an enormous impetus to the awakening of black political agitation in other parts of America and the world.

Summary and restatement of paragraph's central idea

Jervis Anderson, "Profiles: Early Voice," *The New Yorker*

A close examination of these three paragraphs reveals several important features:

1. Each states a single, central idea that develops *unity* within the paragraph and relates it to the other two paragraphs.

2. In each, the individual sentences follow a logical sequence and are clearly related to each other like beads on a string. That principle of internal relationship is called *coherence*.

3. Each contains adequate support, substantiation, amplification, or proof of the central idea. This principle is called *development*.

2

Moreover, within their total context, the three paragraphs reveal what is nearly always true — that paragraphs operate not in isolation but within a context of thought and language.

2c major principles of paragraph forms and development

2c1 paragraph unity

As we have just seen, Anderson's paragraphs in context have unity, achieved and measured by the degree to which all the separate sentences within any of the paragraphs are combined and phrased to establish for the reader one central idea. Just as any sentence must have its subject — a noun or pronoun stated or understood — so any worthwhile paragraph must have a central idea or principle that holds together and justifies the presence of every sentence within the paragraph. As a practical guide to and test for a central thought, most paragraphs contain a *topic sentence*. In its simplest and most familiar form the topic sentence is the most general sentence in the paragraph. It usually comes first; however, it may also turn up in the middle of or at the end of the paragraph. And for many paragraphs, the topic sentence may simply be implied or understood and thus not even actually present. But whether the writer or the reader supplies it, it must be declared or understood in some fashion if the paragraph is to have unity.

Examine the paragraphs below for the identification, placement, or implied presence of the topic sentence.

1. A stated topic sentence at the beginning of the paragraph:

The Post-war Decade was a great sporting era. More men were playing golf than ever before — playing it in baggy plus-fours, with tassels at the knee and checked stock-ings. There were five thousand golf-courses in the United States, there were said to be two million players, and it was estimated that half a billion dollars was spent annually on the game. The ability to play it had become a part of the almost essential equipment of the aspiring business executive. The country club had become the focus of social life in hundreds of communities. But it was an even greater era for watching sports than for taking part in them. Promoters, chambers of commerce, newspaper-owners, sports writers, press agents, radio broadcasters, all found profit in exploiting the public's mania for sporting shows and its willingness to be persuaded that the great athletes of the day were supermen. Never before had such a blinding light of publicity been turned upon the gridiron, the diamond, and the prize ring.

Frederick Lewis Allen, Only Yesterday

2. A stated topic sentence in the middle of the paragraph:

Everybody was reading *All Quiet on the Western Front* and singing the songs which Rudy Vallee crooned over the radio. The literary journals were making a great fuss over humanism. ***But even sun-tan and Ramsay MacDonald's proposed good-will voyage and humanism and <u>All</u> <u>Quiet</u> were dull subjects for talk compared with the Big Bull Market.*** Had not Goldman, Sachs & Company just expressed its confidence in the present level of prices by sponsoring the Blue Ridge Corporation, an investment trust which offered to exchange its stock for those of the leading "blue chips" at the current figures — 324 for Allied Chemical and Dye, 293 for American Telephone, 179 for Consolidated Gas, 395 for General Electric, and so on down the list?

Allen, Only Yesterday

3. A stated topic sentence at the end of the paragraph:

On the morning of March 4, 1921, — a brilliant morning with a frosty air and a wind which whipped the flags of Washington, — Woodrow Wilson, broken and bent and ill,

2

limped from the White House door to a waiting automobile, rode down Pennsylvania Avenue to the Capitol with the stalwart President-elect at his side, and returned to the bitter seclusion of his private house on S Street. Warren Gamaliel Harding was sworn in as President of the United States. *The reign of normalcy had begun.*

Allen, Only Yesterday

4. A stated but divided topic sentence, whose role is divided between two sentences, often the first and the last:

Fear, however, did not long delay its coming. As the price structure crumbled there was a sudden stampede to get out from under. By eleven o'clock traders on the floor of the Stock Exchange were in a wild scramble to "sell at the market." Long before the lagging ticker could tell what was happening, word had gone out by telephone and telegraph that the bottom was dropping out of things, and the selling orders redoubled in volume. The leading stocks were going down two, three, and even five points between sales. Down, down, down. . . . Where were the bargain-hunters who were supposed to come to the rescue at times like this? Where were the investment trusts, which were expected to provide a cushion for the market by making new purchases at low prices? Where were the big operators who had declared that they were still bullish? Where were the powerful bankers who were supposed to be able at any moment to support prices? There seemed to be no support whatever. Down, down, down. *The roar of voices which rose from the floor of the Exchange had become a roar of panic.*

Allen, Only Yesterday

5. A topic sentence not actually present within the paragraph, but implied by the writer and understood by the reader. The controlling idea here is an implied "Here's how the stock market crash happened":

Early in September the stock market broke. It quickly recovered, however; indeed, on September 19th the aver-

ages as compiled by the *New York Times* reached an even
higher level than that of September 3rd. Once more it
slipped, farther and faster, until by October 4th the prices
of a good many stocks had coasted to what seemed first-
class bargain levels. Steel, for example, after having
touched 261¾ a few weeks earlier, had dropped as low as
204; American Can, at the closing on October 4th, was
nearly twenty points below its high for the year; General
Electric was over fifty points below its high; Radio had
gone down from 114¾ to 82½.

                                              Allen, *Only Yesterday*

   Obviously, all five paragraphs have something in
common—aspects of American life in the 1920's. Since
they all were taken from Frederick Lewis Allen's *Only
Yesterday,* an informal history of the United States in that
decade, they ably illustrate how successfully one writer
can achieve variety in the placement of topic sentences.
   They also illustrate the presence within the topic sentence of a *topic* (*what* the paragraph is about) and perhaps
a *controlling idea* (what is *said about* the topic). A good
topic sentence fixes the topic and the controlling idea; the
other sentences carry them along to develop the topic sentence. For example, the first paragraph's topic sentence
presents as topic (a phrase, in this case) the **Post-war
Decade** (that is, the 1920's) and as controlling idea, that it
was a **great sporting era.** Once *topic* and *controlling idea*
have been established as the general idea to be explored,
to be examined in more detail, the nature and function
of the rest of the paragraph are determined—and unity is
the result. Allen is obligated to supply details to illustrate
the controlling idea, **great sporting era,** in the more specific
sentences of the remainder of his paragraph; and as a responsible writer, he does just that. Look at the successive
echoes of **great sporting era: playing golf, golf courses,
players, the game, ability to play, country club, watching
sports, public's mania for sporting shows, great athletes,
the gridiron, the diamond, and the prize ring.** Each sub-

ordinate aspect of **great sporting era** is imbedded within a statement made, statistical evidence offered, or final strong assertion (which, by the way, gives a kind of climactic re-emphasis to the topic sentence).

As a way of testing this concept of *topic* and *controlling idea,* examine each of the other four paragraphs by Allen. Try underlining those parts of the topic sentence which you regard as the topic or the controlling idea, and then checking all subordinate echoes of the topic sentence.

2c 2 paragraph coherence

It is quite possible to have unity within a paragraph (that is, to have all the sentences arising from one topic) without having coherence — without arranging the sentences in a proper order or sequence or without making obvious connections between the sentences. A paragraph is coherent only when a meaningful order of the sentences prevails and when their interrelationships are clearly indicated. The major ways to establish coherence are:

1. *The order of the sentences* — an order of time or space, from the general to the specific, from the specific to the general, from cause to effect, from effect to cause, or toward climax.

2. *Transitional words and phrases* — linking words like **moreover, therefore, first, in addition, however, but, on the other hand.** Such expressions should not be overused, but they are very helpful in guiding readers through a paragraph.

3. *Repetition of key words or ideas* — echoes, variations, renaming, restating important words and phrases, all help to cement the paragraph into a coherent, understandable whole.

4. *Pronoun reference*—turning previously named phrases or words into their equivalent pronouns for the sake of variety and essential specification.

5. *Parallel structures*—conscious efforts to place similar ideas in similar grammatical or sentence forms.

6. *Consistent point of view*—maintenance of a single person, tense, and tone throughout the paragraph (unless circumstances dictate otherwise, as they have dictated occasionally in this book).

All these possibilities are strategic devices for ensuring readers' orderly progress through the paragraph. By using them in appropriate situations, the writer communicates to readers a direction of logic and meaning.

In the following paragraphs, some of these avenues to coherence are marked. You can see that the order of sentences in the first paragraph is from the specific (the founders of science and their deeds) to the general (the importance of the scientific revolution in the total history of humanity). Other devices are indicated in the margin.

The **founders** of modern **science**—**for a instance,** Galileo, Kepler, and Newton— were usually pious men who did not doubt

God's **purposes. Nevertheless they** c **took the revolutionary step** of consciously and

deliberately expelling the idea of **purpose** b

as controlling nature from **their** new c

science of nature. They did **this** on the b   c

ground that inquiry into **purposes** is use- b

a. Transitional words and phrases
b. Repetition of key words or ideas
c. Pronoun references

         b   a
less for ***what science aims at: namely,*** the prediction and control of events. To predict an ***eclipse,*** what you have to know is

 c   b   c   a
not ***its purposes*** but ***its causes. Hence***

b
science from the seventeenth century onwards became exclusively an inquiry into

b   b
causes. The ***conception*** of ***purpose*** in the

                                    c
world was ignored and frowned on. ***This,*** though silent and almost unnoticed, was the greatest revolution in human history, far outweighing in importance any of the political revolutions whose thunder has reverberated through the world.

W. T. Stace, "Man Against Darkness"

    The art of asking oneself critical questions that lead either to new answers or to genuine revitalizing of old answers, ***the art of making*** thought live anew in each generation, may not be entirely amenable to instruction. But ***it is a necessary art*** nonetheless, for any man who wants to be free. ***It is an art*** that all philosophers have tried to pursue, and many of them have given direct guidance in how to pursue it. Needless to say, ***it is an art*** the pursuit of which is never fully completed. No one thinks for himself very much of the time or in very many subjects. Yet the habitual effort to ask the right critical questions and to apply rigorous tests to our hunches is a clearer mark than any other of an educated man.

Wayne C. Booth, "Is There Any Knowledge That a Man Must Have?"

a. Parallel structures
b. Consistent point of view
   1. focus on importance of critical thinking
   2. use of present tense
   3. serious, objective tone

2c3 paragraph development

As a responsible writer, you must accept the obligation to support, illustrate, define, extend, or analyze the controlling idea of your paragraphs. In accepting that obligation, you proclaim your willingness and ability to explore the idea adequately. Although a one- or two-sentence paragraph may sometimes constitute a crisp and effective transition between longer segments of thought, generally the satisfactory paragraph will contain several (three or more) unified, coherent sentences that together form one of the patterns described and illustrated below.

a. Development by Details   This basic pattern actually embraces all other patterns, precisely because virtually any specific development of a general idea is almost bound to offer details or aspects of that controlling idea. More specifically, however, development through details means the presence of concrete aspects of the unifying idea or topic. In the description below of Miss White's second grade classroom, every sentence confirms in a specific way the "aseptic" atmosphere.

Her room, like her person, is aseptic. It is a small class, and the children's movable chairs and desks are spread about the room as far from one another as possible, as if some centrifugal force had flung them apart, each child to be suspended alone in his allotted space. On the side bulletin board, arranged with infinite precision under a frill of yellow and green construction paper, are arithmetic and spelling exercises, with the examples and the words identically positioned on each paper. On the back bulletin board, under a frill of red and blue construction paper, are the results of an art lesson, rexographed outlines of an Easter bunny bearing a basket of flowers colored in with crayons. The bunnies are all white and the baskets all blue, but there is some variation in the colors of the flowers. The children must have spent hours producing those pictures in which the colors remain so obediently within the bounding outlines. Only the irregularly printed names announce them to be products of individual, real-life children.

Miriam Wasserman, "Miss White's Second Grade"

b. Development by Example (or Illustration)   Whereas development by details is limited only by the boundaries, more or less distant, of the topic and its controlling idea, development by example has to be more selective, for it may use *only* such details as are instances or examples of the controlling idea. Ordinarily, the topic sentence of a paragraph that is developed by example introduces the general idea, and the sentences that follow offer particular examples, instances, or illustrations of that general topic.

In the paragraph about the broiling summer of 1934 on page 65, the writer encounters no problems in remembering details of the midsummer heat, but he could easily have substituted other details like the corn shriveling in the sun, the absence of water in the well, the chirping of the locusts, or the discomfort and stoic endurance of the farm families. Development by example is even more restricted than we have just indicated: such a paragraph may develop only *some* typical specific examples of an idea. For example (as we often say as we begin to expand a general *whole* by presenting less general occurrences or examples), the following paragraph about ideas that may dictate a response by action develops by giving examples first of action that would *not* make news and then of action that *would* make news. Desecration of graves and laying curses upon professors are selected as examples of acts that *would* make news if done to support political positions but would merely puzzle people if done without apparent connection to ideas. An "idea" is the *topic;* but the *controlling idea* calls for *a distinction to be made* between acts not apparently dictated by ideology and acts that are understood because they are consequences of ideas. To make that distinction clear to the reader, the writer offers several examples, familiar to anyone who read newspapers or listened to the news on radio in the 1960's, of both kinds of ideas.

An idea in itself may amount to next to nothing, but it becomes news by interfering with something else which is considered to be of public importance. In themselves, a couple of hundred demonstrators somewhere in New York or Chicago would amount to very little; but when fifty students march into a lecture hall, seize control of the podium and broadcast their claims and philosophy to people who came to hear something quite different—then they have made news. If someone advocates urinating on graves (as the Fugs did), or if a few girls dress up as witches and put curses on professors (as they did in Chicago), if they did so without reference to politics, people would rightly wonder about their sanity. But when they do so as a condemnation of the Vietnam war or in the name of some progressive cause, they win the support of many older liberals and enlightened radicals who invariably consider it all very socially significant. When a teen-ager wrestles with the police for the sake of the moral superiority of a future social order, he cannot fail to obtain the sympathetic attention of radio and television editors, if not psychiatrists. The ritualistic invocation of ideology is thus both an alibi and a defense.

Bruno Bettelheim, "The Anatomy of
Academic Discontent"

c. Development by Reasons   Development by reasons is always related to the strategy of argument. Consequently, you can make a quick and simple test of your subordinate sentences by inserting the word **because** before each sentence that seems to tell *why* the more general proposition is valid, or at least *why* you think your proposition is valid. In the following paragraph, try to determine how many sentences will accept a **because** as a preliminary to restating the general proposition that **Christianity does not constitute our best hope:**

Nevertheless I have been arguing that Christianity does not constitute our best hope, at least for our earthly future. An established religion remains by nature a deeply conservative force, not a creative one. The churches have long brought up the intellectual rear of our civilization, and despite their awakened social conscience their claims to spiritual leadership are still weakened by their engrained tendency to resist new knowledge and aspiration. Most are still disposed to a dogmatic supernaturalism that saps the intellectual honesty and courage essential for a responsible idealism. Churchmen persistently narrow our choices by equating "religious" and "spiritual," obscuring all the shriveled, deformed spirituality to be found within the churches and all the healthy idealism to be found outside them. Much of what passes for religious faith today amounts to a side bet, covering a vague belief that "there must be something" or that man needs to believe (especially when in foxholes); often it verges on sentimentality—the indulgence of feeling without commitments in thought and action. Many churchmen are trying to reanimate such faith by exploiting the theology of crisis, the ethos of fear—preaching not merely humility but humiliation. Given the historic record, we cannot be simply heartened by the possibility that the future may belong to the churches again.

Herbert J. Muller, "A Credo"

d. Development by Temporal Order, or Narrative

Whether it is found in a simple recipe or in a formal history, temporal order records events (or steps) in their chronological order—the order in which they happened. The ordering of events is perhaps the easiest kind of development to maintain or to follow; it is, of course, the staple for fiction or personal narrative, although, as the following paragraph indicates, it is often the most economical and clearest pattern for objective, expository narrative also:

By the time of his election to the Presidency in 1801 Jefferson was again considering a national university, perhaps simultaneously with one for his own state. In his annual message to Congress of December 2, 1806, he spoke of a national university, though there is no evidence of his active movement in its behalf. Exactly when he conceived his plan for a new institution in a new place, for Virginia or the nation, it is now impossible to determine. As early as January 18, 1800, he did write to Joseph Priestley concerning his plan for an up-country university. In the same year he was interested in Du Pont de Nemours' plan for a national university. Though he by no means agreed with it, it may have suggested some things he was to use. In 1806–7 he talked over with Joel Barlow that gentleman's plans for a national university. But except for the Geneva episode and the paragraph in his annual message, he did little to foster such an institution, probably because of his growing anti-consolidationist attitudes toward government generally.

Richard Beale Davis, *Intellectual Life
in Jefferson's Virginia, 1790–1830*

Development by process, often considered as a separate form of development, also usually requires a temporal scheme:

When you're ready to make a picture, you press the good-sized, electronically operating red rubber release button on the camera front. An internal mirror flies upward, the shutter mechanism operates, gears whir and a plasticized 3½-in.-square turquoise-colored picture sheet with white borders zips outward from the same slot as the cover did. If you keep pressing the button, you can take pictures at the rate of one every 1.5 sec.

The Editors of *Modern Photography*, "After All the Big Hoopla About Polaroid's SX–70, How Do Results Really Stack Up Against Older Polaroid and Kodacolor????"

e. Development by Spatial Order, or Description   Development by spatial order usually turns out to be description, but description in which the details are supplied in some sequence. The sequence of description may move

2

from left to right, far to near, up to down, or vice versa—or perhaps in a series of relationships of various objects to one important object in the scene. Such paragraphs usually begin with a fairly general statement about the scene or object to be described. Subsequent sentences fill in with details, which the writer selects because of their importance within the scene and because of their essential role in helping readers to form an accurate mental picture.

The first three sentences of the following paragraph act as a kind of camera lens which locates a residential neighborhood before the paragraph focuses on the interior of a typical Creole courtyard. Even after the sentences conduct the reader into the courtyard, more general details form a context of color, plant life, and a drowsy atmosphere. The author then makes a spatial order which we can easily "see" by relating all other details to the door, the fig tree, and the fountain.

An atmosphere of tranquillity and quiet happiness seemed to envelop the old house, which had formerly belonged to a rich planter. Like many of the Creole houses, the façade presented a commonplace and unattractive aspect. The great green doors of the arched entrance were closed; and the green shutters of the balconied windows were half shut, like sleepy eyes lazily gazing upon the busy street below or the cottony patches of light clouds which floated slowly, slowly across the deep blue of the sky above. But beyond the gates lay a little Paradise. The great court, deep and broad, was framed in tropical green; vines embraced the white pillars of the piazza, and creeping plants climbed up the tinted walls to peer into the upper windows with their flower-like eyes of flaming scarlet. Banana-trees nodded sleepily their plumes of emerald green at the farther end of the garden; vines smothered the windows of the dining-room, and formed a bower of cool green about the hospitable door; an aged fig-tree, whose gnarled arms trembled under the weight of honeyed fruit, shadowed the square of bright lawn which formed a natural carpet in the midst; and at intervals were stationed along the walks in

large porcelain vases—like barbaric sentinels in sentry-
boxes—gorgeous broad-leaved things, with leaves fantastic
and barbed and flowers brilliant as hummingbirds. A fountain murmured faintly near the entrance of the western
piazza; and there came from the shadows of the fig-tree the
sweet and plaintive cooing of amorous doves. Without,
cotton-floats might rumble, and street-cars vulgarly jingle
their bells; but these were mere echoes of the harsher world
which disturbed not the delicious quiet within—where sat,
in old-fashioned chairs, good old-fashioned people who
spoke the tongue of other times, and observed many quaint
and knightly courtesies forgotten in this material era. Without, roared the Iron Age, the angry waves of American
traffic; within, one heard only the murmur of the languid
fountain, the sound of deeply musical voices conversing in
the languages of Paris and Madrid, the playful chatter of
dark-haired children lisping in sweet and many-voweled
Creole, and through it all, the soft caressing coo of doves.
Without, it was the year 1879; within, it was the epoch of the
Spanish domination. A guitar lay upon the rustic bench near
the fountain, where it had evidently been forgotten, and a
silk fan beside it; a European periodical, with graceful etch-
ings, hung upon the back of a rocking-chair at the door,
through which one caught glimpses of a snowy table bearing bottles of good Bordeaux, and inhaled the odor of rich
West India tobacco. And yet some people wonder that some
other people never care to cross Canal Street.

Lafcadio Hearn, "A Creole Courtyard"

To be sure, none of us can expect to equal Hearn's literary
artistry in this gem of descriptive prose. But it does serve to
demonstrate the riches that lie within a restricted space,
and it does show the possibilities of even the most trivial
detail. A less formidable, and obviously contemporary,
treatment of spatial order is this paragraph:

[Austin's] leading store is Scarborough's, which was
built up by those Rockdale Scarboroughs. As you walk up
Congress Avenue, the next noteworthy object is the

Stephen F. Austin Hotel, which is rather a nice little hotel except for the perennial and somewhat demoralizing collection of flea-bitten legislators who loaf in its lobby. A few blocks on up the street is the capitol. . . . And a half mile or so farther on is big and rich Texas University, which has latterly begun to build itself skyscrapers, since living space is so restricted in Texas.

George Sessions Perry, *Texas: A World in Itself*

2

f. Development by Definition   No other mode of development is more important than definition. In your writing, you will frequently find it necessary to state clearly the meaning of a word, a concept, a process, an activity. The most basic kind of definition is the logical definition, in which you state the concept to be defined, put it into a category, and then distinguish it from all other members of that category. For example, an *editorial* belongs to the category of *article in a periodical* and may be distinguished from other kinds of periodical articles by noting that it *expresses the opinion of the editor or publisher*. In addition to using logical definition, you will also often employ examples, details, comparisons, and the like to enhance the definition of your subject. In the following paragraph, the writer defines the term **unconscious** by putting it in its category — **all the physiological changes** — and differentiating it from the other **physiological changes** by adding **which escape our notice.** He then restates this definition somewhat more precisely and adds additional observations. The result is an easily understood delimiting of a difficult abstract concept.

The term "unconscious," now so familiar to all readers of modern works on psychology, gives offense to some adherents of the past. There should, however, be no special mystery about it. It is not a new animistic abstraction, but simply a collective word to include all the physiological changes which escape our notice, all the forgotten experiences and impressions of the past which continue to influence our desires and reflections and conduct, even if we cannot remember them. What we can remember at any time is indeed an infinitesimal part of what has happened to us. We could not remember anything unless we forgot almost everything. As Bergson says, the brain is the organ of forgetfulness as well as of memory. Moreover, we tend, of course, to become oblivious to things to which we are thoroughly accustomed, for habit blinds us to their existence. So the forgotten and the habitual make up a great part of the so-called "unconscious."

James Harvey Robinson, "On Various Kinds of Thinking"

g. Development by Analysis and Classification   These two modes are related but differ significantly. Analysis divides *a whole* or *a unit* into its constituent parts, whereas classification arranges *wholes* or *units* into categories according to a selected principle or basis. Thus, we can divide a play into its three acts; the cycle of a piston engine into its four strokes; the life of a human being into childhood, adolescence, adulthood; and the federal government into the administrative branch, the legislative branch, and the judicial branch. In each of these cases, a unit is broken down — analyzed — into its components. On the other hand, we can classify watches, on the basis of where they are carried on one's person, into wrist watches and pocket watches; sports, on the basis of circumstances of payment to players, into professional sports, semiprofessional sports, and amateur sports; persons, on the basis of sex, into men and women; and roads, on the basis of what they are made of, into concrete roads, asphalt roads, dirt roads, and the like. In each of these cases, units are placed into categories according to some useful principle selected by the writer.

1. Analysis

Mine is a striking example of how dependent the individual is upon childhood. My early years allowed me to make a good start. After that it was my luck that no accident occurred to cut short the unfolding of my life; another piece of good fortune was that chance favored me extraordinarily in placing Sartre upon my path. My freedom was used to maintain my very first projects; and it has continually devised and contrived ways of remaining faithful to them throughout the variation of circumstance. Sometimes these inventions have assumed the appearance of a decision, but of a decision that always seemed to me self-evident; I have never had to *ponder* important things. My life has been the fulfillment of a primary design; at the same time it has been the product and the expression of the world in which it developed.

Simone de Beauvoir, "The Woman I Was to Be"

2. Classification

In a bygone day when men lived even more by dogma than they do now, there were two kinds of men whose special office it was to seek for and utter the truth; and they symbolize these two sides of the intellectual's nature. One was the angelic doctor, the learned schoolman, the conserver of old orthodoxies but also the maker of the new, and the prodder at the outer limits of received truths. The other was the jester, the professional fool, who had license to say on occasion for the purposes of amusement and release those things that bordered on lèse majesté and could not be uttered by others who were accounted serious men.

Richard Hofstadter, "Democracy and
Anti-Intellectualism in America"

h. Development by Analogy   Analogy is a special kind of comparison in which essentially unlike things are compared. That is, an unfamiliar concept may be explained or clarified by comparing it with a familiar concept that belongs to another category. For instance, the structure of the atom may be explained by comparing it with the solar system, God may be explained by comparing Him with a loving father, and a political campaign may be explained by comparing it with a professional football team's preparation for the Super Bowl. In the paragraph that follows, a great poet and critic clarifies the nature of the relation of a poem to its author by comparing it with a chemical reaction in the presence of a catalyst.

The analogy was that of the catalyst. When the two gases previously mentioned are mixed in the presence of a filament of platinum, they form sulphurous acid. This combination takes place only if the platinum is present; nevertheless the newly formed acid contains no trace of platinum, and the platinum itself is apparently unaffected: has remained inert, neutral, and unchanged. The mind of the poet is the shred of platinum. It may partly or exclusively operate upon the experience of the man himself; but, the more perfect the artist, the more completely separate in him will be the man who suffers and the mind which creates; the more perfectly will the mind digest and transmute the passions which are its material.

T. S. Eliot, "Tradition and the Individual Talent"

i. Development by Comparison and Contrast   A comparison shows the similarities between things; contrast shows the differences. Two methods are available to you in comparing or contrasting A and B: (1) you may take up all the properties of A and then all the properties of B, or (2) you may take up one of the properties of A and then one of B, a second of A and a second of B, and so forth, alternating between A and B. In the illustrations below, the comparison paragraph uses the second method, and the contrast paragraph uses the first method.

1. Comparison

As I passed from innocent childhood into uncertain adolescence, I became suddenly aware of the totally opposed temperaments of my parents. My father, gentle and absent-minded, liked to read poetry aloud in the evenings and to bring from the public library records of classical

2

music to be played on Sunday afternoons. My mother, always briskly efficient and really contemptuous of the aesthetic enthusiasms, always had about her some kind of handiwork — knitting, mending, sewing on buttons, reversing worn collars and cuffs of our shirts — when she wasn't immersed in kitchen chores or adjusting figures in her household ledgers. He liked to watch the progression from bud to leaf to bloom in his small garden; she was interested only in the herbs and sturdy vegetables that grew in her larger and neater plot. I never heard them quarrel, but neither ever changed. Until his death just before I graduated from high school, Father remained the complete romantic dreamer; Mother, even to this day, deplores any symptom of impracticality or, as she calls my love of ballet and music, "self-indulgence." Under ideal circumstances, perhaps Father would have been a fine artist; and if she could have been whatever she wished, Mother surely would have been the head "efficiency expert" for the erring human race.

Student theme

2. Contrast

In the past it has been only in war, in defense of one's own country or one's ideals, that any people have been able to invoke total commitment. Then it has always been on behalf of one group against another. This is the first time in history, that American people have been asked to defend ourselves and everything that we hold dear, *in cooperation* with all the other inhabitants of this planet, who share with us the same endangered air and oceans. This time there is no enemy. There is only a common need to reassess our present course, to change course, to devise methods by which we can survive.

Margaret Mead, "A Crisis, a Challenge:
Energy and Ecology"

j. Development by Cause and Effect   Determining the causes of effects or the effects of causes is one of the most basic acts of thinking and writing. What caused the South to secede from the Union, what caused Hamlet to delay in avenging his father's murder, what caused the formation of the Mississippi River Valley, what caused my essay to receive an F? Conversely, what effects did basketball's new goal-tending rule have, what effects did his sales pitch have, what political effects did the Watergate scandal have, what effects did Wordsworth's poetry have on nineteenth-century England? The ease with which one asks questions such as these suggests that the cause-and-effect pattern is not only a basic mode of development but also an important means of generating ideas. The first paragraph below states several causes and their effect; the second states a cause and its several effects.

Compaction led to violent collisions of the atoms at the centers of the gas balls. The temperatures became so great that electrons were stripped from protons in the constituent hydrogen atoms. Because protons have like positive charges, they ordinarily electrically repel one another. But after a while the temperature at the centers of the gas balls became so great that the protons collided with extraordinary energy—an energy so great that the barrier of electrical repulsion that surrounds the proton was penetrated. Once penetration occurred, nuclear forces—the forces that hold the nuclei of atoms together—came into play. From the simple hydrogen gas the next atom in complexity, helium, was formed. In the synthesis of one helium atom from four hydrogen atoms there is a small amount of excess energy left over. This energy, trickling out through the gas ball, reached the surface and was formed. There was light on the face of the heavens.

Carl Sagan, "Starfolk: A Fable"

The battle with Mr. Covey was the turning-point in my career as a slave. It rekindled the few expiring embers of freedom, and revived within me a sense of my own manhood. It recalled the departed self-confidence, and inspired me again with a determination to be free. The gratification

afforded by the triumph was a full compensation for whatever else might follow, even death itself. He only can understand the deep satisfaction which I experienced, who has
himself repelled by force the bloody arm of slavery. I felt as
I never felt before. It was a glorious resurrection, from the
tomb of slavery, to the heaven of freedom. My long-crushed
spirit rose, cowardice departed, bold defiance took its
place; and I now resolved that, however long I might remain
a slave in form, the day had passed forever when I could be
a slave in fact. I did not hesitate to let it be known of me, that
the white man who expected to succeed in whipping, must
also succeed in killing me.

Frederick Douglass, "On Slavery"

2c4 opening and concluding paragraphs

Every good essay will have a clear beginning, middle, and
end, but many writers who have no trouble with the middle
often find beginning and ending the essay difficult. Chapter
3, "The Essay," is a detailed discussion of this entire subject; here, let us briefly offer some simple but useful advice about opening and concluding paragraphs, together
with two examples. The opening paragraph of an essay
should accomplish two things: (1) introduce the topic and
(2) interest the reader. The concluding paragraph should do
one or more of three things: (1) finish the matter, (2) summarize, or (3) end gracefully. In the two pairs of illustrations that follow, the opening paragraph both introduces
the topic and interests the reader in it, and the concluding
paragraph both finishes the treatment of the subject and
rounds off the essay.

a. Opening Paragraph

Joey, when we began our work with him, was a mechanical boy. He functioned as if by remote control, run by
machines of his own powerfully creative fantasy. Not only

did he himself believe that he was a machine but, more re-markably, he created this impression in others. Even while he performed actions that are intrinsically human, they never appeared to be other than machine-started and exe-cuted. On the other hand, when the machine was not work-ing we had to concentrate on recollecting his presence, for he seemed not to exist. A human body that functions as if it were a machine and a machine that duplicates human func-tions are equally fascinating and frightening. Perhaps they are so uncanny because they remind us that the human body can operate without a human spirit, that body can exist without soul. And Joey was a child who had been robbed of his humanity.

Concluding Paragraph

One last detail and this fragment of Joey's story has been told. When Joey was 12, he made a float for our Memorial Day parade. It carried the slogan: "Feelings are more important than anything under the sun." Feelings, Joey had learned, are what make for humanity; their ab-sence, for a mechanical existence. With this knowledge Joey entered the human condition.

Bruno Bettelheim, "Joey: A 'Mechanical Boy'"

b. Opening Paragraph

From all available evidence no black man had ever set foot in this tiny Swiss village before I came. I was told before arriving that I would probably be a "sight" for the village; I took this to mean that city people are always something of a "sight" outside of the city. It did not occur to me—possibly because I am an American—that there could be people any-where who had never seen a Negro.

Concluding Paragraph

The time has come to realize that the interracial drama acted out on the American continent has not only created a new black man, it has created a new white man, too. No road whatever will lead Americans back to the simplicity of this European village where white men still have the luxury of looking on me as a stranger. I am not, really, a stranger any longer for any American alive. One of the things that distinguishes Americans from other people is that no other people has ever been so deeply involved in the lives of black men, and vice versa. This fact faced, with all its implications, it can be seen that the history of the American Negro problem is not merely shameful, it is also something of an achievement. For even when the worst has been said, it must also be added that the perpetual challenge posed by this problem was always, somehow, perpetually met. It is precisely this black-white experience which may prove of indispensable value to us in the world we face today. This world is white no longer, and it will never be white again.

James Baldwin, "Stranger in the Village"

2

3

the
essay

The term *essay* may sound forbidding at first, but its root meaning (an attempt or a weighing) and its characteristic form are perfectly in accord with its use in responding to a demanding examination question, writing a unified letter, structuring an argument on paper, or recording directions for a particular process. As we know the essay today, it is nothing more than a form of nonfictional writing usually composed of several paragraphs (although some seventeenth- and eighteenth-century essayists sometimes wrote brief pieces of only one long paragraph). When you take pen in hand or confront the typewriter to write an essay, you accept two obligations:

1. to inform your readers
2. to interest them in the topic you have chosen

Stating those seemingly obvious obligations may risk oversimplifying the actual work and care that go into the writing of an essay, but anything less than constant recognition of those basic obligations usually results in the reader's confusion and boredom. Writing even a bad expository essay takes some time and effort; but with attention to the process and with practice, you can acquire a skill that will become progressively habitual and less agonizing.

3a choosing a subject

You will not be able to write an effective essay unless you can answer "yes" to two basic questions:

1. Do I know enough about my subject to write several pages of expository (that is, informative) prose?
2. Can I summon feelings, attitudes, or tastes adequate for the subject?

The first question may seem elementary enough; indeed, the topic may be assigned to you and embrace a fund of information you've acquired from reading other writers. Yet people will often start on the impossible task of informing others about things they themselves don't understand — a classic case of the blind leading the blind! Generally, having at your disposal more information than you can actually use puts you in the comfortable position of being able to choose details. If you are writing about a movie, for example, don't start writing until you've seen it (preferably, more than once) and know all the details about the characters, setting, plot, direction, photography, technique, and source. If you're writing to inform your readers — the only justification for expository prose — you may need information about the history, purpose, value, and liabilities of the subject. You may choose to take a definite position in an argument; again, you need a large number of details to support your opinion. Often you are asked to write a response to an essay you've read for a class assignment; before you begin to organize your own response, your obligation is to study the piece carefully for both expressed and implied meanings, for the specific details that support those meanings, and for the author's opinion and degree of success in arguing that opinion.

A positive answer to the second question above is equally important. You cannot write engagingly unless you yourself are *engaged* in what you're doing. The dismal alternative is dead prose. Take some time to consider your feelings: are you hostile, indifferent, or attracted to the subject you've chosen (or that has been chosen for you)? Do you care whether an idea about the subject is communicated to other people? Do you have an opinion on a controversial issue? Does it make any difference whether you honestly set forth the facts that will convince or alienate your readers? If your answer is a strong "yes," you are well on the way to grappling successfully with an idea and to sharing it appealingly with a reader.

Expository writing is calculated neither for amusement

nor for boredom. It should always be interesting; and only as your personality and viewpoint are present in your writing will the reader have a sense of sharing experience and thought with you.

3b organization of the essay: beginning, middle, and end

You have surely noticed that objects and processes in the realms of art and nature have structures. Your understanding and appreciation of objects as diverse as a novel and a seashell depend upon your discovery of the structure of each—the principle or system that unifies the various parts into a whole. An essay, too, is an object that should possess a comprehensible structure, and your first task as a writer is to consider the two elements which support and reveal that structure: organization and thesis.

It's conceivable that during your college career you will be asked to write an extended definition of such abstract terms as **beauty, freedom, capitalism, honor, novel of ideas, liberal.** How will you go about treating one of these abstract terms? Happily, although you are perhaps unaware of it, you already understand the basic strategy for dealing with this topic. That is, you know that your fundamental pattern is, quite simply,

I. Beginning
II. Middle
III. End

Aristotle offered this pattern for organizing a subject well over 2,000 years ago, and no later rhetorician has improved on it. Even though it may seem quite obvious, and perhaps even a bit simplistic, you can save yourself much grief, not to mention poor themes, if you will resolve now to make it work for you. Applying it to the problem at hand, we see that your essay defining, say, **liberal,** and indeed all your essays, will consist of three distinct parts, each of which is essential to the whole.

Part I, the Beginning or Introduction, will introduce the topic and inform your readers about the method you will use to handle it. In the case of an essay defining **liberal,** announcing the topic might be no problem, but moving from there probably would be. You may well think, "How much easier writing an essay would be if I could describe something familiar, like one of my golf clubs!" But there *is* no real difference in approaching the two subjects. Very likely you know exactly how to organize a description of a golf club. You simply break it up into its components. Then, your beginning or opening paragraph would introduce the subject and state that the golf club is composed of three main parts — the shaft, the head, and the grip. Your structure would look something like this:

I. Beginning	I. A Golf Club
	A. Shaft
	B. Head
	C. Grip
II. Middle	II. Body
III. End	III. Conclusion

Now common sense tells you that Part II, the Middle or Body, would consist of one or more paragraphs about each of the three main parts mentioned in Part I. If that's the case, the structure would now look like this:

I. Beginning	I. A Golf Club
	A. Shaft
	B. Head
	C. Grip
II. Middle	II. Shaft
	III. Head
	IV. Grip
III. End	V. Conclusion

You have probably noticed that this random order lacks emphasis. It would be more effective to order the three elements according to some significant pattern. For example, you could rank the parts in the order of their importance and then treat them in that order. But this strategy for describing the golf club is rather pointless, for its basic parts are equally important. A more functional ordering principle would be the arrangement of the parts, or the spatiality, of the golf club itself. Thus, you could begin at one end of the club and proceed to the other end, in which case you would start with the part nearest to the golfer, the grip, move on to the shaft, and then to the head. This organization, while not the only one possible, does make sense since it grows out of the subject itself. A writer in search of organization first looks closely at the subject to see how *it* is organized. If the form of an essay is in some way an accurate reflection of the form of its subject, something important has been accomplished already. Your revised structure would now look like this:

I. Beginning	I. A Golf Club
	A. Grip
	B. Shaft
	C. Head
II. Middle	II. Grip
	III. Shaft
	IV. Head
III. End	V. Conclusion

Having devoted a paragraph to each of the fundamental parts, you would then be ready to complete the shape of the essay by adding Part III, the End or Conclusion. This final part, often just a paragraph, is largely a matter of wrapping up the essay and departing as gracefully as possible. This final section may summarize, if a summary is necessary, or enclose the subject for your readers in a convincing and satisfying way. In the case of the golf club, a brief restatement of the description would most likely suffice. The important thing, of course, is to let the reader know that the business of the essay is finished.

But we set out to discover how to cope with the job of defining **liberal.** Is the method for analyzing and organizing a description of a golf club applicable to an essay on this topic? The answer is "yes, indeed," if that method includes one additional and extremely important tactic. Let's observe how. First we think of the essay as a structure composed of three major parts: Beginning or Introduction, Middle or Body, and End or Conclusion. The Beginning, as we have seen, introduces the topic, divides it up into its essential parts or subtopics, and arranges these parts in some significant order. The Middle consists of one or more paragraphs about each of these subtopics in the order established in the Beginning. The End generalizes or summarizes or, at least, informs the reader that the discussion is concluded. Whether the essay is short or long, simple or complex, about a golf club or the term **liberal,** this structure is fundamental.

However, applying this pattern to our term poses a problem not encountered with the previous topic. A description of a golf club is a subject of manageable proportions, but a definition of **liberal** quite obviously soars far beyond the bounds of a 500-word essay. Consequently, you must cut the subject down to a controllable size, or *limit* it severely. Instead of writing a definition of **liberal,** perhaps you should define **American liberal,** using a geographical or spatial limitation. But the topic is still of epic proportions. Let's narrow it further to **American liberal in the 1920's,** using a time limitation. Having got rid of whole continents and centuries full of different types of liberals, you are getting somewhere, but still the subject resists definition in a 500-word essay. On the other hand, you suspect that you have done enough to locate your subject in space and time (who would want to write—much less read—a final essay called "Some Famous Liberals Living in East Springfield, Illinois, on September 26, 1923"?).

3

At this point you recall the success you had with the description of a golf club. In that case, there was no need to limit the topic. And so, working on the principle that the form of the essay should reflect the form of its subject, you broke the golf club down into its components and organized your description around their spatial arrangement. That principle of natural form will also work here—not only for organizing your topic, as was the case with the description of the golf club, but also for further limiting the topic. The term **liberal,** you conclude, has to do primarily with a certain set of attitudes toward life, particularly toward society. If the social sphere is most crucial to the definition of **liberal,** then you could decide to work with one segment of the social structure—the highbrow. By further narrowing the topic to **highbrow American liberal in the 1920's,** you have made yet another improvement, perhaps a more important improvement than you yet realize. In addition to eliminating what you won't say, you have already determined to some extent what you will say and what the form or organization of your essay will be. In other words, limiting the topic and organizing the essay on the topic are closely related.

Having limited your topic to **highbrow American liberal in the 1920's** and determined in the process that the social dimension is most important in your definition, you are ready to begin using the fundamental structure. As we've seen, the Beginning will introduce the topic and direct the reader's attention to the principal subtopics. To point up the social emphasis that you want, you might make the following assertion about your topic: "The designation **highbrow American liberal in the 1920's** means 'exile' and is spelled 'l–o–s–t.'" Notice how this assertion, called the *thesis* (a combination of the *topic* and the controlling idea—see 2c1, page 69), serves to limit your topic still more. That is, while your subject is a definition of **liberal,** your thesis is your assertion about the subject after you have narrowed it to manageable size—the **highbrow American liberal in the 1920's** as social outcast. Here, you see, is the fundamental difference between organizing the essay defining **liberal** and the essay describing a golf club — a difference that is really the key to all effective writing. The need for limiting your subject by *narrowing* and *asserting* cannot be mentioned too often or stressed too much. For, once this process has been carried out, believe it or not, the rest is almost easy. Thus, racking your brain for just a moment would most likely produce at least four subtopics — (1) social attitudes, (2) political attitudes, (3) religious attitudes, and (4) life style (tastes in clothing, entertainment, and other material areas).

Now, what will the ordering principle for these subtopics be? Since time and space are not immediately involved, the most natural organizational principle is the logical movement from the least important of the subtopics to the most important or from the one you want to stress least to the one you want to stress most. And, by previously deciding to deal with these liberals as alienated from society, you have already committed yourself to social attitudes as the main dimension of your essay. But even apart from intrinsic considerations this emphasis is warranted, since whatever else it was, the 1920's was a decade when Americans were "kicking up their heels" and questioning nearly all of the accepted social views. If the most important of the subtopics is social attitudes, then it will be dealt with last, or at the point of climax. The remaining three subtopics can then be ranked in the order of their social significance. Of these, the life-style subtopic is probably the least important because it is the most subject to fad and whim. It is a tossup as to which of the other two — political attitudes and religious attitudes — has the more social significance. Let's say that you settle on a scheme that stresses, with increasing intensity, life style, religious attitudes, political attitudes, and social attitudes. The complete structure of the essay — for either a description of **golf club** or a definition of **liberal** — derived as naturally as possible from the substance and form of the topic itself, becomes finally:

I. Beginning	I. A Golf Club	I. *Highbrow American*
		Liberal in the 1920's
	A. Grip	A. Life style
	B. Shaft	B. Religious Attitudes
	C. Head	C. Political Attitudes
		D. Social Attitudes
II. Middle	II. Grip	II. Tastes in Clothing, etc.
	III. Shaft	III. Religious Attitudes
	IV. Head	IV. Political Attitudes
		V. Social Attitudes
III. End	V. Conclusion	VI. Conclusion

3

The Beginning, or Introduction, broaches the subject and states the thesis; the Middle, or Body, consists of one or more paragraphs about each of the subtopics arranged as shown; and the End, or Conclusion, completes the business in whatever appropriate fashion the writer chooses.

So you see, the basic pattern works as well for a complex and abstract topic like the definition of **highbrow American liberal in the 1920's** as it does for a simple and concrete topic like the description of a **golf club.** Once you have mastered this method, you may use it to organize an essay on *any* topic. Furthermore, as you gain experience, you will learn how to refine and vary this basic organizational pattern. But at the outset, unless you have another scheme for writing tightly structured and logically organized essays, use this general outline form, sometimes called the *five-paragraph theme structure:*

    I. Beginning or Introduction of TOPIC (limited to
       THESIS)
       A. SubTOPIC 1
       B. SubTOPIC 2
       C. SubTOPIC 3
   II. SubTOPIC 1 ⎫
  III. SubTOPIC 2 ⎬ Middle or Body
   IV. SubTOPIC 3 ⎭
    V. End or Conclusion

It clearly demonstrates the properties of all effective writing:

1. Each part contributes to the whole or supports the thesis (unity).

2. All parts are logically arranged and clearly connected (coherence).

3. The parts furnish adequate explanation and illustration of or support for the thesis (development).

This organizational plan will help you get the most out of your ideas.

3c types of development for essays

We have been talking about the structure of the essay—really about the requirement of *unity* and some means of achieving unity. But, as was mentioned, an essay must also have *coherence,* an internal logic or principle by which the parts fit into an understandable sequence of ideas and details. Essential in maintaining coherence is the conscious choice of a pattern of *development.*

An essay, like a paragraph, usually has one dominant mode of development. That is, the basic kind of development within the essay is dictated by the nature of the central idea (telescoped by the thesis) and the writer's decision to handle and arrange the subject in a certain way—to compare two or more things, persons, or ideas; to define a concept; to argue for a position; to illustrate abstractions with specific events or physical details; to show the relationships of parts to a whole; to trace the steps of a process; or simply to chart a series of events or to describe objects, behavior, or scenes.

Of course, we do not mean that *only one* kind of development will ever be present in an essay: it is often hard to separate narrative (a pattern of events in a time sequence) from description (what we have called "spatial order" in Chapter 2), or to distinguish definition from argument, or details from process. When two or more modes of development continue throughout an essay, we can speak of a "mixed mode," although even then one mode is probably more basic than the other mode or modes. The mode you choose, almost automatically in terms of the goal you have set in your thesis statement, is a kind of cement for your essay; it persists from paragraph to paragraph and thus links them in a sequence dictated by the internal logic of the composition.

Since the types of possible essay development are exactly the same as those we discussed for the paragraph (see section 2c3), we see no point in repeating them. We suggest, however, that you review those types and this time try to see them as ways for organizing paragraphs into entire essays. Even the kinds of transitional words or phrases that we pointed out as ways of linking the sentences within a paragraph can operate to provide transitions within the larger form of the essay. The only real difference is that paragraphs now function within the essay as sentences function within the paragraph.

Now, here's a theme written recently by a student to analyze a short poem. As you examine the writing assignment and the student writer's response to it, consider these questions:

1. Does the writer provide a clear beginning, middle, and end?
2. What does the writer do to achieve unity and maintain coherence? What mode of development is paramount? Do the separate paragraphs relate clearly to the whole theme?
3. Do you agree with the commentary that follows the theme?

3d sample student essay

The writing assignment: Read carefully the poem by Delmore Schwartz reprinted below. Your object in writing an essay about the poem should be to partition or analyze the poem in such a way that your essay becomes a statement and explanation of the poem's theme, in 600–1,000 words. Introduce and conclude the essay interestingly and appropriately. Above all, clarify for your reader the essential duality of the human being that Schwartz dramatizes in this poem.

The Heavy Bear Who Goes With Me

"the withness of the body"

The heavy bear who goes with me,
A manifold honey to smear his face,
Clumsy and lumbering here and there,
The central ton of every place,
The hungry beating brutish one   5
In love with candy, anger, and sleep,
Crazy factotum, dishevelling all,
Climbs the building, kicks the football,
Boxes his brother in the hate-ridden city.

Breathing at my side, that heavy animal,   10
That heavy bear who sleeps with me,
Howls in his sleep for a world of sugar,
A sweetness intimate as the water's clasp,
Howls in his sleep because the tight-rope
Trembles and shows the darkness beneath.   15
—The strutting show-off is terrified,
Dressed in his dress-suit, bulging his pants,
Trembles to think that his quivering meat
Must finally wince to nothing at all.

That inescapable animal walks with me,   20
Has followed me since the black womb held,

Moves where I move, distorting my gesture,
A caricature, a swollen shadow,
A stupid clown of the spirit's motive,
Perplexes and affronts with his own darkness,   25
The secret life of belly and bone,
Opaque, too near, my private, yet unknown,
Stretches to embrace the very dear
With whom I would walk without him near,
Touches her grossly, although a word   30
Would bare my heart and make me clear,
Stumbles, flounders, and strives to be fed
Dragging me with him in his mouthing care,
Amid the hundred million of his kind,
The scrimmage of appetite everywhere.   35

"That Inescapable Animal"

"The Heavy Bear Who Goes With Me" by Delmore Schwartz is an anguished cry from the noble spirit which is man seeking relief and separation from his gross body, which also happens to be man. By dividing the human personality into the animal and the spiritual, Schwartz, by means of image and metaphor, closely parallels in the poem the classical theological understanding of man as composed of body and soul. And with the older thinkers, the poet understands the unreasonable demands which the body often makes and the struggles in which the soul or spirit must engage to realize its highest aspirations. Appropriately enough, the metaphor chosen in the poem to convey or suggest the qualities of physical or material man is a bear. Schwartz could have chosen any animal for his purpose, and at first glance, one might suppose that the most apt metaphor would be the most man-like of animals—an ape, for example—but Schwartz sees the exact analogue for man's brutish nature in the bear, indeed a heavy bear. To represent man's higher or spiritual nature, the poet employs only the speaker of the poem, or *persona*, and the poem itself, a lament for the lumbering and irrational tyrant who holds the *persona* prisoner.

The bear of the poem may not be a realistic bear, but no one really cares very much. The brute delights in satisfying his appetites and never seems to be filled up. When he has satisfied his desire for food, he falls asleep, soon to be again awake and full of desires. When blocked from his sensual and gross pleasures, he roars with anger and strikes out wildly and blindly at the sources of his frustrations. But underneath the beastly exterior is a coward of gigantic proportions, matching in every way his other capacities for eccentric and disproportioned behavior. Yet he is master rather than mastered; he directs rather than being directed. Without goals other than low appetites, the bear "stumbles, flounders, and strives to be fed." Such is, as the short epigraph suggests, "the withness of the body." In fact, so overwhelming is this hulking monster, so cataclysmic are his actions, so great is the destruction that he leaves in his wake that one rather finds Schwartz's analysis of the human being unbearably (to use a bad pun) pessimistic. But what of the other part of the human being? What of the voice which laments and would discipline the bear?

That which is not "bear" or material or the senses is the spirit or what is sometimes called the soul. Where the body is irrational, the spirit is rational; where the flesh is gross, the spirit is refined; where the body seeks but low motives, the spirit longs for the ascendant and the noble. The immaterial mind or spirit of man aspires to a much more elevated life than instinctual existence. It would love rather than hate its brother; it would pursue the ideal without distortion or caricature. The mind of man, in short, would rule the unruly passions. To establish clearly this distinction between the realms of spirit and animal, the poet speaks of love between a man and a woman. The *persona* conceives of his love for the woman as existing only on the level of their two minds, such that their motives and desires toward each other are chaste and pure. But even as he would tell her of this love, the bear within him "touches her grossly" and debases his love for her to just another appetite to be fed, another gross delight dragging him away from the undefiled and virtuous. The unruly bear is a "heavy bear" indeed.

The poem's cry for release from the brute echoes the cries of many persons, for as the last two lines of the poem assert, there are literally a "hundred million of his kind" engaged in (to use a very apt metaphor) "the scrimmage of appetite everywhere." It is not only the *persona*'s plight to be plagued by the animalistic, the irrational, and the "descendental"; it is the plight of all men, in whom the mean and the trivial are entangled with the noblest motives, aspirations, and hopes. Nor can the spirit of man, idealistic though it is, contain the beast, which disorders all. But whether or not Delmore Schwartz expects the individual to enforce a change by placing the spirit in command of the passions need not concern the reader much. What does concern him is that the extended metaphor of the "bear" clarifies man's essential double nature and allows him to understand better his nature or "the way things are."

Commentary. In this essay the student has modified the "five-paragraph theme structure" to reflect the structure of his topic. The introduction states that the poet divides the human personality into the body and the soul, and it attempts to engage the reader in this subject. The body of the essay devotes one paragraph to the body and one paragraph to the soul struggling to be free. This order emphasizes, quite appropriately, first the "given" and then the response to the "given." The conclusion reiterates the theme and suggests its importance to the reader. The mode of *development* of the essay, of course, is *analysis:* the writer selects one aspect of the poem, the theme of humanity's dual nature, and divides it into its parts — body and soul — for discussion and explanation. The essay is serious, in keeping with the seriousness of the issue; it is reasonably detailed but focused (never going beyond the boundaries of Schwartz's poem) and confident, assuring the reader that the writer knows what he is talking about; and its length satisfies the requirements specified in the assignment. Although at first glance this essay may seem to be simply a literary paper and thus to belong in Chapter 4, the writer's intention is not literary analysis but rather an examination of an idea that merely happens to be in Schwartz's poem. One minor note: the title of the essay is within quotation marks only because it is a phrase drawn from the poem itself.

the
critical
essay

4

In some ways, writing themes about the literature that you read in a college course involves less uncertainty than writing about subjects of more general interest. For one thing, the subject is more specific: it's a particular novel, short story, play, or poem. For another, it's manageable and handy: the book, the text of the poem, or the script of the play is at hand on your desk and can be consulted as often and as intently as you wish. Finally, you can assume that your readers are interested in the subject, because the book has been discussed in class or because you've picked it as an example of a literary type assigned in the course syllabus.

If your writing experience has not included a "critical paper" or "literary analysis," don't panic. Either term simply means a written evaluation or explanation of one literary work or perhaps a comparable aspect of several works. Such evaluations make use of the principles of good, interesting composition that we've been exploring throughout this book. The only important difference is in the restricted subject matter and in some special ways of looking at literature. This chapter offers suggestions for planning and developing papers about literary works— suggestions that we hope will be useful in writing success- ful critical exposition and will increase your pleasure and competence in reading literature. After a little experience you will discover that the possibilities for interesting and informative literary criticism are virtually unlimited. But while you are learning how to write about literature, you should concentrate on the main approaches.

4a major approaches to writing about literature

4a1 the summary

The simplest approach to a literary work is the condensa- tion of its content—what is often called a *précis*. For fiction, a summary involves little more than a restatement in your own words of what happens to the characters—the *plot* of a short story or a novel. Obviously, you do have to know and understand what goes on within the text of any literary work before you can tackle any other critical approaches. Writing a clear summary might be either a formal assignment or your own means of checking on your grasp of sheer content. Such a summary might become an important step *toward* analysis; however, it should not be offered *as* analysis. In the summary you would concentrate on certain aspects of the work.

a. Lyric Poem   For a summary of a lyric poem (that is, a poem that emphasizes feelings or a response to feeling—that concentrates on an idea or an emotion as opposed to dramatic situations or storytelling in verse, the province of *narrative poetry*), you would reduce the poem's language to your own prose "translation" of the stages of the poem's development. You would consider questions like the following in summarizing a poem:

1. Can a speaker be identified, if not by name perhaps by temperament and manner? If the speaker does not appear to be a rather direct "voice" of the poet, it may be called a *persona*—a voice or character deliberately created by the poet for the occasion of the poem. For example, the *personae* of Robert Frost's more familiar poems— "Birches," "Mending Wall," or "Stopping by Woods on a Snowy Evening"—should not be confused with Frost himself, although Frost and the *personae* he creates have common bonds in the New England rural background and experience, a tendency toward irony, and the brooding over the meaning of a scene or act.

2. To whom—a lover, a friend or foe, countrymen or humanity in general—does the speaker address his or her thoughts, hopes and fears, response to landscape?

3. Is a problem suggested, and does a solution appear likely? The fourteen lines of a sonnet, for example, charac-

teristically establish an issue in the first part of the poem and a response or solution in the second part.

4. Are there identifiable stages in the poem's developing "argument" or "sentiment"?

b. Work of Fiction   For a work of fiction (a short story, a novel, a narrative poem, a film or a play), you would relate the characters in a particular setting of time and place to a series of events (what is usually called *plot*) which have a peak, a crisis or *climax,* and a resolution of the situation. The summary can be as short as a paragraph or two; if, however, the assignment or the work's complexity seems to demand it, the summary might very well require two or three pages.

4a2 the book review

Going at least one step beyond mere summary and into evaluation, this highly popular kind of discussion of books appears in most Sunday metropolitan newspapers and in many popular as well as quality magazines. The book review characteristically includes much summary in the form of considerable revelation of content—especially characters, setting, and plot for a work of fiction—followed by a judgment, preferably with clear reasons for the judgment, about the book's success in achieving the author's purpose or its possibilities for interesting the reader. A review of a minor or ephemeral book may be justifiably short—perhaps no more than two or three paragraphs. A review of an important and interesting book may be extended over several pages. Writing book reviews can be a valuable prelude to writing more complex forms of literary analysis, because it obliges you to *know* your subject, the book, well; to describe its contents and structure; and to make a case for its excellence or shortcomings. In reviewing a book, you should consider these points:

a. The Genre (or Literary Type) Is the book a novel (perhaps a special kind such as science fiction, historical novel, spy or detective thriller, Gothic romance, or novel of manners), a collection of short stories or poems, a drama, a series of essays, a biography or memoir, a history, or a nonfictional presentation of a body of knowledge (science, photography, stagecraft, sex problems, or whatever)?

b. The Structure Is there a time sequence or flashback, an order for imparting information, increasing complexity of plot or knowledge, or a principle of relationship among the parts?

c. The Style Is the use of language characterized by a richness or poverty of expression? Does the writer seek to establish an identifiable relationship with or to appeal to readers? Is language attractively displayed in complex sentence or paragraph structures? Is the language primarily concrete (description, scene-setting, images of particular things and people) or abstract and scholarly?

4

d. The Content Is there a recognizable plot (in a novel) or typical situation (in a collection of short stories), a recurring attitude or body of imagery and symbolism (in a collection of poems), a multiplicity of subjects (in a group of essays)?

e. The Level of Readership Will the book appeal to a special age or interest group? Is it more suitable for the general reader, a particular professional group, or people with a high level of education and experience?

f. A Judgment or Recommendation Why should the book interest a reader? Is it apparently original? Is it just entertainment, or is it a sophisticated, informative book? Should it be taken seriously? (In newspaper and magazine reviews, of course, the question is whether a reader should want to buy the book or look for it in the public library; reviews you write should consider the interests of college students at your level; but any book review should either make readers want to spend time in reading the book or convince them that the book is unimportant or even completely worthless.)

4a3 literary analysis

Instead of merely summarizing the bare content of a literary work, in an analysis you must adopt a point of view toward some aspect of the work. The difference is like that between merely telling chronologically what happened in a football game and explaining the special role of the defensive team or the evidence of the coach's new strategy in Prairie University's startling win over Desert Tech. Some possibilities for analysis are suggested by these considerations:

a. Lyric Poetry 1. What is the poem's tone? Is it melancholy, playful, angry, rhapsodic, enthusiastic, excited, fearful, sentimental, grim, or ironic? Does the poem convey an identifiable attitude toward its subject? These subordinate but necessary questions should be answered to reveal *how* you identified tone:

   a. What clues to tone are found in the choice of words? Is there a pattern of connotation (the emotional or suggestive overtones of a chosen word—for example, **broad** for **female; shepherd** for **poet** in pastoral poetry; **egghead** for **intellectual**)?
   b. Does the language reflect extensive learning (for example, allusions, big or pretentious words, the language of the highbrow), an attitude toward experience (for example, enthusiastic, honest, pessimistic, comic), an expectation of a response from the reader (sympathetic, involved, prejudiced, liberal)?

2. What is the poem's interior "*form*" — the logic or intention that relates the separate parts of the poem to the whole?

   a. What images are central in the poem? Do the images form a pattern of relationships? Do the images point toward something beyond their own literal, concrete meaning?
   b. Does the poem take on the form of argument, definition, explanation, invitation, rejection, glorification, debate, or reminiscence? If so, what are the means by which this form is developed? Can you point out a sequence of steps within the poem that establishes the form?

b. Work of Fiction   Nearly everything said above about lyric poetry is applicable to the analysis of fiction.

Stories of all sorts — even narrative poems (long ones like Homer's *Iliad* or relatively short ones like Robert Frost's "The Death of the Hired Man") — reveal a *tone*, the author's attitude toward the subject and perhaps toward life in general. Homer's epic celebrates Greek ideals of honor, loyalty, courage, endurance, and manhood, and rejects the qualities of dishonor, disloyalty, cowardice, and undisciplined temper; Frost's poem honors an old man's pride in craftsmanship and a farm woman's tenderness even as he ironically lays bare the old hired man's compulsiveness and his need for a home. As in lyric poetry, of course, language is the primary key to tone; but the selection of characters and the events in which they reveal themselves and their motives become even more important in fiction.

Fiction also necessarily contains and reveals an internal "form." The kinds of situations an author selects and the way in which he or she permits a resolution to some conflict reveal a "form" by which all the parts — characters, plot, setting, tone, and theme — manage to become an apparent whole. If the events, their crisis, and their resolution are accounted for by the author too easily despite seemingly serious obstacles, you may properly charge the author with *naiveté,* the kind of gross oversimplification often found in fairy tales, or even with a *sentimentality* that rewards all the good characters, punishes or reforms the wicked, calls for a reaction of tearful pity in the sad parts and sunny smiles at the triumph of virtue. Sometimes the work of fiction may achieve a form that parallels an age-old myth such as the initiation of youth into the tribe (as in Henry Fielding's *Tom Jones,* Nathaniel Hawthorne's "My Kinsman, Major Molineux," and Charles Dickens' *David Copperfield)* or the search for the father figure (as in Herman Melville's *Moby Dick* and *Redburn* and James Joyce's *Ulysses).* Some serious fiction, particularly recent works, more nearly resembles the form and texture of dream than logically developed, realistic narrative (for example, Edgar Allan Poe's "The Fall of the House of Usher" and John Barth's "Lost in the Funhouse"). Often form can be identified by seeing it as a *voyage*—a spatial voyage (for example, Jonathan Swift's *Gulliver's Travels* and Richard Henry Dana, Jr.'s, *Two Years Before the Mast);* or perhaps a psychic voyage (for example, Walt Whitman's *Song of Myself* and Hart Crane's *The Bridge);* as a *process* or *becoming* for the central character (as in Charles Dickens' *David Copperfield* and *Great Expectations);* as an *encounter* that changes him or her forever (for example, Henry James's "The Turn of the Screw"); or as a relationship of character to a symbolic detail—perhaps a building (as in Hawthorne's *The House of the Seven Gables* or Poe's "House of Usher") or an object (Hawthorne's *The Scarlet Letter).*

4a4 kinds of analysis

Although we have conceded that the possibilities of narrative are as numerous and varied as are literary genres, details, devices, techniques, plots, themes, methods of characterization, and forms, we wish to suggest here only some of the most practical kinds of analysis:

a. Analysis of Character Especially in fiction, where characters are paramount, analysis may examine them from a number of viewpoints: their major or minor roles with respect to the central situation or plot, their identification with setting, their psychological problems, their symbolic or allegorical functions, and their interrelationships with other characters. If they are stereotyped ("flat" characters) or highly individualized ("round" characters), you can explain *how* or *why* they are thus made by the author.

b. The Value of Setting In any literary work, we find some indication of time and place, or *setting*. The time may be generalized as merely a broad period—for example, the second half of the twentieth century; and place may be no more restricted than a middle-class living room in the Midwest. If there is a clear sense of place, you might explain how the setting conditions character or colors the central issue of the work. Does the setting play a role in the conflict (for example, in Washington Irving's "Rip Van Winkle" and "The Legend of Sleepy Hollow," most of Thomas Hardy's Wessex novels, James Fenimore Cooper's novels of the American wilderness, or Mark Twain's *Huckleberry Finn*)? Does a particular landscape determine the quality of people and their experiences within it? Does the setting contribute to or necessitate a mythical experience (that is, a recurring human experience, like a hero's pursuit of knowledge, as in Herman Melville's *Moby Dick;* John Steinbeck's *The Grapes of Wrath;* or the initiation of a youth in the ways of the world, as in Twain's *Huckleberry Finn*)?

c. The Identification of Theme Every imaginative literary work has its underlying meaning—its occasionally stated, usually implied, but always somehow present comment about human nature and experience. Although the theme may have to be inferred from the details—a certain kind of experience undergone by a certain kind of character—the theme itself is usually stated in abstract terms by the writer of a critical essay; for example, you might come away from a reading of Irving's "Rip Van Winkle" with the awareness that "An escape from the loud and restrictive world into nature is tempting, but such escape exacts the penalty of losing touch with the passing of time, with possible experience, and even with the self." That would be your statement of the work's theme. If the recognition of the work's underlying idea is to be persuasively advanced to your readers, you must take the responsibility for showing how the parts of the work—characterization, setting, plot, imagery, and structure—support your interpretation of the theme.

For this last kind of analysis, a student wrote a paragraph interpreting the theme of William Carlos Williams' famous little poem "The Red Wheelbarrow," the text of which follows:

> so much depends
> upon
>
> a red wheel
> barrow
>
> glazed with rain
> water
>
> beside the white
> chickens.

And the student paragraph:

In a striking but simple image, which reminds us of a still-life painting, Williams calls the attention of his reader to the importance of seeing things exactly as they are. The wheelbarrow, the chickens, and the rain are named individually: each exists in its own right. But together they form a scene, neither exotic nor remote but familiar and homely. The wheelbarrow and the chickens present to the eye of the speaker — and to the reader through the poem — a scene bright with the primary colors of red and white. The rain, which apparently is no longer falling, has "glazed" the wheelbarrow and thus accented its perceived freshness and brightness. Mere contemplation of the scene, either by the eye of the speaker or the imagination of the reader, is a joy in itself. But the first three words of the poem, "so much depends," suggest caution or warning by speaker to reader. The moment of contemplation must take in the impact and unity of the little scene no matter how common its elements may seem.

4b major approaches to writing longer critical essays

Up to this point we have been stressing ways to look at specific features of literary works and to come to grips with relatively limited questions — usually features and questions that can be dealt with in a good paragraph or two. Now let's discuss some of the many and potentially valuable considerations in planning longer papers (from perhaps four to ten pages) about literary experience.

4b1 relation of the work to the author's life

Mark Twain's childhood in the frontier community of Hannibal, Missouri, and his experiences in young manhood as a riverboat pilot on the Mississippi River supply many of the details, characters, and attitudes in *Adventures of Huckleberry Finn*. Any biography of Twain would reveal some of the correlations between the author's own experiences and the content of his works. Likewise, it is known that John Keats was fascinated by the Elgin marbles, the statuary and other art objects brought from Greece to the British Museum; obviously, his enraptured contemplation of those marvels of classical Greek art is reflected in the tone of excitement and the details of description in his "Ode on a Grecian Urn."

We could choose any author's life for tracing its echoes in his or her work: his or her place of birth and development, awareness of social and political issues, notions of how and for what ends people live and work, understanding of nature and its endless process, store of human types and variety. In short, from their lives, including their reading of other authors, writers select details of plot and theme by which they tell us what experience seems to mean. Jane Austen found English country life as she had experienced it adequate for the materials of all her novels. Walt Whitman remembered virtually every detail of his life, even material found in newspapers and magazines, and recorded it in the imagery of his poems. Hawthorne had in mind a specific house in Salem, Massachusetts, as the model for his *House of the Seven Gables,* and the somewhat gloomy history of his own family as the foundation of his certainty that the past exercises a negative influence on those trying to live abundantly in the present. Of course, an exact transcript of a life gives us an autobiography, but the poet and the fiction writer borrow freely from life even though they try heroically to deny it or transform it into art.

4b2 social, economic, or political context of the work

Closely related to the facts of authors' experiences and to their memories of the past are the ideas that flourish during their lives and to which they feel either commitment or hostility. Writers respond, as all people must in some degree, to the political causes, economic forces, and social issues of their time; and those responses are very likely to be present in their writing. Indeed, some works cannot be satisfactorily understood without some knowledge of the crises that generated or at least animated them. John Steinbeck's *The Grapes of Wrath* vividly reflects the poverty, despair, and dislocation that attended the Great Depression of the 1930's in general, and the plight of sharecroppers in the Southwest and Midwest and their exploitation at the hands of California fruitgrowers in particular. American poets in the late 1920's wrote angry verse in response to the conviction and execution of Sacco and Vanzetti.

If political and social issues interest you, you can gauge the involvement of authors in political, social, even religious causes from biographies of them or their contemporaries, from letters, or from diaries, journals, and notebooks (if they have been collected and published). It will not surprise many people to learn that Thoreau was passionately opposed to slavery and consequently to the Mexican War; but if you take the trouble to discover the issues that divided the American people in the 1840's and 1850's, Thoreau's "Civil Disobedience" and even his masterpiece, *Walden,* will take on additional eloquence and meaning. In such an effort, of course, you would need to read political history of the United States as well as books about Thoreau to establish the social and political implications of his works. Some authors are more obviously political than others: politics did not seem to interest Ernest Hemingway much until he wrote *To Have and Have Not* in the 1930's and *For Whom the Bell Tolls* after the Spanish Civil War. Much English poetry of the eighteenth century requires a knowledge of contemporary political controversy for satisfactory understanding; much American poetry in our own day rarely hints of political implications.

4b3 the literary genre

Literary works, as we suggested earlier, can be profitably considered from the standpoint of their adherence to or deviation from the norms established for and expected in a particular literary *genre,* or category. For example, novels and short stories have conventions of plot, characteriza- tion, and relationships of *narrative* (those parts of works of fiction in which the author simply tells the reader what has happened or what is in the minds of the characters) to *dramatic situation* (the "scenes" of the novel or short story in which the characters talk and act out a particular epi- sode); these fictional conventions require a kind of analysis markedly different from that given to a sonnet or ode. Lyric poetry, however, requires attention to its use of heightened language, to its imagery and possible sym- bolism, to its tone, and to its theme (the "statement" it makes about experience and feeling). Narrative poetry (epics and ballads), depending on length and complexity, shares much common ground with the short story and the novel. But still there are the poetic qualities of intense language, *rhythm* (involving *rhyme* and *meter,* the pattern of stressed and unstressed syllables), and *sound* (patterns of vowel and consonant sounds) that lend themselves to investigation and analysis.

Though we said earlier that genres usually should be treated separately, we do recognize the *occasional* value of considering relationships between one genre and an- other; for example, novels like James Fenimore Cooper's *The Prairie* or *The Last of the Mohicans* display traces of epic treatment and convention, as do Herman Melville's *Moby Dick* and Leo Tolstoy's *War and Peace.* That is, plot, setting, theme, and characters acquire national, racial, or tribal dimensions; upon them depends the fate of a people and perhaps an entire culture (as in Homer's *Iliad*), the triumph or defeat of a whole way of life, perhaps even con- tending forces for the allegiance of humankind (as in John Milton's *Paradise Lost*), Western civilization, American aspirations. The scenery of crucial events is vast and per- haps awe-inspiring; the characters may speak in lofty flights of noble language — language, idiom, allusions that mirror their epic roles (as in *Beowulf*); and large questions of nationality, race, sexuality, or perhaps art itself are at issue. James Joyce's *Ulysses* echoes Homer's *Odyssey* so deliberately that we see Leopold Bloom's hours of wandering about the city of Dublin as a parallel to Odysseus' ten years of wandering about the Mediterranean Sea after the conquest of Troy. Many of the long and complex poems of the twentieth century — T. S. Eliot's *The Waste Land,* Ezra Pound's *Cantos,* Hart Crane's *The Bridge,* and William Carlos Williams' *Paterson* — are sometimes called "neo-epics" in order to justify the narrative structures amid their larger lyrical qualities. In the "neo-epics" of our time, an important consideration for the critical reader is *how* and *where* in the poems are found the echoes of, and the most startling departures from, traditional epic conventions — long serious narrative of the adventures of a national or racial hero; heroic deeds; intervention of supernatural forces like gods or angels; elevated language. In the eighteenth century, burlesques of heroic poetry (for example, Jonathan Swift's *Battle of the Books* and Alexander Pope's *The Rape of the Lock*) treated relatively trivial issues in the grand style of epic for the amusement of readers who would recognize the burlesques.

4b4 patterns of imagery and symbolism

Because of the associations consciously and some perhaps unconsciously suggested by the river and the raft in Twain's *Huckleberry Finn,* particularly as those idyllic associations are obviously contrasted with the deceitful and sometimes sordid life experienced whenever Huck and Jim go ashore, we begin to see that the river and the raft point to something much more complex than a specific river in the heart of the United States or a particular object used to navigate that river. As we come to recognize that the river suggests the greater reality of a free, vital, and spontaneous nature (of which the river is obviously a part), we recognize the *symbolism* of the river. In Keats's "Ode on a Grecian Urn," the urn is symbolic of something like the poetic imagination, which transmits to the receptive spectator a unified "beauty" and "truth"; but the poem is also full of *images* (appeals to one or more of the physical senses) such as the procession of villagers, the ardent lover pursuing a female, and the heifer being led to sacrifice. Patterns, whether of symbols or of images, when established, point toward meaning and form, particularly when we begin to sense that such patterning indicates a "life of its own within the work," the dynamics of a world that was shaped by the particular consciousness of the work's author. Neither Twain nor Keats has to tell us specifically *what* the symbols and images suggest, for we can *know* at least a portion of their meanings by the context that surrounds them, by the ways in which they relate to each other, and by our own responses to them.

4b5 patterns of myth

Certain basic aspects of human experience and human response to the surrounding world recur or seem to recur endlessly. In all societies, from the most primitive to the most sophisticated, the same experiences recur: a youth's movement from childhood into adulthood (the myth of "initiation"), the perception of death and rebirth in the natural cycle (and by hopeful analogy, in the human dimension), the journey of the culture hero (Ulysses, Aeneas, Captain Ahab, Huckleberry Finn)—perhaps through a dark underworld or over treacherous waters to a "home" or to knowledge. These recurring events are formalized into rituals (ceremonial dances, fasting or feasting, offering sacrifices to a deity, and the like) and into narratives that preserve each kind of experience and transmit it from generation to generation. Such narratives are called *myths,* and the recurring figures of hero and natural forces (ocean; summer; the barrier—often a river—that separates life and death; perhaps a white whale or a crucifixion scene) are called *archetypes*—original patterns or models—because they seem to recur in and to have profound meaning for all societies in all eras. The presence of myths of death and re-birth in the modern novel *Moby Dick* resounds as pro-foundly as it does in an ancient Greek narrative of Perse-phone's descent into the realm of Pluto. When Eliot in *The Waste Land* alludes to a fisher-king and his blighted realm, he assumes that we will recall the tales of Adonis, Osiris, and Christ; the associated quest for the Holy Grail adds to the poem all the richness and meaning of Arthurian ro-mance. These echoes within probably the most famous poem in this century reverberate with the initiation of inno-cence into knowledge, the psychic journey into an under-world of darkness and danger, the parallels of sickness and omens of death in humanity and nature, and the loss of a garden and the effort to regain it, the links between mean-ingful sexuality and religious vision. Finally, *Huckleberry Finn, Moby Dick, Heart of Darkness,* and Hawthorne's short story "My Kinsman, Major Molineux" retell in their particular contexts the myth of initiation.

4c conventions and mechanics of quotations in the critical paper

In addition to the mechanics of paragraphing and punctua-tion, which apply to any good prose, in your papers on literature you will undoubtedly have to consider the spe-cial conventions and mechanics of using quotations. (See the more general discussions of paragraphing on pages 63–91 and of punctuation on pages 248–262.)

4C1 justifying the quotation

Because the literary work is made of words—at its best, of striking and memorable words—you will wish from time to time to call attention to the particular language of the work itself in your critical papers. You are justified in quoting passages or parts of passages for the attention of readers whenever you have a significant point to make about that language or whenever only the original words of the work will suffice to say what you want to say.

Most of the time a citation—preferably brief—of a part of the work itself will come by way of direct and exact quotation; and in such a case, you are obligated to establish a suitable context for the quotation. That is, you must introduce it in such a way that your readers will understand perfectly the point of the quotation and will receive from the quotation the insight that you want them to receive. The unassimilated quotation is largely meaningless to the reader: it simply says in effect, "Here's a passage from the work; make what you can of it." In that case, readers might do better simply to read the literary work itself; they are certainly getting precious little help in analyzing it from the writer of the critical essay. Sometimes the careless writer will simply start quoting without any notice at all to readers that there is a point to be made by the quotation, or will make some feeble introduction like "At this point in the poem Keats says" or "To quote from the poem." Neither helps readers at all. But such ineptness, such timidity, such uncertainty need never be a problem if you ask yourself—and in effect answer the question by the way you point up the quotation—"*Why* do I wish or need to quote from the work at this point?" And if you will use good sense in answering that very important question and base your statement to readers on it, you will have succeeded in making clear the significance of and reason for the quotation. Consider some of the following possibilities for introducing quotations:

1. In a paper that aims to explore Keats's use of paradox (apparent contradiction) in "Ode on a Grecian Urn," you might frame—and thus justify—direct quotation in this way:

Keats early hints at the ideal nature of the urn by calling attention to its superiority over ordinary life in its simultaneous eloquence and silence:

> Thou foster-child of silence and slow time,
> Sylvan historian, who canst thus express
> A flowery tale more sweetly than our rhyme (ll. 2–4)

or

Keats immediately establishes the paradoxical nature of the urn and thus its superiority to any human agent by addressing it as a "still unravish'd bride" (l. 1).

2. In a paper that considers the role of nature as the beneficent force opposed to society in Twain's *Huckleberry Finn,* you could cite a famous passage or parts of it in the following ways:

Typically, whenever Huck speaks of the river, he emphasizes its tranquility and repose: "Not a sound, anywheres—perfectly still—just like the whole world was asleep, only sometimes the bullfrogs a-cluttering maybe" (p. 140).

or

For Huck and Jim the river signifies freedom from the restraints of St. Petersburg and of civilization in general:

Here is the way we put in the time. It was a monstrous big river down there—sometimes a mile and a half wide; we run nights, and laid up and hid day-times; soon as night was most gone, we stopped navigating and tied up—nearly always in the dead water under a tow-head; and then cut young cottonwoods and willows and hid the raft with them.

Then we set out the lines. Next we slid into the river and had a swim, so as to freshen up and cool off; then we set down on the sandy bottom where the water was about knee-deep, and watched the daylight come. Not a sound, anywheres—perfectly still—just like the whole world was asleep, only sometimes the bullfrogs a-cluttering maybe" (p. 140).

4C2 the quotation as rhetorical strategy

Used skillfully, the quotation from the literary work can be a great asset to you as you progress through the stages of your paper.

1. The quotation acts as a guide to accuracy and direction by keeping the writer close to the literary text; thus, the quotation is a check on validity and coherence.

2. The quotation keeps the reader thinking along the lines the writer desires; it tends to prevent the development of other patterns of interpretation as it focuses on the pattern you have chosen.

3. The quotation makes the reader consider only your interpretation, suggested by the quotation presented in its proper context, and "turns off" other possible interpretations.

4C3 conventions of quotation

You have probably already observed in the quotations above that there are two different forms. The form is chosen primarily on the basis of the length and nature of the material to be quoted.

a. Quotations Within the Body of the Paper Relatively short quotations—less than 100 words of prose or three or four lines of poetry—can simply be incorporated

into the body of your discourse and set off from your words
by quotation marks. For quotations of more than one line
of poetry, indicate the separation of the lines by a virgule,
or slash mark (/). Consider the following example:

Huck's decision to secede from society is unequivocal:
"But I reckon I got to light out for the Territory ahead of the
rest, because Aunt Sally she's going to adopt me and
sivilize me and I can't stand it. I been there before" (p. 328).

A very short quotation—a part of a line or part of two
lines of poetry or a clause or phrase, sometimes an entire
prose sentence—can be made a part of your own sentence
and thus does not require the very formal colon to set it
off from your words. For example,

Huck has decided that he has "got to light out for the Territory" (p. 328).

Among the other roles of the Grecian urn in communicating insight to men in the modern world, Keats calls it a
"Sylvan historian, who canst thus express / A flowery tale
more sweetly than our rhyme" (ll. 3–4).

b. Quotations Separated from the Body of the Paper

Longer quotations—100 words or more of prose and more
than three or four lines of poetry—are conventionally set
off from the body of the paper by a colon, indented, and
typed double-spaced. Such quotations do not require
quotation marks unless the marks are part of the original
material which you are quoting. Consider the following
example of such formal quotation:

Twain's memories of his childhood in frontier Missouri
became the source of his most profound convictions about
the nature of the world and of the people who inhabit it.
One critic has observed that Hannibal and the river, as remembered and translated into literary setting, contained
all the necessary polarities of the great world beyond:

But in his books about boys—and this partly explains their greatness—he [Twain] accepts the whole of boy nature, good and bad. In Hannibal he had seen both aspects of life. In Hannibal he had witnessed scenes of brutal violence, of absolute terror, of superstitious fear; and, because it remained for him both a summer idyl and a dark ground of horror, Hannibal was always the most fruitful setting for his work. The boy's world that he remembered had been full of charm; and yet his submerged consciousness recognized the dangers that had lurked beneath that surface of charm. Tom Sawyer's St. Petersburg, lying between the forest and the river, seems filled with a slow golden peace. It *seems* so. Jackson's Island was his Shangri-La; but it was not a safe island, for life is not safe. Out of his steady apprehension of the terror of life, he wrote into the book that embodies his village idyl . . . grave-robbing, revenge, murder, robbery, drowning, starvation, witchcraft and demonology, the malevolence of Injun Joe, and the fear of death that grips Tom and Becky lost in the cave and awaiting death in the dark. But after their emergence from the cave, the sun shines again and life goes on, much as before.[1]

c. Inserting Material into Quotations   The quotation must reflect the original source *exactly*, word for word. You can, however, insert explanatory information—the identification of a pronoun (for example, the identification of Twain as the person referred to as **he** in the first sentence of the preceding quotation), a notation that the spelling or the factual basis of the original is incorrect, the insertion of an obvious word accidentally omitted from the original, or the addition of a word needed for grammatical or

[1] Gladys Carmen Bellamy, *Mark Twain as a Literary Artist* (Norman, Okla.: University of Oklahoma Press, 1950), p. 332.

rhetorical sense. You make such an editorial insertion simply by placing it within brackets. The brackets tell the reader that they contain matter not present in the original quotation. The Latin word **sic**, meaning "thus," is inserted within brackets when you wish to inform the reader that an error in spelling, grammar, or fact appears in the original and is not your mistake. Because frequent use of **sic** is tiresome for your reader, you should consider paraphrasing any sentence or passage that would otherwise be weighted down with **sic.**

d. Omitting Material from Quotations   The visual signal for omissions from an otherwise exact quotation is the *ellipsis* — three spaced periods (. . .). If the omission occurs after a complete sentence of quoted material, put the original end mark of punctuation (period, question mark, or exclamation point) in its proper place, immediately after the last word, and then follow it with the three spaced periods. If the quoted sentence ends in a period, there would be four periods — one for the ending of the sentence as a part of the quotation followed by the three spaced periods to indicate ellipsis.

If you are omitting words from the end of a sentence, insert the three spaced periods where the omission occurs, and then add the period, question mark, or exclamation point that punctuates the sentence.

Suppose, for example, we decided to omit parts of the quotation about Mark Twain. We might use ellipsis in the following manner:

> But in his books about boys . . . he [Twain] accepts the whole of boy nature. . . . In Hannibal he had seen both aspects of life. In Hannibal he had witnessed scenes of brutal violence, of absolute terror, of superstitious fear; and, because it remained for him both a summer idyl and a dark

> ground of horror, Hannibal was always the most
> fruitful setting for his work. . . . Tom Sawyer's
> St. Petersburg, lying between the forest and the
> river, seems filled with a slow golden peace.

This passage contains omissions from within a sentence, from the end of a sentence, and after a complete sentence.

4d sample student critical essay

Usually the assignment for a critical paper on literature is very specific, and accordingly you should follow very closely the terms of the assignment. The important requirements — kind of paper, length of paper, critical approach — must be met fully. Carol Salvo, an undergraduate student at the University of Kansas, accepted as her assignment a careful explication (interpretation of the main verbal features — diction, tone, imagery, sound, rhythm, and the interrelationships of all these) of the following poem:

[anyone lived in a pretty how town]

> anyone lived in a pretty how town
> (with up so floating many bells down)
> spring summer autumn winter
> he sang his didn't he danced his did.
>
> Women and men(both little and small)
> cared for anyone not at all
> they sowed their isn't they reaped their same
> sun moon stars rain
>
> children guessed(but only a few
> and down they forgot as up they grew
> autumn winter spring summer)
> that noone loved him more by more

when by now and tree by leaf
she laughed his joy she cried his grief
bird by snow and stir by still
anyone's any was all to her

someones married their everyones
laughed their cryings and did their dance
(sleep wake hope and then)they
said their nevers they slept their dream

stars rain sun moon
(and only the snow can begin to explain
how children are apt to forget to remember
with up so floating many bells down)

one day anyone died i guess
(and noone stooped to kiss his face)
busy folk buried them side by side
little by little and was by was

all by all and deep by deep
and more by more they dream their sleep
noone and anyone earth by april
wish by spirit and if by yes.

Women and men(both dong and ding)
summer autumn winter spring
reaped their sowing and went their came
sun moon stars rain

                                    e. e. cummings

The Cycle of Life

by

Carol Salvo

English 322
Mr. Henderson
6 May 1978

The Cycle of Life

In "anyone lived in a pretty how town," e.e. cummings presents, on one level, a definition of society, the attitudes and behavior of the men and women who compose that society, and the convention—bound cycle of their existence; on a more specific level, the poem is concerned with two individuals, "anyone" and "noone," their problems among "someones" and "everyones," and their great love for one another which culminates in a rich spiritual existence after death.

The poem begins with the introduction of "anyone" in the first stanza. The second stanza defines the difference between "anyone" and the rest of the people in the "pretty how town":

> Women and men(both little and small)
> cared for anyone not at all
> they sowed their isn't they reaped their same
> sun moon stars rain

The other people in the town do not care for "anyone," probably because he is different from everyone else: where they are concerned with the practical limits of conventional existence, "anyone" is capable of experiencing a childlike joy in life and his surroundings. The sterile nature of the commonplace existence led by the people of the "how town" is revealed by the contrast between the poet's descriptions of them and his description of "anyone." For example, "anyone's" ability to respond fully and naturally to life and to love is contrasted with the fact that the women and men of the town "cared for anyone not at all." This line suggests that not only do the people mistrust

the character called "anyone" in the poem,
but they are also incapable of experiencing a
deep love of the sort that gives meaning to
the lives of "anyone" and "noone" in this
poem. The absence of love which gives a
spiritual dimension to the relationships
between women and men leads to the practical
and rather meaningless sexuality implied
by the bawdy pun contained in "Women and
men(both dong and ding)," and also perhaps in the line "they reaped their sowing
and went their came." This sexuality is practical because it makes possible the new cycle
of life that is implicit in the poem's final
stanza, but its limits are indicated by the
fact that the final stanza ends with the refrain "sun moon stars rain," which is used
throughout the poem to mark the narrow, practical aspect of the concern that "Women and
men(both little and small)" feel for their
dull, everyday business. The refrain that is
used to differentiate "anyone's" perception
of his existence from the conventional conception of the townspeople is "spring summer
autumn winter," which suggests a larger, more
expansive response to life. The "dong and
ding" that is associated with the "Women and
men" of the final stanza also recalls the "up
so floating many bells down" that charac-
terizes "anyone's" life. The lilting music of
his bells is emphasized by contrast with the
dullness of the bells in the last stanza.

   In "Anyone's How Town: Interpretation as
Rhetorical Discipline,"[1] S. John Macksoud
suggests that "pretty how town" can be interpreted to mean a town that is concerned with

_____

   [1]S. John Macksoud, "Anyone's How Town: Interpretation as Rhetorical Discipline," Speech Mono-
graphs, 35 (March 1968), 73.

the pragmatic "how" of life, with questions
of function rather than of essence; thus,
"pretty" would act as an adverb, modifying
"how" and conveying the sense of "rather,
quite," instead of an adjective modifying the
noun phrase "how town." This reading seems to
be more consistent with the way the townspeople are presented in the poem. Still, we
can have it both ways: "anyone," with his
natural ability to find beauty in life, is
surely capable of finding beauty even in a
"how town."

Throughout the poem "anyone's" understanding of and joy in life are shown to be those
of a child, but a child who does not "forget
to remember" the magic he had recognized when
he viewed the world through fresh eyes. This
childlike personality is, perhaps, that of
the artist, the creative personality. David
R. Clark notes that the phrase "he sang his
didn't" suggests that "anyone" is capable
of taking the disappointments and frustrations
of life and turning them into music, or art.[2]

Every affirmation that "anyone" makes, it
seems, is countered by a negation on the part
of the townspeople. Whereas "anyone" "sang
his didn't" and "danced his did," the people
of the town "sowed their isn't they reaped
their same." The result of their sowing and
reaping is predictable: they sow negation and
reap the same—i.e., they reap what they sow,
which in this case is a lifeless, conventional mode of existence, marked by sameness
rather than by individuality. This idea is
echoed in the next to the last line of the
poem by "reaped their sowing and went their
came." This line not only reminds us that

[2] David R. Clark, "Cummings' 'anyone' and
'noone,'" Arizona Quarterly. 25 (Spring 1969), 38.

these people are bound to reap what they have
sown;it also ties in this cycle of sameness
and negation with the recurring cycle of life
that operates on the most general level of
the poem: "they went their came" suggests
that the common folk of the pretty how town
are trapped into retracing their own foot-
steps instead of breaking out of their dull
routine into a fresh, individual existence
such as that achieved by "anyone" and
"noone."

The main reason for "anyone's" and
"noone's" ability to escape this cycle of negation is simply that they share an honest
and selfless love. In fact, "noone" so completely merges her identity with that of
"anyone" that she becomes anyone only, and no
one in her own right. Paradoxically, though
"noone" seems to be a "nobody" to the "someones" and "everyones" who make up the popu-
lation of the how town, her relationship with
"anyone" gives a meaning both to her life and
to his that is lacking in the lives of everyone else in the town. Although the rest of
the townspeople obey conventional standards
of behavior ("someones married their everyones"), which seem to lead them to the love-
less sexuality of the last stanza, there is
no mention made of marriage for "anyone" and
"noone." Yet their union is so profound and
so complete that "anyone's" death (if it even
can be called "death"—the speaker of the poem
is not quite sure about it) becomes "noone's"
death:

    one day anyone died i guess
    (and noone stooped to kiss his face)
    busy folk buried them side by side
    little by little and was by was

Her physical existence ceases with his. The thoughtlessness of the townspeople may be indicated by the fact that they "bury" "noone" alongside "anyone," even before she has died, it seems. This suggests not only that "noone" does not exist without "anyone," but also that those who have always viewed her as a no one deny her existence even more thoroughly after the death of "anyone." The view the townspeople take of what they have buried is presented in the final two lines of this stanza: what has been was very little, and it is all over and in the past now. Yet the next stanza carries us beyond the physical death of the lovers to suggest the spiritual culmination of their love:

> all by all and deep by deep
> and more by more they dream their sleep
> noone and anyone earth by april
> wish by spirit and if by yes.

Their love and the meaning it gives to their lives continue to grow even beyond death. The suggestion of spiritual rejuvenation and its relation to the natural life cycle is conveyed by "earth by april / wish by spirit and if by yes." All the uncertainties of life, "wish" and "if," are replaced by spiritual affirmation. "They dream their sleep" now, which suggests that this culmination is eternal and cannot be touched again by death.

The present tense of "they dream their sleep" contrasts sharply with the past tense used in "they / said their nevers they slept their dream." The negations in the lives of the townspeople become realities, they are articulated; but the dreams, those seeds of beauty that are contained within each soul

4

and which are most clearly recognized by
children, are never realized but are left
dormant. The cycle that "anyone" and "noone"
have traced has led them to a state of fulfillment. But the cycle followed by the other
people in the poem, "(sleep wake hope and
then)," is incomplete, broken by the negation
that is articulated in the very next line.

The essential movement of "anyone lived in
a pretty how town" seems to operate, then, on
two levels. The general cycle of life is contained in the refrains and in the open-ended
structure of the poem. The first stanza introduces "anyone"—he is "born," so to
speak. The stanza ends with a period and is
followed by a capitalized initial letter in
the next line, which signals that a new cycle
is about to begin. The poem, in a sense,
zooms in for a close-up of the lives of "anyone" and "noone," follows them to death and
then beyond that to the spiritual fulfillment that is the result of their great love.
The stanza that marks the completion of this
individual cycle ends with a period, and a
new cycle is begun with the opening line of
the final stanza, which echoes the opening of
the second stanza and is also capitalized. In
this stanza, the process of birth that is
necessary to the new cycle is suggested by
the words that imply the sexual relationship
between men and women, although our interpretation of what this cycle will mean to
most people is colored by the difference
we have seen between the meaning that
"anyone" and "noone" find in their lives
and the emptiness that the other people
in the town find in theirs. The seasonal
refrain ends with "spring," a further
sign of the imminence of the new cycle, and

```
the daily refrain ends with "rain," which
also suggests the fertilization of the earth.
     The fact that two people have managed to
separate themselves from the emptiness that
characterizes the lives of most people and,
by becoming one, to find meaning in a deep
and selfless love suggests that there is hope
in future cycles also for people who can
learn to love. As cummings shows in his poem
"if everything happens that can't be done,"
it is love that gives meaning to everything
else in life and that separates the indi-
vidual from the masses. And love consists of
the merging of two people into a single iden-
tity, as "anyone" and "noone" have done:
     "there's nothing as something as one"
```

                      BIBLIOGRAPHY

```
Clark, David R. "Cummings' 'anyone' and 'noone.'"
   Arizona Quarterly, 25 (Spring 1969), 36-43.

Macksoud, S. John. "Anyone's How Town: Interpreta-
   tion as Rhetorical Discipline." Speech Monographs,
   35 (March 1968), 70-76.
```

Ms. Salvo relied very little on secondary, or outside, critical commentary; therefore, she was obligated to use only a minimal number of footnotes and very short bibliography for her paper. Forms of footnotes and bibliography are covered thoroughly in the next chapter, on the research paper.

4

5

the research paper

In many courses in college you will be asked to write a "term paper" or "research paper." Quite often your ability to gather facts, judge their value, and put them together convincingly will be a significant measure of your progress in the course, of your readiness to handle and interpret information, of your willingness as one educated person to communicate knowledge to other educated people. We need not linger on the "practical" aspects of learning to do research, for you already know that professions, vocations, and even serious hobbies rely heavily on the interchange of valid information. As a reliable citizen in a community, you may be asked from time to time to make a speech before a civic club or organization or to write an article for the local newspaper or a study group. In short, throughout your college years and afterward you will need skill in using libraries, securing the most pertinent information, and assembling that information into an orderly and convincing whole.

5a selecting a topic

In college your instructors may assign a topic for the research paper. But if you have any choice at all, try to select a topic which you already know a little about, which you have some interest in, which perhaps promises you a valuable learning experience. Your hobby, major academic subject, intended vocation, or simple curiosity may direct your choice of a subject. The more experience you bring to research, the greater will be your satisfaction in gathering material—facts, opinions, arguments, or various sides of a controversy. It can be very exciting to gather information and then shape it into a paper of your own.

5a1 assessing your prior interest and knowledge

Let's say your freshman English instructor presents your class with this list of possible topics for a research paper:

America's energy crisis
Nationalization of the railroads
Ghetto poetry
Equal rights for women
Stock theater in the 1970's
Posthumous restoration of citizenship for Robert E. Lee
The community college movement in your state
The rise of Pop Art
American ragtime music
The single-lens reflex camera
Whale hunting in the 1970's
The case for gun controls
The influence of Common Cause
Louisiana Cajun culture today
Strip mining
The history of the local "little theater"
"Adult" movies: art or pornography?
American Indian art
Italic calligraphy

This list taps several areas of knowledge — sociology, politics, the fine and popular arts, technology, history, economics, science. You are probably already somewhat interested in one or more of these topics. But before committing yourself to a choice, you should ask yourself about the depth of your interest and the extent of your present knowledge (if any). Even casual reading of a daily newspaper or a weekly newsmagazine will open up topics that engage your interest — perhaps some aspects of the topics listed above.

Let's say you're interested in black composer Scott Joplin's ragtime music. As you assess your interest in and present knowledge of the topic, try writing a few sentences for your own use about your reasons for interest and your present fund of information. Such an inventory might look something like this:

Liked Joplin's music used in sound track of *The Sting*
Bought an album of Joplin's rags

Read news story about last summer's ragtime festival at
Sedalia, Missouri
Heard broadcast of Joplin's opera, *Treemonisha*

Such a relaxed consideration of your interest in and basic
knowledge of a topic will certainly help you to determine
the degree of your enthusiasm and the prospects for successful pursuit of additional information and intellectual
profit.

5a2 restricting the topic

The topics, as they stand, are typically rather broad. The
usual length of a college research paper is 3,000 to 4,000
words, or ten to twelve double-spaced typed pages (more
pages for handwitten papers, usually). If your instructor
recommends that length, you would have to divide or
refine any of the hypothetical topics listed above and almost any topic that you might think of. To cut down the
scope of a paper, you might restrict the topic in *time* (for
example, ghetto poetry in the 1920's), in *place* (ragtime
at the Sedalia festival), or in *number,* by focusing on an
individual's role within the larger subject (Scott Joplin's
role in the development of American ragtime). Any reasonably restricted scope will help to make the topic manageable in a paper; otherwise, you'll be struggling with a
massive subject that might require hundreds of pages or
perhaps even volumes for adequate treatment. You probably don't want to write a book on the numerous efforts
made between 1870 and 1975 to restore General Lee's
citizenship, and your instructor wouldn't have time to
read it anyway. You could handle much more successfully the efforts made on Lee's behalf within the last ten
years. So, realistic restriction of the topic is sensible and
necessary before you can make an outline of or begin to
write the paper.

But maybe you don't know offhand how you can restrict the topic. Let's say that you've decided to write

5

about Scott Joplin and ragtime; you've heard the sound-track of *The Sting* and some of the many recent recordings of Joplin's rags, and now you want to know more about Joplin's career. Before you can settle finally on the scope of the paper, perhaps you'll do a little preliminary reading to discover the possibilities for restricting the subject. In any case, you can follow a procedure somewhat like the one used in *partitioning* a topic (see pages 93–102): you can break the more general topic into its increasingly more specific parts. And those parts may simply not be available to you until you've done some preliminary reading.

Nor can you plan to write on a given topic unless you're sure your library contains adequate reference material on it. You may need to check the resources not only of your college library but also of any nearby public or other college library. Moreover, you can seek information from fellow students or people in the community who might be able to give you enough information to set you on your way. Perhaps a local pianist or a collector of records of Joplin's music could tell you something useful about the history and technical aspects of ragtime.

5b using the library

Rather soon, of course, you'll have to start gathering reference material, and that means going to the library and finding sources of information. Libraries do have their individual arrangements of material, methods of classifying it, physical layouts, and staffs. But nearly every library has certain basic resources.

5b1 encyclopedias

Before you begin to read whole books, chapters of books, or even magazine articles, you can save much time and effort by first reading a basic discussion of your subject in one or more of the general encyclopedias:

Chambers's Encyclopaedia, 15 volumes
Collier's Encyclopedia, 24 volumes
Columbia Encyclopedia, 1 volume
Encyclopaedia Britannica, 24 volumes
Encyclopedia Americana, 30 volumes
Lincoln Library of Essential Information, 1 volume

These encyclopedias give you a concise, dependable orientation to your topic and often offer a bibliography following the article to send you on your way to more extensive information. Jot down for later search the names of any books or articles mentioned.

5b2 other reference works

In addition to the general encyclopedias, the reference room of most libraries will contain such reference books as the following:

Art	Bernard S. Lyers, ed., *McGraw-Hill Dictionary of Art*
Business	G. G. Munn, *Encyclopedia of Banking and Finance*
Drama	Phyllis Hartnoll, *The Oxford Companion to the Theatre*
Education	*Encyclopedia of Educational Research*
History	Richard B. Morris, *Encyclopedia of American History*
	William L. Langer, *An Encyclopedia of World History*
Literature	Lillian H. Hornstein, ed., *The Reader's Companion to World Literature*

5

	Alex Preminger *et al.,* eds., *Princeton Encyclopedia of Poetry and Poetics*
Music	Percy Scholes, *The Oxford Companion to Music*
Mythology	*Larousse Encyclopedia of Mythology*
Philosophy	James M. Baldwin, *Dictionary of Philosophy and Psychology*
Religion	*The New Catholic Encyclopedia*
	Cecil Roth, ed., *The Standard Jewish Encyclopedia*
Science	*Van Nostrand's Scientific Encyclopedia*
Social Sciences	Bert F. Hoselitz, ed., *A Reader's Guide to the Social Sciences*
	John T. Zadrozny, *Dictionary of Social Science*

There are also such collections of useful facts as *The World Almanac and Book of Facts.* After you have spent some time looking for reference books, you will see of course that we are offering here only a sample listing of "ready reference" books; there are many subject encyclopedias, dictionaries, guides, and almanacs. The zealous reference librarian can help you to find some of these useful reference tools, which generally take you one step beyond the more general encyclopedias.

5b3 the card catalog

After you've made a satisfactory search for information in the reference collection, you're ready to work with longer and more detailed sources—that is, *books.* The library's card catalog is the guide to its book collection. Most American libraries file in the catalog separate cards for author, title, and subject or subjects of each book. The various subject headings relating to your subject are very important, for they can steer you to all the library's books on your topic. The author card is called the "main card," and it usually lists toward the bottom (sometimes on the back) of the card the additional entries for a particular book—the subject, title, and additional author cards (if there are any). A typical author card, with its listings of other cards for the book, is reproduced below.

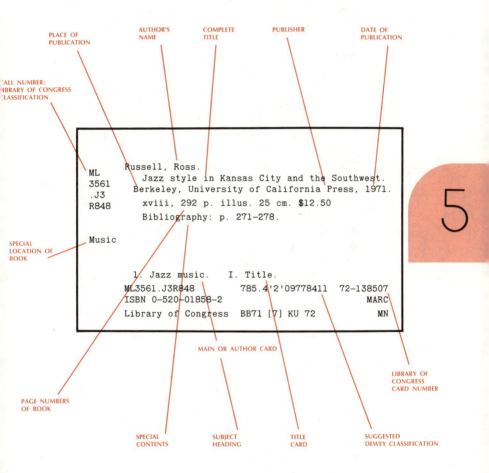

PLACE OF PUBLICATION

AUTHOR'S NAME

COMPLETE TITLE

PUBLISHER

DATE OF PUBLICATION

CALL NUMBER: LIBRARY OF CONGRESS CLASSIFICATION

```
ML
3561
.J3        Russell, Ross.
R848           Jazz style in Kansas City and the Southwest.
           Berkeley, University of California Press, 1971.
               xviii, 292 p. illus. 25 cm. $12.50
               Bibliography: p. 271-278.

Music

               1. Jazz music.   I. Title.
           ML3561.J3R848          785.4'2'09778411   72-138507
           ISBN 0-520-01858-2                        MARC
           Library of Congress   BB71 [7] KU 72      MN
```

SPECIAL LOCATION OF BOOK

PAGE NUMBERS OF BOOK

SPECIAL CONTENTS

SUBJECT HEADING

TITLE CARD

MAIN OR AUTHOR CARD

SUGGESTED DEWEY CLASSIFICATION

LIBRARY OF CONGRESS CARD NUMBER

5

In the United States two systems for classifying books are widely used: the Dewey Decimal System and the Library of Congress System. Each has the same aim—to shelve together books on the same subject. The Dewey System accomplishes this purpose by numbers and decimal points; the Library of Congress makes its divisions of knowledge primarily by letters and combinations of letters and numerals.

The author card will send you straight to the book in its proper place on the shelves of the library. But you can't find author or title cards unless you already know the author's name or the book's title—that is, unless you've found them in a bibliography (perhaps one following an encyclopedia article) or unless someone has told you about the book. But since you *do* know what the subject is, you can locate books under the right subject heading. And if you have in mind a term for the subject which the catalog apparently does not use, you may find a *cross-reference* card directing you from the subject under one name to the same subject under a different name or to approximately the same subject or a related subject under a different name. In one library, for example, we found that the catalog refers us from "Rag time" to "Ragtime." In a very large catalog, the two terms might be rather widely separated, because the two-word term would precede the one-word term.

5b4 indexes to newspapers and periodicals

Newspaper stories and magazine articles are other important sources of information. Fortunately, there are keys to unlock yesterday's newspapers and magazines, not to mention those of another decade or century, many of which are on permanent file in the library or libraries you use.

Periodical Indexes   There are three important guides to the contents of a wide range of American periodicals, or magazines:

Readers' Guide to Periodical Literature (1900–the present). This best-known and most useful of the indexes to magazines annually lists articles in approximately 135 general-circulation magazines alphabetically by both author and subject, with helpful cross-references. Sample entries are these:

RAGTIME music
Musical events: concert of S. Joplin's works at Columbia university. W. Sargeant. New Yorker 48:110-12+ Mr 25 '72
Rebirth of ragtime. il Life 73:46-7+ Jl 21 '72

AUTHOR ENTRIES

JOSEFSSON, Lars. See Fernlund, P. jt. auth.
JOSELOW, Beth
NRC volunteer tutor-training under way. il PTA Mag 66:11 Je '72
JOSEPH, James
This Indian art still saves lives. il Pop Mech 138:134-7 S '72
JOSEPH, Jenifer S.
Questions; poem. Negro Hist Bull 35:181 D '72
JOSEPH, Maxwell
He wants Watney's. por Time 99:78 Je 19 '72 *
JOSEPH, Richard
Travel notes. See issues of Esquire

CROSS-REFERENCES

JOSEPH Pulitzer, Jr, collection. See Art—Private collections
JOSEPH Schlitz brewing company. See Schlitz, Joseph, brewing company
JOSEPHSON, Hannah
Nominating Miss Rankin. Nation 215:165-6 S 11 '72

SUBJECT HEADINGS

JOPLIN, Scott
From rags to rags. por Time 99:89-90 F 7 '72 *
Joplin: professorial genius of frontier saloons, brothels. por Ebony 27:90-1 Ap '72 *
Musical events. W. Sargeant. New Yorker 48: 110-12+ Mr 25 '72 *
Scott Joplin renaissance. A. Shaw. il por Hi Fi 22:81-3 O '72 *
Scott Joplin's Treemonisha. V. B. Lawrence. il por Hi Fi 22:MA10-12 My '72 *
Second coming of Scott Joplin. I. Kolodin. Sat R 55:18 Ap 1 '72 *
Treemonisha. Criticism
Ebony il 27:84-6+ Ap '72 *
Hi Fi por 22:MA10-12 My '72 *
Newsweek il 79:46 F 7 '72 *
Sat R 55:62 S 2 '72 *

Poole's Index to Periodical Literature (1802–1907). As the dates show, this index is a helpful guide to magazines of the previous century and a few years of the twentieth century.

Social Sciences and Humanities Index (1907–the present). This annual index, more specialized than either *Readers' Guide* or *Poole's Index,* lists only articles in scholarly journals within the two large fields of knowledge.

The New York Times Index Since 1913, *The New York Times Index* has supplied to the researcher a guide to what has been published in that major American newspaper. And when you consider that much of any large daily newspaper consists of wire services news or features, the date on which an Associated Press, United Press, or International News Service story appeared in the *Times* probably will be the same date on which the same story appeared in other metropolitan newspapers.

Other and more specialized indexes, whose titles reveal their subject areas, are:

Abstracts of English Studies (1958–the present)
Agricultural Index (1916–64; succeeded by *Biological and Agricultural Index* (1964–the present)
Art Index (1929–the present)
Biography Index (1946–the present)
Biological Abstracts (1926–the present)
Book Review Digest (1905–the present)
Business Periodicals Index (1958–the present)
Chemical Abstracts (1907–the present)
Current Anthropology (1960–the present)
Current Index to Journals in Education (1969–the present)

Economic Abstracts (1953–the present)
Education Index (1929–the present)
Engineering Index (1884–the present)
Historical Abstracts (1955–the present)
Index to Book Reviews in the Humanities (1960–the present)
Industrial Arts Index (1913–57); succeeded by *Applied Science and Technology Index* (1958–the present); *Business Periodicals Index* (1958–the present)
Music Index (1949–the present)
Popular Periodical Index (1973–the present)
Psychological Abstracts (1927–the present)
Public Affairs Information Service (1915–the present)
Science Abstracts (1898–the present)
United States Government Publications: Monthly Catalog (1895–the present)

5b5 keeping track of your bibliography

5

As you search out information—first, let's say, in encyclopedias and other reference books; second, in the books you've located through the card catalog; and finally, in newspaper and magazine articles you've found through indexes—you should be recording on a separate card or paper slip (usually 3″ x 5″) all the publication information you need about each source (if you want to return to it later to check a point or two, when you cite the source in a footnote, or when you are ready to make the complete bibliography for your paper). That information should include author (if one is named), title, facts of publication, and date. Especially if you use more than one library, you should note on the bibliography card the location of the book or magazine; and in all cases, you'll want to record the library's call number to save time when you want to return to the book or article. And because the card or slip is made primarily for your use during the writing of the paper, you might want to note on it something about the special strengths or weaknesses of the source to guide you if you decide to check back on it during the planning, writing, or completion of the paper's first draft.

   a. Book   A typical bibliography card for a book looks like this:

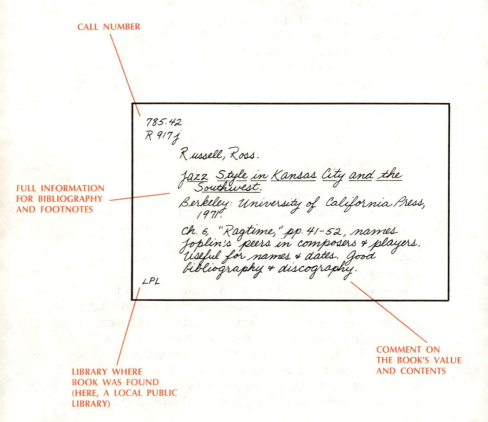

CALL NUMBER

FULL INFORMATION
FOR BIBLIOGRAPHY
AND FOOTNOTES

785.42
R 917 j

Russell, Ross.

Jazz Style in Kansas City and the
         Southwest.
Berkeley: University of California Press,
         1971.

Ch. 6, "Ragtime," pp. 41-52, names
Joplin's peers in composers & players.
Useful for names & dates. Good
bibliography & discography.

LPL

LIBRARY WHERE
BOOK WAS FOUND
(HERE, A LOCAL PUBLIC
LIBRARY)

COMMENT ON
THE BOOK'S VALUE
AND CONTENTS

b. Magazine Article   The bibliography card for a magazine article takes a form like this:

AUTHOR OF THE
ARTICLE

INFORMATION
ABOUT THE MAGAZINE
AND THE LOCATION
OF THE ARTICLE

ITLE

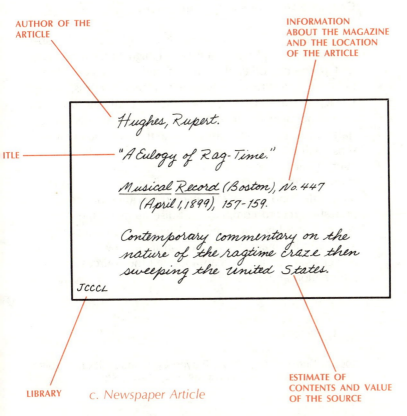

Hughes, Rupert.

"A Eulogy of Rag-Time."

Musical Record (Boston), No. 447
(April 1, 1899), 157-159.

Contemporary commentary on the
nature of the ragtime craze then
sweeping the united States.

JCCCL

5

LIBRARY   *c. Newspaper Article*

ESTIMATE OF
CONTENTS AND VALUE
OF THE SOURCE

Haskell, Harry. "'Ragtime': A Bacchanalia of Fabulous
Imagery," rev. of *Ragtime*, by E. L. Doctorow, *Kansas City
Star*, 27 July 1975, pp. 1D, 3D.

d. Pamphlet   In general, the bibliographical form for a
pamphlet is the same as that for a book. However, many
pamphlets do not indicate an individual author but instead
a foundation, governmental agency, or institution under

whose auspices it appeared (examples: U.S. Department of Agriculture; University of Kansas Libraries; Common Cause; Sedalia, Missouri, Chamber of Commerce).

   e. Other Media   Sometimes (as in research on a subject like Scott Joplin or ragtime) you might find it expedient to tap sources other than books and magazines. Maps, films or film strips, unpublished letters, records, sheet music, and the like might be quite as pertinent to a discovery about your subject as conventional printed material would be. In such cases, a little thought and common sense will tell you that you need to provide yourself — and, later, your reader — with the essential facts about the source: author, composer, agency, firm; correct or formulated title; and identification of origin (film studio, map publisher, record company and disc number) and date (if you can possibly determine it). A few examples of citations for non-print material will demonstrate how to tell your reader as much as you can about all the sources of your information and ideas:

1. Record

Joplin, Scott. *Piano Rags.* Played by Joshua Rifkin. 2 vols. Nonesuch Records, H–71248, H–71264, 1972.

2. Program notes on a record album

Rifkin, Joshua. Program notes. *Piano Rags.* By Scott Joplin. Vol. II. Nonesuch Records, H–71264, 1972.

3. Interview with a person of authority on the subject

Rifkin, Joshua. Personal interview. 24 May 1976.

5C note taking

Completely separate from the record keeping that goes on
the bibliography cards is the taking of notes as you read
your source materials. Again, you will find it most convenient to use cards or slips of paper (however, some
people prefer to use a different size from the bibliography
cards — say, 4" x 6", or even 5" x 8" — in order to keep the
two operations completely separate).

Resolve to put no more than one point or idea on each
card, and resist steadfastly any temptation to combine several ideas from even one source. Otherwise, you'll find
yourself frustrated when it's time to spread out note cards,
to discover what you've got, to fit the cards into a logical
order or system, or even to make an outline. Moreover, we
urge you not to consider taking notes on sheets of looseleaf
or typing paper, which suddenly become very unwieldy
when you're ready to plan the structure of your paper.

We recommend that you convert the information you
find into your own words most of the time; exact quotations from a source should be written down only when the
language is particularly memorable or when you need the
authority of the writer's own words. When you quote, of
course, you should indicate that you have quoted by en-
closing all of the writer's own words in quotation marks
and record it *exactly* as it appears on the printed page, even
when a word is misspelled or the punctuation is odd. As
we noted in Chapter 4, you can insert for obvious omissions or for errors of fact, spelling, grammar, or punctuation the Latin word **sic** ("thus") in brackets to show your
recognition of the error and the accuracy of your transcrip-
tion.

We recommend strongly that you follow these procedures as you take notes:

1. Always identify a source somehow — either by the
last name of the author (and a shortened title if you have

more than one source by the same author or if no author's name is given) or by a number that corresponds to a number you have given to the bibliography card (in which case you will have to keep a separate master list of sources and numbers).

2. Check every note for accuracy, especially if it is a direct quotation, before you return the book or magazine to the shelves.

3. Be sure to put down the page numbers of the source, whether you quote or paraphrase the material. The purpose of this absolutely necessary step is to enable you to give proper credit to the source of your facts and to avoid any question of conscious or unconscious *plagiarism* — the presentation of another person's words as your own.

4. Because a long time may elapse between your reading and your use of the gathered information in writing the paper, make sure you understand what you have written on the note card.

5. Be as concise as possible without sacrificing or distorting meaning; use phrases and condensed sentences that are loaded with facts. You may even wish to use a system of abbreviations (for example, **RT** for **ragtime; SJ** or **J** for **Scott Joplin; comp** for **composition** or **composer** — but not for **compare,** for which only the established abbreviation **cf.** should be used). Just be sure you will be able to remember what all your abbreviations mean later, even if you have to make a key to these abbreviations to refer to when you write the paper.

6. Keep your note cards in good order and in safe storage.

7. Write your notes in ink (or with a ballpoint pen) because pencil marks tend to smudge and become in time hard to read.

8. Make sure you have made a separate bibliography card for each source of notes.

9. As you collect notes, give each card a brief *subject heading* that in a word or short phrase summarizes or

points up anything special (a controversial opinion, an unusual insight, or a striking way of making a point) about the quotation. These subject headings, invented and put somewhere at the top of the card (we recommend the upper right portion of the card, as in the example below), will greatly facilitate the tasks of arranging cards according to their subjects and of making an outline for the paper.

10. For a long quotation or for a guarantee of exactness, you may want to photocopy some material instead of writing a note card. Many libraries make such duplicating machines available and charge only five or ten cents per page for copying.

Below is a sample of a note card (which an experienced writer would condense by abbreviating, omitting **a** and **the,** and so on).

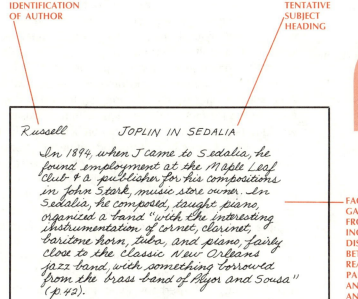

IDENTIFICATION OF AUTHOR

TENTATIVE SUBJECT HEADING

Russell   JOPLIN IN SEDALIA

In 1894, when J came to Sedalia, he found employment at the Maple Leaf Club & a publisher for his compositions in John Stark, music store owner. In Sedalia, he composed, taught piano, organized a band "with the interesting instrumentation of cornet, clarinet, baritone horn, tuba, and piano, fairly close to the classic New Orleans jazz band, with something borrowed from the brass band of Pryor and Sousa" (p. 42).

FACTS GATHERED FROM READING, WITH DISTINCTION BETWEEN READER'S PARAPHRASES AND REMINDERS AND RUSSELL'S EXACT WORDS

5

5d outlining

Once you have gathered as many notes as you can on the subject you have chosen, you are ready to think about the assembling of those notes into one unit—the research paper itself. First, however, you should arrange the note cards by putting together the cards on the same divisions of the subject—for example, Scott Joplin's activities in Sedalia, Missouri; Joplin's career in St. Louis; and Joplin's failures in New York. Thus, the many note cards begin to form clusters or units that together make up the total subject. When they have been arranged by clusters, you should be able to see within one cluster a set of relationships (perhaps a sequence in time or process, a progression from cause to effect, or an evaluation of some aspect of your topic). Such arrangements within one cluster and the relationship of that cluster to another will indicate to you the structure and sequence of a working outline—that is, an outline that will help you stay on the track as you write the first draft of your paper.

As you did research for a paper on Scott Joplin and American ragtime, you would discover that several reference sources offer facts or theories on the origins of ragtime. As you arranged those facts within a cluster, you would notice very quickly a distinction between influences within black American culture and influences from outside that culture. Moreover, there is a chronological order in which those influences arose. Clearly, then, one segment, or main division, of the paper can be devoted to the origins and influences that combined to produce American ragtime in the 1890's. Once you make such a start in the classification of note cards on one fairly important division of the subject, other divisions of the total subject will begin to stand out—particularly if you have assigned brief subject headings and perhaps even tentative numbers or letters for a possible place in the sequence of the outline. Less important details will begin to show up as subheads or subtopics of more important or larger ideas.

There are not really any "rules" for making outlines, but a few words of advice will help you to make the best possible outline and thus a kind of "blueprint" or "map" for your paper before you begin to write it. We recommend a "system" like this:

1. After you have made note cards of all the information you can find on your subject, arrange the cards in groups or clusters. If you've given summary captions to each card, arranging the cards will be quite easy. For example, all your cards on Joplin's years in Sedalia will end up in the same cluster.

2. Decide what subjects logically come first. In the case of a person's life or the evolution of an institution, a chronological order will logically suggest itself. If you're working on an analysis of a thing or an idea, probably the largest or most immediately apparent aspect or thought will come first. For example, the characteristics of ragtime as it suddenly appeared out of nowhere in the early 1890's might logically precede information about its sources or about Joplin's role in the development of ragtime.

3. Conventionally, if one heading is assigned to a certain level within the familiar outline pattern — roman numerals, capital letters, arabic numerals, small letters, arabic numerals within parentheses, small letters within parentheses — at least one other heading or subheading at that same level should appear. Thus, if we assign to one part of our subject the main heading of *I*, we should allow for at least one other main heading of *II*. As it turns out, the investigation of the subject of Joplin and American ragtime generates several main headings that take roman numerals. Student papers rarely require more than three levels in the sequence:

I.
   A.
   B.
   C.
      1.
      2.
      3.
II.
   A.
      1.
      2.
   B.

4. Once you've got your cards under the control of a few closely related, rather general categories — for example, "sources of ragtime" — you've tentatively established the shape of an outline. Now go one step forward by trying to arrange the subdivisions of the more general headings (remember that *at least two headings at each level* are desirable). Thus, Joplin's life in Sedalia might be subdivided like this:

C. Life in Sedalia
   1. Connections with the "district"
   2. Formal study of music
   3. Composing and publication

5. At this point you are probably able to formulate a *thesis sentence* that will embrace all the general divisions of the outline. A good thesis statement summarizes and encloses the boundaries of your total subject and establishes (primarily for your own guidance, as a check against allowing extraneous matter to creep into the paper and a constant reminder to carry out the task set by the assignment) any particular purpose or argument proposed within the paper. The student who chose to write on Joplin and American ragtime finally came to this statement of his paper's subject and its approach to that subject: Scott

Joplin's life mirrors or parallels the ups and downs of American ragtime music.

6. Decide whether you wish to use phrases or sentences in your outline. Do not mix the two.

7. After you've made the divisions and less general subdivisions, try to write out an outline that accommodates your subject and to whose headings and subheadings each note card can be related. Of course, you will not make an outline subheading for every card in your file; but every card, if you intend to use its information, ought to fit into some part of the outline. Otherwise, you will risk violating unity and perhaps coherence. In short, don't be uneasy if your plan cannot accommodate all those note cards you assembled: a successful researcher nearly always has more material than he or she can use.

After careful examination of his material and the interrelationships, our student writer wrote this outline for his topic, "Scott Joplin and the Rise and Fall of American Ragtime":

I. The renaissance of ragtime in the 1970's
  A. Film *The Sting*
  B. Reissue of Joplin's works
  C. Concerts
  D. Records
  E. Best-selling novel *Ragtime*
II. The beginnings of ragtime
  A. The American world's fairs of 1893–1904
  B. The "districts" of Missouri towns
    1. Jobs for pianist-composers
    2. The pianist's detachment from sordid surroundings
  C. Black American experience
    1. African rhythms
    2. Plantation life
    3. White ballads
  D. The repertoire of the minstrel shows
    1. "Coon songs"
    2. The cakewalk

5

III. Definition of ragtime
    A. Formal characteristics
        1. Beat and melody
        2. Structure
        3. Syncopation
        4. Other devices
    B. Origin of the name
        1. Connotations of "rag"
        2. "Ragging" as a mode of piano playing
IV. Life and career of Scott Joplin
    A. Childhood and early talent
    B. Wanderings before 1893
    C. Life in Sedalia
        1. Connections with "the District"
        2. Formal study of music
        3. Compositions and publications
    D. Move to St. Louis
        1. Separation from "the District"
        2. Continuing composition and publications
        3. Desire to expand ragtime
           a. Ballet
           b. Opera
        4. Serious view of ragtime
        5. Growth of interest in ragtime
           a. Improvement in arrangements
           b. Inexpensive sheet music
           c. Joplin's reputation
        6. Impact of St. Louis Fair of 1904
    E. Joplin's last years in New York (1907–1917)
        1. Growing frustrations and bitterness
           a. Struggles with *Treemonisha*
           b. Break with John Stark
           c. Impact of imitators and plagiarists
           d. Commercial adulteration of ragtime
        2. Mental illness and death
V. The finale for ragtime
    A. Replacement by jazz
        1. Orchestras
        2. Gramophones
        3. New dance styles
    B. Ragtime's stubborn, "underground" survival

8. Notice that this outline scheme employs this order for the various levels as it moves from the most general to the most specific parts of the subject:

Roman numerals—largest and most general divisions of the topic and its thesis statement.
Capital letters—the main subdivisions of each of the largest divisions of the topic designated by the roman numerals.
Arabic numerals—the next smaller divisions.
Small letters—still smaller (therefore, more specific) subdivisions.

9. Make a final check of your outline. Has every part been assigned to the right level of generality or specificity? Do you have enough material from the note cards to justify every head and subhead? Do the headings show distinctions between the highly general and highly specific parts of your essay?

10. Finally, remember that you have constructed the outline mainly for a guide in the writing of the paper. Unless your instructor specifically requires you to hand it in, it need not be a part of the final paper. In any case, it should be detailed enough to prompt you as you write, to send you back to the appropriate batch of cards, and to keep you from straying from the subject.

5e writing the paper

Preparing the paper which you will submit to your instructor is, of course, the act to which everything else—gathering notes, making an outline, devising a thesis statement—has pointed. If you've been responsible and resourceful in the earlier steps, you will naturally want to write the best possible paper to get the most possible benefit from your careful earlier work. Perhaps your instructor will give explicit instructions about the number of drafts and the format of the completed paper. In the absence of such specific instructions, we recommend that you proceed as follows.

1. Always write your paper in rough draft first — perhaps even in pencil for ease in making corrections. Make all the changes that will improve the paper — making more precise statements, "beefing up" paragraphs, correcting errors in facts or mechanics, editing to make the final draft represent your best effort. After you've read the paper very critically, ask an honest friend to read it and give you his or her reactions to the paper as a whole or in parts.

2. For the final draft, write on lined 8½" x 11" paper or type on white unlined paper of the same size. Leave wide margins — at least one inch at top, bottom, and both sides of the page.

3. If you type, double-space the body of the paper.

4. Before you hand the paper in to your instructor, read the final draft for slips of pen or typewriter.

5f documentation

5f 1 footnote vs. bibliography forms

Footnote and bibliography forms are often confused; therefore, we should point out the main differences between them before you examine the sample forms below.

Footnote	*Bibliography*
1. All the items of information — author, title, publication data, and volume or page numbers — are separated only by commas and parentheses; thus their unity is stressed.	1. Basic parts of a bibliography are separated strongly by periods after author, after title, after publication data.

Footnote	*Bibliography*
2. Author's name appears in the usual order: first name, middle name or initial, and last name.	2. Author's name appears with last name first (for alphabetizing), followed by a comma and first and middle names or initials.
3. Parentheses set off publication data.	3. No parentheses surround publication data except for the date of a magazine's or newspaper's issue.
4. Specific page number or inclusive page numbers are required in a footnote.	4. No page numbers are needed unless the entry is only for a particular essay or chapter in a book, or for the location (*i.e.,* particular pages of a magazine or newspaper article).
5. Footnotes are identified by superscript or raised numbers in the text which correspond to raised numbers at the bottom of the page, followed by the appropriate citation of author, title, required publication data, and page number(s).	5. Bibliography entries appear on a separate page or pages at the end of the paper. They are not numbered but are recorded in alphabetical order by authors' last names.

Thus:

Footnote	*Bibliography*
[1] David A. Jasen, *Recorded Ragtime* (Hamden, Conn.: Archon Books, 1973), p. 21.	Jasen, David A. *Recorded Ragtime.* Hamden, Conn.: Archon Books, 1973.
[Fn. no.] Author, Title (Place: Publisher, Date), page number.	Author. Title: Subtitle if Any. Place: Publisher, Date.
[28] Winthrop Sargeant, "Rags and Riches," *New Yorker*, 25 March 1972, p. 112.	Sargeant, Winthrop. "Rags and Riches." *New Yorker*, 25 March 1972, pp. 110–12, 115.
[Fn. no.] Author, "Title," Name of Magazine, Date, page number.	Author. "Title," Name of Magazine, Date, inclusive page numbers.

5f 2 footnotes

You must give proper credit to your sources for every important fact, opinion, paraphrase, and direct quotation you gathered in your research and later incorporated into your paper. Rather obvious facts or generally known information — such as the discovery of America by Columbus in 1492 or the approximate span of ragtime's popularity — needs no documentation, but facts or arguments not so well known or widely accepted — for example, differing opinions about the essential characteristics of ragtime — *do* need documentation, that is, *footnotes* which give the essential facts about the source of your information. The footnote tells your readers where you got a fact or idea and invites them to check that source if they wish. Conventionally, an arabic number typed one-half of a space above the line of text (see the student paper on pages 134–141 for the format) signals readers to seek complete information about the source at the bottom of the page. (Sometimes, especially if there are lengthy or numerous notes, they may be better placed on their own separate pages at the end of the paper.) The sample footnotes below illustrate the situations you are most likely to encounter in your documentation of a research paper.

Sample Footnote Forms
BOOKS

Book with a single author

[1] Ross Russell, *Jazz Style in Kansas City and the Southwest* (Berkeley: University of California Press, 1971), p. 15.

Book with two authors

[2] William J. Schafer and Johannes Riedel, *The Art of Ragtime* (Baton Rouge: Louisiana State University Press, 1973), p. 215.

Book with more than two authors

[3] Wilfred Guerin and others, *A Handbook of Critical Approaches to Literature* (New York: Harper & Row, 1966), p. 59.

Note: Some people prefer to use the abbreviated Latin phrase *et al.* instead of the English "and others."

Book with an editor

[4] Luke Foster, ed., *Essays on Ragtime* (El Paso, Tex.: Domino, 1930), pp. 108–11.

Book in a second or later edition

[5] Rudi Blesh and Harriet Janis, *They All Played Ragtime,* rev. ed. (New York: Oak Publications, 1966), p. 28.

Essay within a book

[6] Rudi Blesh, "Scott Joplin: Black-American Classicist," in *The Collected Works of Scott Joplin,* ed. Vera Brodsky Lawrence (New York: New York Public Library, 1971), I, xxii.

5

ARTICLES

Newspaper

[1] Jess Ritter, "From Sedalia Ragtime to Kansas City Jazz," *Kansas City Star,* 17 August 1975, Section E, p. 1.

Magazine

[2] A. Shaw, "Scott Joplin Renaissance," *Hi Fi,* 22 (October 1972), 82.

For a popular weekly magazine you can omit the volume number:

　　³ "From Rags to Rags," *Time*, 7 February 1972, p. 90.

Note that the above citation is to an unsigned article; therefore, it is a title entry. In the bibliography it will be alphabetized under *F,* for "From."

Encyclopedia

　　⁴ "Joplin, Scott," *World Book Encyclopedia*, XI, 126.

Informational Footnotes Sometimes you find additional information about a point in your paper that is too pertinent or interesting to discard but too restricted in scope or too marginal to be presented coherently in the body of your paper. Samples of informational footnotes in the sample research paper on Scott Joplin are numbers 6, 9, 12, 17, 26, 29, 30, and 32. Notice that often the source of such side issues or amplification of a point appears as part of the entire note. You may want to use fewer informational footnotes than did the author of the paper on Joplin; but they are handy ways to communicate to your reader another side of a question or your wider grasp of the subject which would be out of place in the body of the paper.

5f3 bibliography

The bibliography you have compiled on bibliography cards as you discovered sources and began to take notes is simply a record of what materials you have used in writing the paper. You may choose to include works that have benefited your paper but have not been mentioned in the text or in a footnote. Another reason for listing sources separately from the body of the paper is to give readers a list of works to consult in order to verify the information presented in your paper or to pursue the topic further if they wish. Usually, as we've indicated on page 154, bibliography entries are arranged alphabetically according to authors' last names. The first line of an entry begins at the left margin, and subsequent lines of the same entry are indented five spaces. Although for a research essay intended for publication you would double-space the lines of a specific entry, most college papers can have single-spaced bibliography entries with double-spacing only between entries. Unless your instructor prefers other placement, the bibliography is on separate pages following the conclusion of the paper's body, under the heading BIBLIOGRAPHY.

Conventional bibliographical forms appear on page 15 of the sample research paper. Notice that the author's last name comes first, that the full title (with the subtitle, if there is one), and the complete publication information—place, publisher, and year of publication—plus page numbers only for articles (not for books) are given.

5f 4 abbreviations used in documentation

ed.	editor, edited by, or edition
eds.	editors
rev. ed.	revised edition
ibid.	literally, "in the same place" (for a work cited immediately beforehand). If the page number is the same, it is not repeated; otherwise, a page number would follow *ibid*. The abbreviation is underlined (or italicized when typeset) because it is a foreign (Latin) term.
op. cit.	literally, "in the work cited." Used for a work previously but not immediately beforehand cited. If there is an author, his or her last name precedes the abbreviation. Example: Blesh, *op. cit*.

5

loc. cit.	literally, "in the place cited." Used for an identical passage previously but not immediately beforehand cited; thus no page number is necessary. Example: Blesh, *loc. cit.*
p., pp.	page, pages. When a volume number is given for a book or a magazine, this abbreviation is not used. Example: II, 267 *or* 23 (January 1932), 114.
vol., vols.	volume, volumes
pt.	part
ch.	chapter
et al.	literally, "and others." Used after first author's name in footnotes and bibliography entries for works with three or more authors.

Note: The abbreviations for the Latin terms mentioned above — *ibid., op. cit.,* and *loc. cit.* — are gradually disappearing from research paper documentation in favor of short author or title references like the following:

[5] Ritter, p. 1.
[6] Shaw, p. 83.
[7] "From Rags to Rags," p. 89.
[8] "Joplin, Scott," p. 126.

5f 5 quotations within the paper

In section 4c we mentioned the conventions and reasons for using direct quotations from another writer. Choosing apt and effective quotations that amplify and strengthen your own language, and meticulously quoting exactly from your sources, reinforce your claim to be a responsible writer.

Quotations from your reference sources may be more valuable than your own words in establishing proof, giving historical or stylistic flavor to your paper, specifying the exact nature of a controversy, or simply allowing an author to speak for himself or herself. Quotations should not be used for padding the paper, relieving you from your primary responsibility to know and interpret your material to your trusting reader, or saving you the effort of thinking through your subject and organizing it. The quotation on page 186 in the student research paper is a good example of a proper and interesting quotation: Joplin himself speaks to tell us what ragtime meant to him and explains a major point about the technique of playing rags.

When quotations are used, they must be exact and thus must be checked and rechecked for absolute accuracy. Even misspellings, grammatical errors, oddities of punctuation must be reproduced exactly as they are found in the original source. To assure your reader that the errors are the original author's and not yours, you place after each such error the Latin word **sic,** which means ''thus,'' in brackets.

Short quotations of only two or three lines or one sentence or part of a sentence may simply be set off by quotation marks within the body of your paper. Footnote 13 on page 181 is an example of such a quotation within the body of the paper. Notice that omissions from the quotation are indicated by ellipsis (. . .).

5

Scott Joplin and the Rise and Fall
of American Ragtime

by

Peter J. North

English 101
Mr. Jameson
14 May 1978

Scott Joplin and the Rise and Fall of
American Ragtime

   Early in the 1970's the American ear began to respond to the glorious music of another era——the ragtime of the late 1890's and
the first two decades of the twentieth century. Indeed, the national ear had never entirely forgotten ragtime, for certain pianists like James Johnson had continued to play
rags during the 1920's and 1930's; and tunes
like Scott Joplin's "Maple Leaf Rag" had
endured throughout the successive reigns of
jazz, swing, and rock. But a series of events
precipitated in the 1970's a genuine revival
of ragtime and a belated acknowledgment that
ragtime is a serious, original, and entirely
native American art form. Probably the most
influential and certainly most obvious event
was the highly successful use of several of
Joplin's rags on the sound track of a popular movie, The Sting, in 1973. Admittedly,
one can question the suitability of music
from an earlier day as background for fictional events set in the 1930's, but the producer of the movie recognized at once the
parallels between the tone and tempo of the
music and the tempo, urban setting, under-
world hijinks, and gaiety of the movie. Certainly the film and an immediately forth-
coming record album of the movie's sound
track set an entire nation to humming and
playing once more the lilting, "toe-tap-
ping" tunes that had once conquered the
hearts of another generation. A well-known
concert pianist, Vera Brodsky Lawrence, had
persuaded the New York Public Library to
publish in two handsome volumes the extant

5

–2–

works of Joplin, for which she served as
editor.[1] Thus serious students of music at
last had the music of a man who is being increasingly recognized as a rarity among American composers—a completely original creator
of music rooted in American experience. Also,
suddenly there were concerts of Joplin's
music; productions of his ragtime opera,
Treemonisha; new recordings from old player-
piano rolls and by a few fortunately still
living ragtime pianists and composers. The
New England Conservatory of Music formed a
ragtime ensemble, which gave concerts in
Boston and Washington in 1972 and 1973 and
made recordings of orchestral versions of
Joplin's music.[2] Joshua Rifkin, the pianist,
has toured the United States playing ragtime
music to enthusiastic audiences and has recorded two albums of Joplin's rags for Nonesuch Records. In 1975, an American novelist,
E. L. Doctorow, named his best seller Ragtime, not only to emphasize its temporal setting in the first two decades of this century but also to suggest the novel's formal
similarity to the structure and effect of a
rag.[3] In such ways have ragtime and Scott
Joplin been restored to the American people.

---

[1] The Collected Works of Scott Joplin, ed.
Vera Brodsky Lawrence, 2 vols. (New York:
New York Public Library, 1971).

[2] Program Notes for Scott Joplin, The Red
Back Book, played by the New England Conservatory of Music Ragtime Ensemble, conducted by Gunther Schuller. Angel Record
S-36060, c1973.

[3] George Stade, review of Ragtime by E. L.
Doctorow, New York Times Book Review, 6 July
1975, pp. 1–2; R. Z. Sheppard, "The Music

-3-

Although in a sense it had been in the
black American consciousness for a long time,
ragtime gradually and at first imperceptibly
emerged as a distinct musical genre during
the decade of four American world's fairs--
the Chicago Columbian Exposition of 1893, the
Trans-Mississippi Exposition at Omaha in
1899, the Pan-American Exposition at Buffalo
in 1901, and the Louisiana Purchase Exposition at St. Louis in 1904.[4] When a host of
itinerant pianists, especially those from the
South and Midwest, came to Chicago in 1893
to enter piano-playing contests, to exchange
ideas and techniques, to hear and be heard by
other pianists, the sounds of pure ragtime
were probably first heard.[5]

But Missouri, during the next decade,
was to be the principal seedbed of American
ragtime. For St. Louis, Kansas City, and
smaller towns like Sedalia, Joplin, Carthage,
and St. Joseph all had their corps of
talented pianists, most of them young black
men, who would jointly launch ragtime. Each
town had its "District" of bawdyhouses,
gambling halls, and saloons, where gifted
performers could play innovative piano without being at all involved in the diversions
offered to white customers. Thus the fairly
rigid segregation of the 1890's actually
stimulated an emerging ragtime because the
pianist-composers could weave their elegant
rags in almost total detachment from the

5

of Time," review of Ragtime by E. L.
Doctorow, Time, 14 July 1975, p. 64.
   [4]Rudi Blesh and Harriet Janis, They All
Played Ragtime, rev. ed. (New York: Oak
Publications, 1966), p. 4.
   [5]Ibid., p. 87.

-4-

rowdy life around them. Also, the madams and
the saloon keepers offered steady employment
to good pianists, who were consequently able
to devote much spare time to creativity. But
none of these conditions would have suf-
ficed without the intensively imaginative
drive of the black pianists of Missouri to
create a music of complex structure and lyric
beauty.

Ragtime was not wholly a product of the
imagination, however; for it did have deep
roots in Afro-American experience before,
during, and after slavery. West African
rhythms still display a basic characteristic
of the rag—a steady, regular beat on one
drum contrasting with the irregular or syncopated rhythms of other drums, combined
mainly to support and stimulate dancing. Preserved in the black culture of Southern plan-
tations and of cities like New Orleans and
passed on to new generations, these rhythms
and dances were never lost but were merely
altered to encompass new experiences in
North America, including parody of white manners and music. After the Civil War, the very
popular minstrel shows featured "coon
songs," scurrilously comic songs sung mainly
by white performers in blackface and portray-
ing the Negro as childlike, roguish, lazy,
and unquestionably inferior.[6] No matter,
however, how racist the lyrics of the songs

---

[6] Such "coon songs" were even composed by
blacks also, faced as they were with the
necessity of catering to white tastes and
prejudice. See William J. Schafer and
Johannes Riedel, The Art of Ragtime: Form
and Meaning of an Original Black American
Art (Baton Rouge: Louisiana State University
Press, 1973), pp. 18, 24-29.

−5−

were, behind the words was a bright, spark-
ling music that had evolved from folk experience and had a strong rhythm that encouraged dancing. Also, the "coon songs"
introduced pronounced syncopation into
printed popular sheet music.[7]

The popularity of the "coon song" and the
rag coincided with an irresistible dance
craze of the 1890's—the cakewalk, another
offshoot of minstrel repertoire. The cakewalk took its basic rhythm from the march and
was sometimes called the "march and two-
step" or "patrol," after the terminology of
the big brass bands, like Sousa's, of that
era.[8] And like the rag and the "coon songs,"
the cakewalk originated in antebellum plantation experience—the "walk-around."[9] By 1897
everyone in America, and shortly afterward

---

[7] Blesh and Janis, They All Played Ragtime, p. 93.

[8] Schafer and Riedel, The Art of Ragtime,
p. 29.

[9] Shephard N. Edmonds, once a prominent
black entertainer, described the walk-around
as "just a happy movement [the slaves] did to
the banjo music because they couldn't stand
still. It was generally on Sundays when
there was little work that the slaves both
young and old would dress up in hand-me-down
finery to do a high-kicking, prancing walk-
around. They did a take-off on the high
manners of the white folks in the 'big
house,' but their masters, who gathered
around to watch the fun, missed the point.
It's supposed to be that the custom of a
prize started with the master giving a cake
to the couple that did the proudest movement." Quoted in Blesh and Janis, They All
Played Ragtime, p. 96.

5

–6–

in Europe, was strutting around dance floors
and doing the cakewalk.

When, then, native and popular forces con-
verged to produce ragtime and the triumphs
of artists like Scott Joplin, an impatient
public immediately and enthusiastically embraced ragtime. By the mid–1890's, ragtime
had acquired distinctive characteristics—
highly stylized composition, primarily for
the piano, combining a regular bass beat with
"an off–beat treble."[10] It usually has, like
a march, four or five themes with a <u>reprise</u>,
or repetition, of the first theme right
after the second theme.[11] Rudi Blesh and
Harriet Janis argue that syncopation, a
shifting of the stress from the normally accented first and third beats of a measure to
the normally unaccented second and fourth, is
the essential single quality of ragtime, but
William J. Schafer and Johannes Riedel insist
that syncopation is merely one of several devices—"devices like the break, stoptime,
various complex bass patterns beyond the
usual march or oompah bass line and many
other methods of varying and contrasting
rhythmic patterns."[12] A more technical defi-

---

[10] Blesh and Janis, p. 107.

[11] Rudi Blesh, "Scott Joplin: Black Amer-
ican Classicist," <u>The Collected Works of
Scott Joplin</u>, ed. Vera Brodsky Lawrence
(New York: New York Public Library, 1971),
I, xvi.

[12] Blesh and Janis, p. 107; Schafer and
Riedel, p. 10. The latter team think that a
narrow view of ragtime as simply "syncopated
music" obscures the fact that ragtime is a

–7–

nition of American ragtime mentions "duple
meter (2/4 or 4/4); functional harmony
stressing tonic, dominant, subdominant, and
applied dominants in a major totality; compounded song-form structures with 16 or 32-
bar periods and shorter introductions, vamps,
and codas; a syncopated treble melody which
operates in opposition to a harmonic and
nonsyncopated bass line; and a bass line
which moves approximately at half the speed
of the melody. . . ."[13]

The name "rag" seems to have been the in-
vention of a Chicago newspaperman and apparently implied disdain for what earlier had
been called merely "jig piano."[14] When early
players syncopated marches, ballads, hymns,
and even waltzes, they often said they were
"ragging up" a tune.[15] Joplin disliked the
name "rag" because he felt keenly an implication of contempt for what many people, especially those of the white musical establish-
ment who recommended veneration and imita-
tion of European classical music, regarded as
a vulgar art form of an inferior people. But

5

"style" as much as it is a "genre" and that
the style, present in banjo songs, string
bands, minstrel shows, and buck dances—"a
method of organizing folk materials"—preceded the form and even called it into being
(pp. 12-13).

[13] John Vinton, ed., _Dictionary of Contemporary Music_ (New York: E. P. Dutton, 1974),
p. 368.

[14] Blesh and Janis, p. 100.

[15] David A. Jasen, _Recorded Ragtime_,
_1897-1958_ (Hamden, Conn.: Archon Books,
1973), p. 1.

-8-

"rag" and "ragtime" appealed to the popular
fancy; thus the terms were fixed and given
complete respectability. Ironically, however,
the black pianist—composers had to accept
second place in the founding of American ragtime: "Mississippi Rag," by a white band-
master, William Krell, was the first published rag; Ben Harney, a white pianist from
Kentucky, was the first performer to make
ragtime a "hit" in a New York theater; and
such was the racism of that era that a white
composer inevitably found it easier than his
black counterpart to sell rags.[16]
     The life and career of Scott Joplin
typify those of most of the other great black
American ragtime artists. Born in a small
river town——Texarkana, Texas——in 1868 to poor
but musically talented parents, Joplin early
showed exceptional musical leanings, including the ability to play by ear. After his
father somehow scraped together the money to
buy an old square grand piano and a kindly
old German teacher of music offered to give
the gifted boy free lessons in sight—reading
and harmony, Joplin was on his way to a life
committed to music. When his father realisti-
cally argued that the boy ought to learn a
useful trade or vocation, Joplin left home at
the age of fourteen to wander about the
South and the Midwest as an itinerant pianist
and sometimes as an accompanist for vocal
groups.
     Like many of his peers, Joplin went to
the Chicago Fair in 1893 to enter the contests for pianists but he won no prizes.
But he won something even greater than

---

[16] Blesh and Janis, pp. 100, 93—94.

–9–

prizes, for he heard the sounds of emerging ragtime in the fairgrounds and in Chicago's red light district. Taking to the road once again as an entertainer, Joplin settled in Sedalia, Missouri, in 1896, to earn a living playing at the Maple Leaf Club and to study music at the George Smith College for Negroes.[17]

The choice of Sedalia as at least a temporary home was fortunate for the unfolding of Joplin's creativity. Though Sedalia was segregated, as were all Missouri towns of that day, its sporting clubs and saloons employed black piano players and thus indirectly encouraged expanded repertoires and playing techniques.[18] For Joplin the Maple Leaf Club performed an even greater service when one day his playing pleased the ear of John Stark, owner of a local music store, who had dropped into the club for a beer. When Stark offered to pay Joplin fifty dollars for one of his compositions and in

---

[17] Additional details of Joplin's life can be found in Blesh and Janis, Schafer and Riedel, and Blesh's "Scott Joplin: Black-American Classicist." Although Peter Gammond's Scott Joplin and the Ragtime Era (New York: St. Martin's Press, 1975) offers a convenient body of background and lists of Joplin's compositions, there is as yet no definitive biography of Joplin, and only one general encyclopedia has an entry for his name (Gilbert Chase, "Joplin, Scott," World Book Encyclopedia, 1973, XI, 126).

[18] Ross Russell, Jazz Style in Kansas City and the Southwest (Berkeley: University of California Press, 1971), pp. 41–42.

5

-10-

addition to give him a royalty from sales, a
long and mutually profitable association between the black composer and the white publisher began. The composition was "Maple
Leaf Rag," an instant popular success which
catapulted Joplin, John Stark and Son, and
Missouri ragtime generally to fame in 1899.

The phenomenal success of "Maple Leaf
Rag" (it sold in the hundreds of thousands
during the first dozen years) convinced Stark
that, as a successful publisher of sheet
music, he needed to be in a larger city;
consequently he moved his new firm to St.
Louis in 1900. Joplin, newly married to
the widowed sister-in-law of a close
friend and fellow musician in Sedalia,
soon followed. The two departures ended
Sedalia's role in ragtime and signaled the
rise of St. Louis as the capital city of
American ragtime. Soon other pianists and
composers--Arthur Marshall, Otis Saunders,
Scott Hayden, Brun Campbell, James Scott, and
Tom Turpin--turned up to form something like
a St. Louis "school" of ragtime.[19]

In St. Louis, Joplin chose to be essentially remote from the red light district. By
supplementing his income from composing and
teaching with operating a rooming and board-
ing house, the serious and dedicated Joplin
and his wife managed to live very comfort-
ably. And the marvelous rags--"Peacherine
Rag," "Easy Winners," "Augustan Club
Waltzes," as well as collaborations with
friends ("Swipesy Cakewalk" and "Sunflower
Slow Drag")--continued to flow from his
pen.[20]

---

[19] Jasen, Recorded Ragtime, p. 3.
[20] Blesh and Janis, pp. 52-53.

-11-

But Joplin's creative drive demanded larger scope than the individual rag. Before he left Sedalia, Joplin had written and produced, in one performance only, The Ragtime Dance, "a kind of ragtime ballet based on Negro social dances of the time, with sung narration."[21] Published against Stark's better judgment, The Ragtime Dance was not a successful publishing venture, though even today it gives proof of Joplin's interest in larger forms of the instrumental rag piece. Issued later in a shortened form, The Ragtime Dance has become a significant indication of Joplin's genius.

Joplin's high hopes for the recognition of ragtime's right to be compared with the greatest European classical music met another reversal when he failed to find a publisher for his first ragtime opera, A Guest of Honor, performed only once at St. Louis in 1903 and apparently now totally lost.[22] Meanwhile, he continued to compose and publish more individual rags—"Weeping Willow," "Palm Leaf Rag," "Chrysanthemums," "The Favorite," "The Sycamore," "Eugenia," "Leola Two-Step," "Binks," "Bethena," "Rosebud," and his lyrical tribute to the electrically lighted waterways of the St. Louis Fair, "The Cascades." Although he had withdrawn from the easy camaraderie and sensational life of the bawdyhouses and saloons, Joplin continued to receive, teach, encourage, and even collaborate with aspiring pianist-composers who sought him out.

5

[21] Blesh, "Scott Joplin: Black-American Classicist," p. xxii.
[22] Blesh and Janis, pp. 70-71.

-12-

Claiming for ragtime an essential seriousness, Joplin knew that it was difficult for
the average pianist and that much of the
music being passed off to the public as genuine "ragtime" was worthless and cheap. In
his notes accompanying his book of exercises,
School of Ragtime (1908), he stated his
awareness of both problems:

> What is scurrilously called ragtime is
> an invention that is here to stay. That
> is now conceded by all classes of musi-
> cians. That all publications masquerading
> under the name of ragtime are not the
> genuine article will be better known when
> these exercises are studied. That real
> ragtime of the higher class is rather
> difficult to play is a painful truth
> which most pianists have discovered. Syn-
> copations are no indication of light or
> trashy music, and to shy bricks at "hate-
> ful ragtime" no longer passes for musical
> culture.[23]

Although, at first, published arrangements
were awkward because white arrangers for
established music publishers did not know
how to handle syncopation and other intrica-
cies of black piano rags, they gradually
learned. Inexpensive sheet music very quickly
poured from the presses to meet the feverish
demands of a delighted public. And ragtime
offered a "pleasant alternative to Czerny
exercises and the parlor classics, a relief
to thousands of small boys and girls driven
to daily practice, a boon to the semiskilled

---

[23] The Collected Works of Scott Joplin, I,
284.

-13-

housewife looking for something to whet her
appetite."[24] By 1905, ragtime was America's
favorite music, and Scott Joplin could reasonably be called by his publisher and by
other ragtime artists the "king of ragtime."[25]

St. Louis's Louisiana Purchase Exposition
of 1904 coincided with the apex of ragtime's
first decade. As they had gravitated eleven
years earlier to the Chicago Fair, pianists
and composers poured into St. Louis; and pol-
ished ragtime could be heard everywhere.
"Cutting contests," tournaments of piano vir-
tuosity, although not on the fair's official
agenda, displayed new tunes and refined techniques. A host of black pianists formed
around Tom Turpin, operator of the Rosebud
Saloon, a pioneer player-composer, and creator of "Harlem Rag," "The Bowery Buck," "A
Ragtime Nightmare," "St. Louis Rag," and "The
Buffalo Rag."[26]

In 1906, Joplin's first marriage ended in
separation. His wife had no interest in his
creative achievements and aspirations; but
Joplin felt increasingly compelled to justify
ragtime and his own devotion to it. New York
seemed to be the proper place for a serious
American musician, and there Joplin, hoping
still for proper recognition, went in 1907.
In that same year he wrote four rags--"Non-
pareil," "Searchlight," "Gladiolus," and
"Rose Leaf"--and collaborated with friends on
"Heliotrope Bouquet" and "Lily Queen."

5

---

[24] Schafer and Riedel, p. 33.
[25] This appellation often appeared on the
covers of Joplin's rags published by Stark.
[26] Schafer and Riedel, pp. 109-10.

-14-

In the last decade of his life (and, quite appropriately, the final decade of rag-time's supremacy before the arrival of jazz), Joplin turned toward another major effort: the writing of his second ragtime opera, Treemonisha, published at his expense in 1911 but performed only once, in Harlem in 1915, without scenery or orchestra and with no suc-cess at all.[27] What was to have been the cli-max of his career and a complete justifica-tion of American ragtime as a serious art form ended in failure and obscurity, although serious students of music in the 1970's can unhesitatingly refer to Treemonisha as "the first demonstrably great American opera."[28]

At about the same time he was struggling to complete Treemonisha, to which he was tying all his hopes, Joplin broke with John Stark, who wanted to buy Joplin's composi-tions outright and no longer pay royalties. In the floods of rags coming from all parts of the country and from all kinds of com-posers, both black and white, Joplin saw not only imitations of his "classic ragtime" but also outright plagiarisms without any sort of acknowledgment. John Stark, who had by this time opened a New York office, and the established publishers in New York's Tin Pan Alley were reaping wealth from the pio-

---

[27] Winthrop Sargeant, "Rags and Riches," New Yorker, 25 March 1972, p. 112.

[28] Schafer and Riedel, p. 205. Irving Ko-lodin, however, prefers to call Treemonisha a "musical" (a distinctly American genre) rather than an "opera": "The Second Coming of Scott Joplin," Saturday Review, 1 April 1972, p. 18.

-15-

neers of ragtime, but Joplin was barely eking
out a living.[29] Despite a happy marriage to
his second wife, Lottie Stokes, Joplin suffered increasingly frequent bouts of depression and was finally admitted to the Manhat-
tan State Hospital for the insane in the fall
of 1916. By then hardly remembered in the
realm of entertainment, he died there on
April 1, 1917, just a few days before the
United States entered World War I.[30]

By 1917, the great days of ragtime were
over and with them Joplin's dreams and hopes.
After the war, jazz was America's new musical
craze. The solo piano gave way to the orchestra; the gramophone, unable in its in-
fancy to record solo piano very well, sup-
planted the pianola; the elegant cakewalk of
ragtime was forgotten as the public warmed to
the Charleston, the Lindy Hop, and the Black
Bottom in the Jazz Age of the 1920's; ragtime composition gave way to jazz improvisa-
tion.[31] Ahead lay approximately fifty years

5

---

[29] The commercial exploitation of ragtime
is traced in David Ewen, The Life and Death
of Tin Pan Alley: The Golden Age of American
Popular Music (New York: Funk and Wagnalls,
1964), pp. 168-78.

[30] Ortiz M. Walton, Music: Black, White &
Blue (New York: William Morrow & Co., 1972),
p. 45.

[31] Gunther Schuller relates "improvisa-
tion" to the essence of jazz in Early Jazz:
Its Roots and Musical Development (New York:
Oxford University Press, 1968), p. 378. According to Winthrop Sargeant, jazz is mainly
"an improvised music," whereas ragtime was
mainly composed and written down: "Rags and
Riches," p. 110.

of neglect for ragtime, the Rip Van Winkle--
or, perhaps better, the Sleeping Beauty--of
American music, and for Joplin, the greatest
exponent of "classic ragtime."

Ragtime may have gone underground but, unlike Joplin, it would not die. On into the
1920's, John Stark and Son, contemptuous of
jazz, continued to publish ragtime exclusively. A few great artists, like James Scott
in Kansas City and James P. Johnson in New
York, continued to play and record rags. And
much of ragtime's innovation and vitality,
through relatively young disciples like Jelly
Roll Morton of New Orleans, passed into the
idiom of jazz. But the best proof of pure
ragtime's refusal to lie down and die has
been its resurgence in the 1970's and the
growing conviction of music scholars and general public alike that it represents a major
development in American music and is a delight in and of itself.

-17-

BIBLIOGRAPHY

Blesh, Rudi. "Scott Joplin: Black American Classicist." The Collected Works of Scott Joplin. Ed. Vera Brodsky Lawrence. New York: New York Public Library, 1971. I, xiii-xl.

Blesh, Rudi, and Harriet Janis. They All Played Ragtime. Rev. ed. New York: Oak Publications, 1966.

Chase, Gilbert. "Joplin, Scott." World Book Encyclopedia, 1973 ed. XI, 126.

Ewen, David. The Life and Death of Tin Pan Alley: The Golden Age of American Popular Music. New York: Funk and Wagnalls, 1964.

Gammond, Peter. Scott Joplin and the Ragtime Era. New York: St. Martin's Press, 1975.

Jasen, David A. Recorded Ragtime, 1897-1958. Hamden, Conn.: Archon Books, 1973.

Joplin, Scott. The Collected Works of Scott Joplin. Ed. Vera Brodsky Lawrence. 2 vols. New York: New York Public Library, 1971.

Kolodin, Irving. "The Second Coming of Scott Joplin." Saturday Review, 1 April 1972, p. 18.

Program Notes for Scott Joplin, The Red Back Book, played by the New England Conservatory of Music Ragtime Ensemble, conducted by Gunther Schuller. Angel Record S-36060, c1973.

Russell, Ross. Jazz Style in Kansas City and the Southwest. Berkeley: University of California Press, 1971.

Sargeant, Winthrop. "Rags and Riches." New Yorker, 25 March 1972, pp. 110-12, 115.

Schafer, William J., and Johannes Riedel. The Art of Ragtime: Form and Meaning of an Original Black American Art. Baton Rouge: Louisiana State University Press, 1973.

5

-18-

Schuller, Gunther. <u>Early Jazz: Its Roots and
    Musical Development</u>. New York: Oxford Uni-
    versity Press, 1968.

Sheppard, R. Z. "The Music of Time." Review
    of <u>Ragtime</u> by E. L. Doctorow. <u>Time</u>, 14
    July 1975, p. 64.

Stade, George. Review of <u>Ragtime</u> by E. L.
    Doctorow. <u>New York Times Book Review</u>, 6
    July 1975, pp. 1-2.

Vinton, John, ed. <u>Dictionary of Contemporary
    Music</u>. New York: E. P. Dutton & Co.,
    1974.

Walton, Ortiz M. <u>Music: Black, White & Blue</u>.
    New York: William Morrow & Co., 1972.

two handbook

grammar 6

For many persons, just hearing or reading the word **grammar** causes feelings of anxiety, inadequacy, and perhaps boredom, as they recall classroom drills and exotic terms such as **subjunctive** and **gerund,** the importance of which they perhaps did not understand or appreciate. This reaction seems unnecessary, however, if we realize that the grammar of the English language, or indeed of any language, is simply a body of principles that work to ensure clear and effective communication. Moreover, many persons who have not formally studied these principles possess the bulk of them naturally, simply as a part of their heritage in growing up, in hearing and reading the language. A child just beginning to speak can often utter grammatically complex statements, though he or she would obviously not be able to understand, much less describe, their structures. And indeed, describing the workings of a language is not an easy task, as many contemporary linguists have found.

Until relatively recently, we have had only one anatomy of English to guide our speaking and writing: traditional or *prescriptive grammar,* which received its essential form as early as the eighteenth century from the model of Latin. Prescriptive grammar tried to fix the language and thus codified its principles into rules that governed *correct usage.* But in the twentieth century, as the authority of "the King's English" broke down, linguists recognized that much effective speaking and writing deviated from the older prescriptions. Consequently, these students of language developed an alternative grammar: *structural grammar,* which, basically, described how the changing language was being used and insisted that any attempt to fix it was unrealistic and ultimately futile. Even more recently, another alternative grammar has developed called *transformational grammar.* Still in the formative stages, this system attempts to show how very basic patterns can, through certain kinds of transformations, produce every

conceivable statement in English. The proponents of this
method of looking at grammar hope to reduce the use of
language to a few basic formulas capable of generating
and describing the most complex utterances and, at the
same time, to show how the mind itself works in the use
of language. Despite the multiplication and elaboration of
systems, the various grammars usually agree; but we have
chosen in this chapter to rely essentially on the traditional
system of grammar because it is simply more familiar to
most of us. However, we shall draw on elements of the
more recently developed systems when they seem useful
to a college writer.

6a parts of speech

All words are divided into nine parts of speech: noun,
pronoun, verb, adjective, adverb, preposition, conjunction, article, and interjection. These parts of speech may
be defined in various ways; perhaps the most practical
definitions are the following, taken from *The American
Heritage Dictionary of the English Language* (1969).

Noun: A word that names a person, place, thing,
quality, or act.

Examples: John F. Kennedy, Nashville, typewriter, beauty,
kindness

Pronoun: A word that substitutes for a noun and denotes a person or thing asked for, previously specified, or
understood from the context.

Examples: he (the opposing pitcher), they (the scholarship
holders), her (Mary's) bicycle, it (the defeat)

Verb: A word that expresses existence, action, or occurrence.

Examples: be, was, hasten, love, collide, slip, win, shoot

Adjective: A word used to modify a noun by limiting, qualifying, or specifying.

Examples: few, second, gray, undying, modern, literacy, physical, imaginative

Adverb: A word that modifies a verb, adjective, or other adverb.

Examples: slowly, wildly, too, very, highly, extremely, exceedingly

Preposition: A word that indicates the relation of a noun to a verb, an adjective, or another noun.

Examples: over, under, for, in, by, with, at, of, before, to

Conjunction: A word that connects words, phrases, clauses, or sentences.

Examples: and, or, but, however, although, because, consequently, moreover, nevertheless

Article: A word used before a noun to signal a noun and to specify its application.

Examples: a, an, the

Interjection: A word of exclamation, capable of standing alone.

Examples: ouch! mercy! oh! help! ah! outrageous!

6a1 nouns and pronouns

Case   Nouns and pronouns in English may be used as subjects, complements, or objects. If a noun or pronoun is used as a subject or subjective complement, it is in the nominative *case;* if an object or objective complement, the objective case. Possessive case of nouns and pronouns shows ownership, origin, or relationship.

The *book* stressed the importance of the frontier in America. (nominative case)

John returned the *book* to the library. (objective case)

In the first sentence **book** is the subject of the sentence; in the second, **book** is the direct object of the verb **returned.** The form of the word is the same in either case, and this is always true in English if the word is a noun. For example:

The *magazine* contained two articles about President Ford. (*magazine* is the subject of the sentence)

She took the *magazine* on her trip to Oklahoma. (*magazine* is the object of the verb *took*)

The first *mechanic* found nothing seriously wrong with the car. (*mechanic* is the subject of the sentence)

Mr. Johnson distrusted the *mechanic* at Marion Autos. (*mechanic* is the object of the verb *distrusted*)

The *boxes* were stored for one year at the Delaware warehouse. (*boxes* is the subject of the sentence)

The company stored the *boxes* for one year at the Delaware warehouse. (*boxes* is the object of the verb *stored*)

The spring *picnic* this year had a fine turnout of teen-agers. (*picnic* is the subject of the sentence)

We scheduled the spring *picnic* early in order to attract as many teen-agers as possible. (*picnic* is the object of the verb *scheduled*)

If the word is a pronoun, however, its form in the nominative case is usually different from its form in the objective case.

He found himself wandering toward the cottage by the lake. (nominative case)

His father found *him* wandering toward the cottage by the lake. (objective case)

In the first sentence, **he** is the subject of the sentence; in the second, **him** is the object of the verb **found.** Here are the subject and object forms of the personal pronouns:

Nominative case	*Objective case*
I	me
you (singular)	you (singular)
he	him
she	her
it	it
we	us
you (plural)	you (plural)
they	them

I found that I couldn't trust her with the money. (subject of the sentence)

She trusted *me* before I told her what I knew. (object of the verb *trusted*)

You will find him easy to work with once you get to know him. (subject of the sentence)

I saw *you* before you left for Texas. (object of the verb *saw*)

We hope to buy a new car next year. (subject of the sentence)

The children found *us* at the dealer's looking at new cars. (object of the verb *found*)

They marched quickly into position and began firing. (subject of the sentence)

The enemy met *them* as they emerged from the woods and opened fire. (object of the verb *met*)

A common problem is the failure to use the objective case for the pronoun **who** when it is called for. Notice the proper uses in the following instances:

Who called while I was out? (subject of sentence)

The student *who* studies will succeed. (subject of subordinate clause)

Whom can I trust with the manuscript? (object of verb phrase *can trust*)

To *whom* will you go if the letter doesn't come? (object of the preposition *to*)

Increasingly in speech **who** is used for both the nominative and the objective cases, but the distinction between the forms should be preserved in written discourse.

In addition to being used as both subjects and objects of verbs, as was mentioned above, nouns and occasionally pronouns can also be used as *subjective complements* and *objective complements* — that is, they can echo the meaning of the subject of the sentence, although they follow the verb; or they can follow the direct object and rename that direct object as a consequence of the action of the verb.

John Steinbeck was a great *novelist.* (subjective complement *novelist* echoes or renames the subject *John Steinbeck*)

His most famous novel was a *tale* of migrant workers. (subjective complement renames, restates *novel*)

She called her husband *Spanky.* (objective complement renames and completes the direct object, *husband*)

The firehouse gang, however, called him *Teddybear.* (objective complement follows and completes the meaning of the direct object, *him*)

The Chamber of Commerce named him *"Man of the Year"* for his fearlessness at a fire. (objective complement completes and renames the direct object, *him*)

So familiar is this use of subjective and objective comple-

6

ments that sentences in which they occur make up one of the basic sentence patterns, as described in section 1d, "*The Sentence.*"

Possessive case for nouns nearly always involves the use of the apostrophe (**John's** book, **Keats's** poetry, **Henry James's** novels, the **Joneses'** new car, **Harry Jones's** filling station); for pronouns there is usually inflection, a change of form (**her, hers, its, theirs, ours, yours, whose**), rather than any use of the apostrophe. The possessive case is usually a modifier, but it may also take the role of complement.

Joan gave me **her** book. (modifier)

The book is now **mine**. (complement)

Once it was **hers**. (complement)

Number   Both nouns and pronouns have *number*— either singularity or plurality. Most nouns form the plural number by adding **–s** or **–es** to the singular forms. Thus, **cards, pencils, baseballs,** and **boxes, buses, tomatoes.** Some use the same form for both the singular and plural: **fish, deer, pair.** Many change the form significantly: **child, children; life, lives; duty, duties; criterion, criteria; datum, data.** If you are unsure of the correct plural form of a noun, look up the word in the dictionary. Any deviation from the simple addition of **–s** to form the plural will be noted there. The plurals of pronouns are the same as the singulars, except for two demonstrative pronouns (**this, these; that, those**) and the personal pronouns, as follows:

Singular		*Plural*
I		we
you	(same)	you
he, she, it		they

Since a verb used with a noun or pronoun must agree with it in number, the writer must be sure to recognize the relationship. In the following sentence, for example, the relative pronoun **that** is plural because it refers to the plural noun **styles** and therefore requires a plural verb **were:**

The styles *that were* available did not interest her.

One of the common mechanical errors in writing — lack of agreement between subject and verb — occurs because the writer has failed to observe the number of the noun or pronoun in choosing the form of the verb used with it.

6a 2 verbs

The fundamental form of the verb is the infinitive — **to** + verb — as in the following: **to walk, to study, to dance, to shoot, to think, to procrastinate, to wonder.** The *conjugation* of a verb is the various forms the verb can take to indicate variations in *person, number, tense, mood,* and *voice.* The most important of these forms are the first three — person, number, and tense.

Person, Number, and Tense   *Person* refers to the relationship between speaker(s) and person(s) or thing(s) spoken of: first person is speaker(s) (**I, we**); second person is person(s) addressed (**you, you**); and third person is individual(s) or thing(s) spoken of (**he, she, it, they**). Once again, *number* refers to singularity or plurality of person(s). **I, you, he, she, it** are singular; **we, you, they** are plural.

The *tense* of a verb indicates the time (past, present, or future) and continuance or duration (progressive) or completion (perfect) of the action or state. There are six tenses: *present, past, future, present perfect, past perfect,* and *future perfect.* Thus the verb **to work** (or any other *regular verbs* which in English form simple past tense and past participle by adding the suffix **–ed** to the present infinitive) is conjugated as follows:

	SINGULAR	PLURAL

Present tense

	SINGULAR	PLURAL
First person	I work (am working)	we work (are working)
Second person	you work (are working)	you work (are working)
Third person	he, she, it works (is working)	they work (are working)

Past tense

	SINGULAR	PLURAL
First person	I worked (was working)	we worked (were working)
Second person	you worked (were working)	you worked (were working)
Third person	he, she, it worked (was working)	they worked (were working)

Future tense

	SINGULAR	PLURAL
First person	I shall work (shall be working)	we shall work (shall be working)
Second person	you will work (will be working)	you will work (will be working)
Third person	he, she, it will work (will be working)	they will work (will be working)

Present perfect tense

	SINGULAR	PLURAL
First person	I have worked (have been working)	we have worked (have been working)
Second person	you have worked (have been working)	you have worked (have been working)
Third person	he, she, it has worked (has been working)	they have worked (have been working)

Past perfect tense

	SINGULAR	PLURAL
First person	I had worked (had been working)	we had worked (had been working)
Second person	you had worked (had been working)	you had worked (had been working)
Third person	he, she, it had worked (had been working)	they had worked (had been working)

Future perfect tense

	SINGULAR	PLURAL
First person	I shall have worked (shall have been working)	we shall have worked (shall have been working)
Second person	you will have worked (will have been working)	you will have worked (will have been working)
Third person	he, she, it will have worked (will have been working)	they will have worked (will have been working)

Note: many writers insist on the use of the helping verb **shall** in the first person singular and plural (**I shall, we shall**), and **will** in the remaining forms of the conjugation for formal written prose. Informal use, now widespread, however, permits the use of **will** for all of the forms.

Some verbs — *irregular verbs* — in English do not simply add endings like **–s** and **–ed,** as in the case of the verb **to work,** but rather change the form of the word itself. An example of this is a verb like **to ring,** which is conjugated as follows:

	SINGULAR	PLURAL
	Present tense	
First person	I ring	we ring
Second person	you ring	you ring
Third person	he, she, it rings	they ring
	Past tense	
First person	I rang	we rang
Second person	you rang	you rang
Third person	he, she, it rang	they rang
	Future tense	
First person	I shall ring	we shall ring
Second person	you will ring	you will ring
Third person	he, she, it will ring	they will ring
	Present perfect tense	
First person	I have rung	we have rung
Second person	you have rung	you have rung
Third person	he, she, it has rung	they have rung
	Past perfect tense	
First person	I had rung	we had rung
Second person	you had rung	you had rung
Third person	he, she, it had rung	they had rung
	Future perfect tense	
First person	I shall have rung	we shall have rung
Second person	you will have rung	you will have rung
Third person	he, she, it will have rung	they will have rung

You will have observed that the progressive forms, future tense, and all the perfect tenses require an *auxiliary (helping) verb.* These verbs in English are **will, shall, would, should, can, could, may, might, must, ought.** Even when these helping verbs appear alone, as in a question or conversation, the main verb is always implied.

Principal Parts   As the table on p. 205 shows, the three essential forms of the verb **to ring** are **ring, rang, rung** — called, respectively, the present infinitive (without **to**), the past tense, and the past participle. Because these three forms, always provided in the dictionary entry, are the bases of all tenses, you should have no trouble conjugating any verb.

Mood   The remaining two properties of verbs — mood and voice — are less important to our understanding, but we need this knowledge rather more frequently than we might at first think. *Mood* refers to the writer's attitude toward the factuality or likelihood of the action or condition expressed. The *indicative mood* expresses statements of fact or declarations; the *subjunctive mood,* statements contrary to fact or of hypothesis (possibility); and the *imperative mood,* commands, directions, or injunctions. Here are several examples:

Many fans *continue* to maintain that Babe Ruth *was* the greatest home run hitter who ever *lived.* (indicative mood)
Many young men and women *find* a tour of duty in the armed services valuable. (indicative mood)
If this *were* 1958, we *would be listening* to the Diamonds and Little Richard. (subjunctive mood)
If an exhibit *be held* in the Union, I'll bring my pet whale. (subjunctive mood — an exhibit is possible, but unlikely)
Should you *go, buy* three extra copies for use in the dormitories. (*should go,* subjunctive mood; *buy,* imperative mood)
Go! (imperative mood)

Finish the first task before you **begin** the second. (**finish,** imperative mood; **begin,** indicative mood)

Once again, notice that formal prose calls for the use of **were** in the subjunctive rather than **was,** though in informal situations you may use **was.** Then, too, notice that the subject **(you)** is always understood in the imperative mood — **(You) go!**

Voice   *Voice* indicates the relation between the subject and the action expressed by the verb. There are two voices: *active* and *passive*. In the active voice of a verb the subject acts, whereas in the passive voice the subject is acted upon.

       S   V
The **poet found** just the right image to convey his idea. (active voice)

       S   V
Over **half** of the class **failed** the examination. (active voice)

  S   V
Applicants for the position of clerk-typist **should fill out**

              V
Form 20A and **submit** it at Window 3. (active voice)

  S   V
St. Louis was the departure point for many travelers west. (active voice)

S V
She ran toward the dock, hoping to see him before he sailed. (active voice)

             S   V
Just the right **image was found** by the poet to convey his idea. (passive voice)

         S   V
The **examination was failed** by over half of the class. (passive voice)

  S   V   V
Form 20A should be filled out and **submitted** at Window 3 by applicants for the position of clerk-typist. (passive voice)

<pre>
S   V   V
</pre>
Apartments are sometimes ***rented*** for three months rather than a full year. (passive voice)

<pre>
       S   V
</pre>
The ***Civil War was ignited*** when the Confederacy fired upon Ft. Sumter. (passive voice)

Notice that the first three active-voice sentences can easily be rewritten in the passive voice because they follow the pattern of subject-verb-direct object (discussed in section 6b1 and in section 1d, "The Sentence"). The last two active-voice sentences cannot be similarly rewritten because they follow the pattern of subject-verb but do not take direct objects. You will find suggestions for effective use of the active and passive voice in section 1d.

Verbals From verbs are fashioned *verbals: gerunds,* which function as nouns; *participles,* which function as adjectives; and *infinitives,* which serve as nouns, adjectives, or adverbs. Although they function as parts of speech other than verbs, verbals retain some of the properties of verbs: they possess voice and tense, and they may take subjects or objects.

Gerund: always ends in **–ing** and functions as a noun.

Reading books makes a complete person. (gerund phrase; subject of the sentence)

Participle: ends in **–ing, –ed, –d, –t** and functions as an adjective.

All elementary school students receive ***reading*** books. (participle; modifies ***books***)

Infinitive: begins with **to,** either stated or implied, and functions as a noun, an adjective, or an adverb.

To read three books a week is a modest ambition. (infinitive phrase; used as noun and subject of sentence)

The best books *to read* are always the last *to be reviewed*. (*to read* is infinitive as adjective; *to be reviewed* is infinitive as adverb—note the passive voice)

6a3 adjectives

Attributive Adjectives, Subjective Complements, and Objective Complements Adjectives usually precede the nouns they modify, as in the following instances:

    ADJ   NOUN   ADJ NOUN
American humor is a *native genre* that has become a part of
ADJ NOUN
world literature.

        ADJ   NOUN
The *preliminary report* lacked details about the cause of the accident.

                ADJ NOUN   NOUN
Let us now praise *famous men* and *women.*

Adjectives of this kind are called *attributive adjectives*—that is, they attribute some quality to the following noun or nouns they modify. But adjectives can also appear elsewhere in the sentence, as follows:

NOUN   ADJ
She is *beautiful* when she smiles.

        NOUN   ADJ
The *salesman* was *rude* to the secretary who refused to let him see Mr. Thompson.

        NOUN
The *selection* of Adams to play quarterback may be
    ADJ
unpopular with the alumni and fans.

In each of these sentences the adjective modifies the noun but appears after the noun in the predicate and is therefore called a *predicate adjective,* or *subjective complement.* Sentences which contain a predicate adjective or subjective complement constitute one of the basic sentence patterns in English (discussed in section 1d).

Adjectives can also appear after a direct object and modify that object as a consequence of the action of the verb. In such cases the adjectives are called *objective complements.*

           DO OC
The jury found **him guilty** as charged.

         DO   OC
He sanded the **grain smooth.**

         DO OC
The manager turned the **air blue** when the umpire called the batter out.

All objective complements are not adjectives, but the adjective is so commonly used this way that this pattern is another of the basic sentence kernels described in section 1d.

Degree   Every adjective has three degrees: *positive, comparative,* and *superlative.*

Adjective	Positive degree	Comparative degree	Superlative degree
blue	blue	bluer	bluest
tense	tense	tenser	tensest
accurate	accurate	more accurate	most accurate
inept	inept	more inept	most inept
gross	gross	grosser	grossest
simple	simple	simpler	simplest
lovely	lovely	lovelier	loveliest
serious	serious	more serious	most serious

As you see, some adjectives form the comparative and superlative degrees by adding **–er** and **–est,** respectively, to the positive degree or basic form, whereas others add **more** and **most,** respectively, before the positive form. When they are appropriate, the dictionary provides the **–er** and **–est** forms; their absence indicates that **more** and **most** are to be used in forming the comparative and superlative forms of that adjective.

6a4 adverbs

Adverbs, like adjectives, also have three degrees: *positive, comparative,* and *superlative.*

Adverb	Positive degree	Comparative degree	Superlative degree
wildly	wildly	more wildly	most wildly
carefully	carefully	more carefully	most carefully
quickly	quickly	more quickly	most quickly
cleanly	cleanly	more cleanly	most cleanly
ferociously	ferociously	more ferociously	most ferociously

Adverbs usually end in **–ly** and usually form the comparative and superlative with **more** and **most,** respectively. Many common adverbs, however, form their comparative and superlative degrees irregularly.

Adverb	Positive degree	Comparative degree	Superlative degree
well	well	better	best
badly	badly	worse	worst
fast	fast	faster	fastest

Writers often confuse adjectives and adverbs, as in the following cases:

He plays third base *good,* even though he is a rookie. (incorrect)

He plays third base *well,* even though he is a rookie. (correct)

(*Well* is an adverb modifying *plays; good* is an adjective.)

The kitchen looks *well* since you painted it blue and white. (incorrect)

The kitchen looks *good* since you painted it blue and white. (correct)

(*Good* is a predicate adjective completing the verb of being *looks; well* is an adverb which, if it modified *looks,* would indicate sharpness of sense—a meaning clearly not intended here.)

She felt *badly* because Tim wouldn't admit that she had won fairly. (incorrect)

She felt *bad* because Tim wouldn't admit that she had won fairly. (correct)

(*Bad* is a predicate adjective completing the verb of being *felt; badly* is an adverb which, if it modified *felt,* would indicate sense impairment—a meaning clearly not intended here.)

She finished the concerto *bad,* and then burst into tears. (incorrect)

She finished the concerto *badly,* and then burst into tears. (correct)

(*Badly* is an adverb modifying *finished; bad* is an adjective.)

This drink you made for me tastes *bitterly.* (incorrect)

This drink you made for me tastes *bitter.* (correct)

(*Bitter* is a predicate adjective completing the verb of being *tastes; bitterly* is an adverb which, if it modified *tastes,* would indicate, absurdly, that the drink had the sense of taste—and an emotional one, at that.)

Before he left the room, he spoke *bitter* about the treatment he had received. (incorrect)

Before he left the room, he spoke *bitterly* about the treatment he had received. (correct)

(*Bitterly* is an adverb modifying *spoke; bitter* is an adjective.)

You must always determine whether the word modifies a noun or pronoun (in which case it is an adjective) or a verb, an adjective, or an adverb (in which case it is an adverb), and then use the appropriate part of speech.

6a5 prepositions

A prepositional phrase—consisting of a preposition and the noun(s) or pronoun(s) it governs—generally functions either as an adjective or an adverb.

The reporter **for the Daily Planet** is waiting in the lobby. (adjective phrase)

Many of the automobiles **of the 1920's** are classics. (adjective phrase)

He went **across the river** to look at the wheat field. (adverb phrase)

Marian paused **for an instant** and then left the room. (adverb phrase)

In using prepositions, you must remember to use these connectors idiomatically—that is, as they are normally or characteristically used in English. Consider the following examples:

The teacher should indicate a grade **of** every student (incorrect)

The teacher should indicate a grade **for** every student. (correct)

Carson has been a fugitive **of** the law since he was fourteen years old. (incorrect)

Carson has been a fugitive **from** the law since he was fourteen years old. (correct)

In throwing ability he is equal **with** Bob Shaw, who usually plays third base. (incorrect)

In throwing ability he is equal *to* Bob Shaw, who usually plays third base. (correct)

Her skirt and blouse were made *with* gingham. (incorrect)

Her skirt and blouse were made *of* gingham. (correct)

In comparing the figures of the first project *to* these, I find that we must cut down on the materials used. (incorrect)

In comparing the figures of the first project *with* these, I find that we must cut down on the materials used. (correct)

Even so seemingly minor an error as the wrong preposition causes writing to appear semiliterate. Consequently, the writer who does not have a good ear for the way in which prepositions are used idiomatically may consult a dictionary or a handbook of English usage, many of which give useful guidance.

6a6 conjunctions

Conjunctions are basically of two kinds: *coordinating conjunctions,* which link words, phrases, and clauses of equal grammatical weight; and *subordinating conjunctions,* which link subordinate clauses with main clauses. Familiar coordinating conjunctions are **and, but, or, nor, for, yet;** familiar subordinating conjunctions are **although, because, unless, after, when, where, if, while, since** (and many more). A third category can also be described — *correlative conjunctions,* which indicate reciprocal or complementary grammatical relationship. This kind consists of paired conjunctions such as **neither-nor, either-or, not only-but also.** A fourth category of words functioning conjunctively is *conjunctive adverbs,* which link ideas or make transitions from one clause to another: **however, moreover, nevertheless, thus, consequently, furthermore, likewise, then, also, besides.** The writer will find ample use for all of these conjunctions, as the following examples illustrate:

Reading *and* writing fiction are her two favorite pastimes. (coordinating conjunction linking parallel nouns used as subjects)

I arrived shortly before noon, *but* the bus had already left for Junction City. (coordinating conjunction linking two independent clauses)

He quit his job *because* he wanted to spend more time with his wife and two sons. (subordinating conjunction linking the main clause of the sentence to a following dependent clause, which modifies it)

The house, *which* my father used to own, became a boy's club and recreation center. (relative pronoun linking the subordinate clause to the subject of the sentence, itself the object of the infinitive *to own*)

Either you turn in the key issued to you *or* I will report this matter to the dean. (correlative conjunctions linking the two independent clauses)

During the semester I worked *not only* eight hours a day at the restaurant *but also* three hours in the evening counseling delinquent teen-agers. (correlative conjunctions linking the two parallel direct objects of the verb *worked*)

The contractor has failed for the third straight month to complete the scheduled work; *moreover,* according to our inspectors, the completed work has been slipshod. (conjunctive adverb logically connecting the idea of one clause to another idea but specifying their relationship—in this case, making more intense the judgment of the contractor's work)

The Chiefs had a losing season last year; *however,* the prospects for next year, since the addition of Johnny Simpson, are indeed promising. (conjunctive adverb connecting one clause to another and showing that the second qualifies the first)

Even a quick glance at these examples reveals quite clearly the important role conjunctions play in showing exact relationships between grammatical parts. You should become familiar with the various conjunctions available to you—and put them to work for you.

6

6a7 articles

In English, articles are of two types: the definite article, **the,** and the two indefinite articles, **a** and **an.** The definite article specifies or fixes the identity of the noun that follows it, whereas the indefinite article does not. Thus, in the case of the former, we have **the dog, the book, the umbrella, the typewriter, the porch, the telephones, the data, the paintbrush**—in all of which **the** limits or restricts the noun to a certain one. In the case of the latter, we have **a chair, a girl, a card, an angel, an inquest, an oval, an herb**—in all of which **a** or **an** points to one nonspecific person or thing. Notice that **an** is used before nouns that begin with the vowels **a, e, i, o, u** or with an unpronounced **h,** such as **heiress.** Definite articles precede either singular or plural nouns; indefinite articles, only singular nouns. Lapses in the proper use of articles are embarrassing and suggest to the reader that the writer either is careless or has limited language skills.

6a8 interjections

The interjection is a burst of emotion in writing that is unconnected grammatically with what precedes or follows it. Nearly any part of speech that expresses this explosion of feeling may be an interjection:

Damnation! (noun)
Hers! (pronoun)
Punt! (verb)
Help! (verb)
Beautiful! (adjective)
Exceedingly! (adverb)
Over! (preposition)
Or? (conjunction)
Ouch! (interjection)

Only articles—*a, an, the*—are unlikely to serve as inter-jections. The interjection may simply be a sound, as in **Oof! Pow! Oh! Ah! Ugh! Ow!** Generally the interjection requires an exclamation mark (!), but if it is mild, a comma linking it to a statement may be sufficient:

Oh, I don't know whether I want to go or not.

Oh, really?

My, my, how some people do get around.

In writing expository prose, you should use the inter-jection infrequently. Even in writing prose fiction, you should beware of its overuse, which reduces the emotional force or impact upon the reader.

6b common problems in grammar

6b1 basic concepts of grammar: a brief review

In section 1d, we presented the sentence primarily from the standpoint of rhetoric or effectiveness, but much of that discussion implied the grammar or correctness of the sentence as well—in particular, the extended treatment and illustration of fundamental grammatical concepts such as *phrase, clause, sentence, sentence types* (including *fragment*), and *modifier*. To review briefly, let us define and illustrate each of these concepts.

a. Phrases A *phrase* is two or more words, not having both a subject and a verb, that form a unit.

American literature **to the Civil War** is the area **of knowledge** that the test **will cover in depth.** (**to the Civil War:** preposi-tional phrase modifying **literature,** therefore functions as an adjective; **of knowledge:** prepositional phrase modifying *area,* therefore functions as an adjective; ***will cover:*** verb phrase; ***in depth:*** prepositional phrase modifying ***will cover,*** therefore is an adverb)

Seeing a cabin far ***up to his right,*** he tried ***to climb up the side of the mountain.*** (***seeing a cabin:*** participial phrase modifying ***he,*** therefore is an adjective; ***up to his right:*** prepositional phrase modifying ***far,*** therefore is an adverb; ***to climb:*** infinitive phrase used as the direct object of the verb ***tried,*** therefore is a noun; ***up the side:*** prepositional phrase modifying the verb ***climb,*** therefore is an adverb; ***of the mountain:*** prepositional phrase modifying ***side,*** therefore is an adjective).

Helping our companions is a duty we all ***must share on this trip.*** (***helping our companions:*** gerund phrase, therefore is a noun; ***must share:*** verb phrase; ***on this trip:*** prepositional phrase modifying ***must share,*** therefore is an adverb)

As you can see, there are five kinds of phrases:

> prepositional phrase
> verb phrase
> participial phrase
> infinitive phrase
> gerund phrase

They may be used as

> an adjective
> a verb
> an adverb
> a noun

b. Clauses A *clause* is a group of words containing both a subject and a verb.

    S   V
Jesus wept.

The working ***relationship*** between the two companies ***has*** continually ***improved.***

Pitching for the Angels against the Royals, ***Nolan Ryan*** ***struck out*** fourteen and ***walked*** five, one of the better performances of the season.

In each of these examples, the clause is an *independent* or *main clause* because it can stand alone. Another way of saying this is that it does not modify any other element in the sentence.

In the following examples, however, the clause is a *dependent* or *subordinate clause* because it cannot stand alone. That is, it serves in each case, respectively, as an adjective, a noun, or an adverb—the three basic functions of the dependent or subordinate clause.

The car ***that passed us at Allentown*** later careened off a high curve. (has both a subject ***that*** and a verb ***passed***—making it a clause—and the clause modifies ***car***—making it an adjective clause)

Whoever sent us that information deserves a reward of some kind. (has both a subject ***whoever*** and a verb ***sent,*** and because the clause functions as the subject of the sentence, it is a noun clause)

When I learned of the forfeit, I sat down and wrote the commissioner of the league a letter of protest. (has both a subject ***I*** and a verb ***learned,*** and because the clause modifies the main clause which follows it, it is an adverb clause, or sentence modifier)

Generally, sentences in good writing contain both independent and some dependent clauses, as in the following examples in which (1) main clauses are in bold italic type

and subordinate clauses are in brackets, (2) their subjects and verbs are marked, and (3) the functions of the
dependent clauses are indicated:

      S   V   V

[If you have never seen the sights and sounds at the Grand

               S   V   V

Ole Opry], *you have missed one of life's great pleasures.*
(The dependent clause—in brackets—modifies the independent clause—in bold type—and is therefore an adverb
clause, or sentence modifier.)

         S   V V   S

The course in auto mechanics will begin [when ten persons

  V   V   V

have signed up for it]. (The dependent clause—in brackets
—modifies the independent clause and is therefore an adverbial clause or sentence modifier.)

         S   S   V   V

My brother, [who practices law in Cleveland], *was an outstanding scholar and athlete in college.* (The dependent
clause modifies the subject *my brother* and is therefore an
adjective clause.)

        S   V   S   V

[*Whether I play tennis this weekend*] *depends* on [how

              S   V   V

many household chores I must do]. (The first dependent
clause is the subject of the entire sentence. It names *what*
depends, and is therefore a noun clause. The second dependent clause is a noun clause because it forms the object
of the preposition *on;* the entire prepositional phrase, however, functions as an adverb modifying the verb *depends.*)

                            S   V   V

Most television programs [that describe and analyze social

                                       V

and political events and conditions] seldom *receive* the

                   S   V

recognition [they deserve]. (The first dependent clause
modifies the subject of the independent clause—*programs*

—and is therefore an adjective clause. The second dependent clause modifies the noun **recognition** and is therefore an adjective clause.)

S   S   V   S
Colleges and universities report [that the percentage of

                    S   V
incoming students (who need remedial work) in basic

          V   V
English skills has increased significantly]. (The first dependent clause is the direct object of the verb **report** and is therefore a noun clause. The second dependent clause— **who need remedial work**—modifies the noun **students** and is therefore an adjective clause.)

c. *Sentences*   A *sentence* is a group of words, containing both a subject (perhaps only implied) and a verb, that can stand alone. In other words, a sentence is, at the very least, an independent or main clause, but of course can contain any number of words, phrases, and clauses in addition to this independent or main clause. For example:

V
Help! (subject *you* implied)

V S   V
May I borrow your car? (one main clause)

    S   V   V   S   V
[If he can serve in Germany], **Tom plans to reenlist in the Army.** (one subordinate clause, one main clause)

          S   V   S
Mr. Richards drove to Mexico City in April, and **his wife**
        S   V   S   V
and children flew down in May [when school was out]. (two main clauses and one subordinate clause)

Sentence types: grammatical forms defined by the presence and number of independent and dependent clauses in the sentence. A full discussion of these types, as well as of other ways of describing sentence types, may be found in section 1d. For our purposes here, the following definitions and examples will suffice:

1. *Simple sentence:* contains one independent clause and no dependent clauses.

      S   V
The Old Testament is an exciting book to read.
According to an announcement last week, **this year's**
   S   S   S   V   V
Humanities Lecture Series will present a literary critic, an historian, and a sculptor.

2. *Complex sentence:* contains one independent clause and one or more dependent clauses.

         S   V   V
Our Chamber of Commerce is sponsoring a winter carni-
     S V V V
val, [which will be held during the first week in December] on the campus of the junior college.
    S   S   V   V   V
The paint [that you bought on sale] **does not cover well.**

3. *Compound sentence:* contains two or more independent clauses and no dependent clauses.

     S   V
Michael Russell, Chief Engineer, **wrote the rough draft of**
            S   S
the report, and **Robert Miller,** Head of Technical Com-
          V
munications, **revised it for publication and distribution.**
 S V   S V
He asked me to work for him Saturday morning, but **I had**
       V
already made other plans.

4. *Compound-complex sentence:* contains two or more independent clauses and one or more dependent clauses.

S   V   S   V   S
He attended M.I.T. and *she attended Radcliffe* [until they

V   V
were married].

    S   V
The party began at Howard's hotel room, but *around mid-*

        S   S   V
night Howard and several of his guests drove downtown

                              S   V
to the Casino Royale, [where they celebrated until dawn].

5. *Fragment:* contains no independent clause, though it may contain one or more dependent clauses or phrases.

                                            S   V
Our thanks, then, to the committee [whose efforts made this special day possible]. (contains no independent subject and independent verb, only a dependent clause, in brackets; it can be argued, of course, that an understood *we give* precedes *our thanks.*)

                                  S   S
A story, in short, in which [the comedy and tragedy of life

V
are inextricably mixed]. (contains no independent subject and independent verb, only a dependent clause, in brackets)

Notice that both of these fragments, as is often the case, depend for any legitimacy they may have on a previous statement that has been omitted.

d. Modifiers   A *modifier* is a word or group of words (phrase or clause) that limits or qualifies another word or group of words. Modifiers are of two basic kinds: (1) ad-

jectival modifiers — those which modify nouns and pronouns — and (2) adverbial modifiers — those which modify
verbs, adjectives, and adverbs.

1. *Adjectival modifiers:*

ADJ NOUN
The ***weary hiker*** motioned to us. (one-word adjective)

NOUN ADJ
The ***car*** is ***new.*** (one-word adjective)

ADJ   PRONOUN
Laughing hysterically, she turned down his proposal. (participial phrase used as adjective)

NOUN   ADJ
The ***speaker*** sat down, ***hoping for the best.*** (participial
phrase used as adjective)

NOUN   ADJ
The ***catcher, whom the Aeros purchased a week ago,*** is a
weak hitter. (relative clause used as adjective)

NOUN   ADJ
The ***newspaper that printed the story*** has often been
charged with irresponsibility. (relative clause used as adjective)

2. *Adverbial modifiers:*

V   ADV
The woman ***spoke sharply*** to her child. (one-word adverb)

ADV ADJ
She is a ***highly paid*** consultant. (one-word adverb)

ADV ADJ
Editors can be ***very helpful*** to authors. (one-word adverb)

V   ADV
The robber ***threw*** his handgun ***into a trash barrel.*** (prepositional phrase used as adverb)

V   ADV
I'll ***go when I have finished this job.*** (clause used as adverb)

     V   ADV
Leave the key *where I can find it.* (clause used as adverb)

                  ADV
                 ADV ADV ADV
[*Before a traveler goes very far north,*] he begins to see the mountains surrounding Santa Fe. (clause used as an adverb and containing a phrase used as an adverb)

    With this brief review of some basic concepts in mind, we can now isolate some of the main grammatical problems that writers have in writing correct and effective sentences.

6b2 agreement of subject and verb

Subjects and verbs must agree in person and number.

   S   V
Students need their own personal dictionaries.

       S   V
Whoever finds the coin wins the prize.

  S V
You are the only one whose judgment I can trust.

 S V
I wonder if everyone is as puzzled about John Brown as I am.

If the subject does not begin the sentence or if words intervene between the subject and the verb, the writer needs to be especially careful in matching the subject properly with its verb. For example:

Since he hasn't played more than three or four innings this
        S   V
season, *Harry,* after considerable thought, *has decided* to quit the team.

     S   V

The ***dogs*** that my brother bought from the farmer ***were*** of little use to him in hunting.

              S

According to one of my teachers, ***books*** on the history of

         V

the United States ***are being sold*** at half price at the university bookstore.

  Collective Nouns Certain nouns, called collective nouns (**cast, team, group, fraternity, crew**), require singular verbs when they denote a group considered as a unit and plural verbs when they refer to individual members of the group.

     S   V

The ***couple was vacationing*** in Hawaii when the bad news arrived. (two people considered as one)

     S   V

The ***couple were having*** marital problems because of the constant interference of their parents. (two people considered as individuals)

     S   V

The ***faculty demands*** its right to participate in the governance of the university. (college teachers considered as a body within the university)

     S   V

The ***faculty have voted*** 45–21 in favor of the Dean's controversial proposal. (college instructors acting as individuals)

       S   V

The ***committee is charged*** with studying the present curriculum and recommending changes for next year. (the group as a whole is given one assignment)

       S   V

The ***committee were debating*** the issues that had been discussed the day before in subcommittees. (individual members have different points of view)

Irregular Plurals   Some nouns are plural by definition and require plural verbs, such as **data, criteria,** and **media:**

S   V
The **data were taken** from the second test run.

V   S
There **are** three **criteria** for selecting an engine: cost, performance, and emission control.

S   V
The **media have been** antagonistic to Senator Roberts' views.

Nouns denoting weights and measures are, by convention, construed as singular and thus require singular verbs:

S   V
Twelve pounds of cement **was added** to the mixture.

S
According to the handbook, **12,000 revolutions per minute**

V
is permissible.

S V
If you want my opinion, **$12 is** too high a price to pay for this purse.

Occasionally the intention of the writer will determine the number of the noun and therefore its verb, as in the following:

S   S V
Every **boy** and **girl has** an obligation to help keep the area clean and neat. (every individual in the group is stressed)

S   S   V
Each **writer** and **editor was told** to eliminate the deadwood from his or her work. (each individual in the group is stressed)

Since the heart of the sentence is the subject and its verb, you must be sure that they agree. Lack of agreement generally suggests carelessness, which in turn has a negative rhetorical effect.

6b3 pronoun reference: agreement and consistency

Pronouns, used to replace nouns or other pronouns, must agree with those nouns or pronouns in number and gender:

I found the tennis *rackets* late yesterday afternoon on the bench where you had left *them.* (plural noun, plural pronoun)

The *dog* had found *his* way home after escaping from the yard of a boy who had found *him* and penned *him* up.

Everybody has a right to protect *himself* from an attack upon *his* person.

A demonstrative pronoun, such as **this** and **that** (plurals: **these** and **those**), must match what it specifies or singles out:

This candy is the kind that always makes me sick. (singular noun, singular pronoun)

These are the *kinds* of errors that do not greatly bother most managers. (plural noun, plural pronoun)

P   N
That is the ***bear*** that suffered a gunshot wound last fall. (singular noun, singular pronoun)

P   N
Those are the ***bears*** that live in the woods just north of Wakefield. (plural noun, plural pronoun)

Relative pronouns like **who, which, that** must agree with their antecedents in person and number, and likewise the verbs which follow them must agree with the antecedents of the relative pronouns:

     N   P   V   V
That movie, which is now ***showing*** at the Granada, has a poor story line. (singular noun, singular pronoun, singular verb)

   N   P   V
Engineers who have experience in constructing roads and bridges are nearly always in demand. (plural noun, plural pronoun, plural verb)

        N   P   V
The old ***songs that linger*** in our minds for years are my favorites. (plural noun, plural pronoun, plural verb)

You will want to be careful to use intensive and reflexive pronouns, such as **himself, myself, herself, ourselves,** properly. An **intensive pronoun** emphasizes the noun or pronoun to which it refers; a **reflexive pronoun** receives the action of the noun or pronoun to which it refers:

   N   P
Tom himself was to blame for the accident last December. (intensive)

P   P
I myself ought to be the one to go to the convention. (intensive)

After wandering for three days, **Marie** found **herself** in a farmyard. (reflexive)

We forced **ourselves** to finish our work. (reflexive)

6b4 dangling or misplaced modifiers

As we saw in section 1d, generating sentences from a kernel or basic pattern is largely a matter of adding structures of modification — words, phrases, and clauses that modify what they are attached to. And here we have another principal rule of grammar to ensure clarity and precision: subordinate structures, since they modify what they are connected to, must be placed with care and not allowed to dangle or wander in the sentence, to modify ambiguously or erroneously an element of the sentence. Notice the following flawed sentences and the suggested revisions which make this point clear.

I mailed him the letter on July 10 from Milwaukee, **which contained my estimate of the total cost.** (adjective clause, as positioned, incorrectly modifies the noun **Milwaukee**)

I mailed him the letter, **which contained my estimate of the total cost,** on July 10 from Milwaukee. (adjective clause, as positioned, now correctly modifies the noun **letter**)

Judging from the response of the parents, the Little League this summer has been popular and successful. (participial phrase, as positioned, incorrectly modifies the noun **Little League**)

Judging from the response of the parents, we can conclude that the Little League this summer has been popular and successful. (participial phrase, as positioned, now correctly modifies the noun **we**)

He mentioned that he *only* had fourteen players report to baseball practice. (adverb, as positioned, incorrectly modifies verb *had*)

He mentioned that he had *only* fourteen players report to baseball practice. (adverb, as positioned, now correctly modifies the adjective *fourteen*)

The girl whom he dated *occasionally* called him on the phone. (adverb, as positioned, ambiguously modifies either the verb *dated* or the verb *called*)

The girl whom he *occasionally* dated called him on the phone. (adverb, as positioned, now modifies the verb *dated*)

OR

The girl whom he dated called him *occasionally* on the phone. (adverb, as positioned, now modifies the verb *called*)

In each of the sentences above, the revision simply repositions the modifying structure so that, attached to what it modifies, its purpose and meaning are clear.

6b5 sentence fragments

A complete sentence consists of at least one main clause — that is, a group of words which has both a subject and a verb and which can stand alone. A sentence fragment lacks either the subject or the verb, or is a dependent rather than an independent group of words.

Sentences:

S V   V
I did not *begin* reading the novels of Henry James until I was a graduate student.

V   V
Pick up your materials from the storeroom and *go* directly to the laboratory. (subject *you* is understood)

When the report first came out, *it provoked* little or no discussion.

My mother's *poems,* which she has written over a period of some forty years, never *fail* to move me.

Neither the *man* in the store nor the *girl* in the car *could identify* the alleged thief when each was shown his picture.

Fragments:

The Carroll Company, which has offices in some thirty states and over seventy-five cities. (This fragment has only an independent subject; the **which**-clause is dependent because it modifies this subject.)

In addition to the rules **that govern the dress and behavior of students at Madison High School.** (This fragment has neither an independent subject nor an independent verb; the **that**-clause is dependent because it modifies the noun **rules,** which in turn is a part of the phrase that modifies the noun **addition,** which in its turn is part of a phrase that merely dangles.)

Perhaps the most skillful at making the lob-shot, **Bill Warren, who won last year's open tennis tournament.** (This fragment has only an independent subject; the first group of phrases modifies the independent subject; the **who**-clause is dependent because it modifies this subject.)

The **crime was committed** in broad daylight in the busiest part of downtown Hill City. **Which is quite surprising.** (The first statement is a sentence; the second group of words is not. It is a dependent clause modifying the main clause that constitutes the preceding sentence.)

               S   V

Our *vacation* this past summer *was* a trip to the Smoky Mountains in Tennessee. *Which have practically virgin forests and wildlife of all kinds.* (The first statement is a sentence; the second group of words is not. It is a dependent clause modifying the pronoun *Smoky Mountains* in the preceding sentence.)

All these examples are unintentional fragments, produced by a careless or uninformed writer. An occasional deliberate use of a sentence fragment for special effects like suspense, summary judgment, or obvious qualification, can, however, be effective, as in the following cases.

The short story is a literary form which nearly all students enjoy. *Nearly all.* A distressing number of students do not like to read anything at all. (refinement or qualification)

First came his career as a musician. *A disaster!* He simply had no real talent, as several of his teachers had tried to make clear to him. (emphatic judgment)

After the mixture has set for five minutes, pour it slowly into the beaker. *Slowly.* Rapid pouring might alter the chemical and physical properties of the mixture. (emphasis)

You should use the fragment sparingly, only for stylistic effect. Extensive or whimsical use of the fragment is always suspect. The use of fragments for which no rationale exists suggests the writer's failure to understand the basic act of writing — predication or assertion.

6b6 comma splices and fused sentences

Main clauses may be connected in only three ways, as follows:

Fundamentals of Speech I is a prerequisite for Debate I, *and* English I is a prerequisite for Introduction to the Drama.

(clauses connected by a comma and a coordinating conjunction; the comma may be omitted when clauses are short and parallel)

Fundamentals of Speech I is a prerequisite for Debate I; English I is a prerequisite for Introduction to the Drama. (clauses connected by a semicolon)

Fundamentals of Speech I is a prerequisite for Debate I. English I is a prerequisite for Introduction to the Drama. (a period and capitalization make separate sentences of the two clauses)

A *comma splice* occurs when main or independent clauses are joined only by a comma; a *fused sentence,* or *run-on sentence,* occurs when main or independent clauses are joined by no punctuation at all.

Fundamentals of Speech I is a prerequisite for Debate I, English I is a prerequisite for Introduction to the Drama. (comma splice)

Fundamentals of Speech I is a prerequisite for Debate I English I is a prerequisite for Introduction to the Drama. (fused, or run-on, sentence)

Of these two basic sentence errors, the comma splice is the more common, since the writer generally sees that some kind of division between the clauses is necessary, but isn't quite sure just what kind of punctuation is required and consequently employs the familiar comma indiscriminately. Following are several additional examples of comma splices and fused sentences, and revisions of them.

Writing the rough draft of a theme is easy for me, the difficult part is revising it. (comma splice)

Writing the rough draft of a theme is easy for me; the difficult part is revising it. (revision with a semicolon)

Mary brought iced tea for the picnic, John as usual brought nothing. (comma splice)

Mary brought iced tea for the picnic, **but** John as usual brought nothing. (revision with a comma and a coordinate conjunction)

The fate of the American Indians is an indictment of our nation **we** have consistently failed to live up to our agreements and treaties with them. (fused, or run-on, sentence)

The fate of the American Indians is an indictment of our nation. **W**e have consistently failed to live up to our agreements and treaties with them. (revision with a period and capitalization — that is, separate sentences)

If you wish, however, you may join short, parallel independent clauses with commas:

I found the hockey stick, she found the puck.

Taking the picture is easy, developing it is hard.

I watched, I practiced, I dedicated myself.

Generally, though, the writer will use conventional punctuation, which indicates for the reader the grammatical and rhetorical relationships between main clauses.

6b7 faulty parallelism

Section 1d, ''The Sentence,'' stresses that parallelism — giving similar grammatical units similar structure — produces economical and clear prose, and that you should be alert to opportunities to cast your thoughts into such functional, and pleasing, structures. You must, however, guard against a parallelism that is only approximate or inexact, which may not only waste words but also confuse rather than clarify meaning. Below are examples of faulty parallelism and possible revisions.

Gordon found the girl appealing and with a fine sensitivity. (confused meaning — is it Gordon or the girl who has the sensitivity? — and wordy)

Gordon found the girl appealing and sensitive. (clear meaning and economical construction)

She likes performing the laboratory experiments in electricity and to write up the reports about them. (awkward, "jolting" prose; a gerund and an infinitive are mismatched)

She likes to perform the laboratory experiments in electricity and to write up the reports about them. (identical structures — infinitives — for identical thoughts; the effect is exact and pleasing)

OR

She likes performing the laboratory experiments in electricity and writing up the reports about them. (identical structures — gerunds — for identical thoughts; the effect is exact and pleasing)

He finally learned to field strip his rifle and the technique of reading maps. (awkward, "jolting" prose; an infinitive and a noun are mismatched)

He finally learned to field strip his rifle and to read maps. (identical structures — infinitives — for identical thoughts; the effect is exact and pleasing)

OR

He finally learned the techniques of field stripping his rifle and of reading maps. (identical structures — the noun **techniques** and prepositional phrases — for identical thoughts; the effect is exact and clear)

"The Path to Independence" is the title of one of the chapters in *Words That Made American History,* and "The Wrong of Slavery" is another one. (meaning is clear, but the prose is needlessly wordy; parallel clauses are used when parallel phrases are called for)

"The Path to Independence" and "The Wrong of Slavery" are the titles of two of the chapters in *Words That Made American History*. (identical structures—the two chapter titles—for identical thoughts; the titles are used as dual subjects of the same main clause rather than as subjects of their own individual main clauses; the effect is exact and informative)

Washing the car, painting the fence, and a clean-up of the garage are three jobs my wife insists that I do during my vacation. (awkward, "jolting" prose; two gerunds and a noun result in a slight mismatch)

Washing the car, painting the fence, and cleaning up the garage are three jobs my wife insists that I do during my vacation. (identical structures—gerunds—for identical thoughts; the effect is exact and clear)

A special case of faulty parallelism occurs when the writer employs correlative conjunctions such as **not only– but also** and **either–or** inexactly. For example:

Not only is the trip down the river invigorating, it is educational. (the sentence breaks in two and lacks emphasis)

The trip down the river is not only invigorating but also educational. (the revision tightens the sentence and emphasizes the two adjectives describing the trip)

You will either have the work completed by next Monday or I shall take my business to Kennedy Electric. (awkward, "jolting" prose; the second of the two correlative conjunctions introduces its clause, while the first of the two is imbedded within the clause it should introduce)

Either you will have the work completed by next Monday or I shall take my business to Kennedy Electric. (revision makes the two clauses exactly parallel, clearly indicating their relationship to one another and imparting a pleasing balance)

6

As these examples clearly show, the conscious use of parallelism reflects the control that the writer has over his expression. Always proofread your writing carefully to detect and eliminate faulty parallelisms.

6b8 incomplete expressions and omissions

Carelessly omitted words will, of course, confuse the reader. But here we are concerned about more serious omissions and incomplete expressions than these merely inadvertent lapses. Make sure that comparisons are always logical and completely presented:

She is more talented than anyone in the class. (Since **she** is a member of the class, the writer has illogically stated that she is more talented than herself, which is of course absurd.)

She is more talented than anyone else in the class. (The revision which adds **else** sets her off from the rest of the students and thereby permits a legitimate and sensible comparison.)

Gatorade tastes better. (It is unclear what it tastes better than—apple pie, fried chicken, grass?)

Gatorade tastes better than any other thirst-quencher on the market. (The revision indicates the relationship of **Gatorade** to other drinks and therefore allows for comparison.)

If you omit words for the sake of brevity, be careful that the omission doesn't result in grammatical error or ambiguity in meaning.

The books are on the shelf and the typewriter on the desk. (**books** takes a plural verb **are,** but **typewriter** is singular and therefore takes the singular verb **is**)

The books are on the shelf and the typewriter is on the desk. (revision adds **is** so that subject and verb agree)

The antique vase was Early American and bought by the Smithsonian Institution. (The first verb, **was,** is linking or copulative, whereas the second verb, **[was] bought,** is passive; therefore, the writer may not correctly omit the auxiliary **was** used with **bought.** Notice, too, that the sense of the sentence as written is not quite clear.)

The antique vase was Early American and was bought by the Smithsonian Institution. (revision adds the auxiliary verb **was** so that each verb is complete, and the sense is clear)

I want you to see what I have. (quite apart from the ambiguity in meaning, the omission implies that the omitted verb that goes with **have** is **see,** which is grammatically incorrect)

I want you to see what I have seen. (revision adds the proper verb **seen**)

Ken saw the girl knew who had been hiding in the cabin. (initially the reader thinks that **girl** is the direct object of the verb **saw** but then realizes that this is not the case; the clause **the girl . . . cabin** is the direct object)

Ken saw that the girl knew who had been hiding in the cabin. (revision adds the relative pronoun **that** to introduce the subordinate clause, or the direct object of the verb **saw**)

A common error, combining incomplete comparison and omission, is the following:

This mower is as good if not better than the one we rented last summer.

We can see that the predication is inexact, and although we can make out the sense of the sentence, such a statement forces us to pause and supply the omitted words

6

necessary to make the comparison complete and exactly stated. In other words, we have to do the writer's job, an unwelcome task that at the very least is exasperating. The revision should look like this:

This mower is **as good as if not better than** the one we rented last summer.

This error is perhaps typical of this entire category of errors. Even slight carelessness can result in, at worst, illogical and ambiguous statements and, at best, irritating statements.

6b9 awkward expressions

The possibilities for awkward or unnatural expressions are practically unlimited; they are therefore difficult to categorize into a few readily identifiable types. However, one of the most obvious of these is the mangled meaning that results from *"upside-down subordination"*—that is, from putting main thoughts into subordinate structures and subordinate thoughts into main structures. (Section 1d also discusses this error, from a rhetorical point of view.) Here are several examples of this kind of error of awkwardness, which seriously distorts meaning.

As the audience became restless and bored, the speaker droned on about energy shortages in the future.

When Willa Cather was most successful as an author, her writing was most autobiographical.

Passing the medical examinations with highest distinction, he was gifted with a fine mind.

Each of these sentences makes some sense, but even the rather hurried reader will do a "double-take," realizing that something is not quite right. The problem is, of course, that the clauses within each sentence have been awkwardly inverted—independent or more important material and dependent or less important information have been interchanged—a flaw that is obvious when the sentences are revised as follows:

As the speaker droned on about energy shortages in the future, the audience became restless and bored.

When her writing was most autobiographical, Willa Cather was most successful as an author.

Gifted with a fine mind, he passed the medical examinations with highest distinction.

Always make sure that your sentence structure shows the proper relationships between clauses.

Another common kind of awkwardness is the *rambling sentence,* one that is overloaded, lacks emphasis, and continually shifts its point of view. Even experienced writers, seeming to be unaware that sometimes "more is less," are susceptible to this weakness. Consider the following rambling statements:

If you have read any of Emerson's essays, you know how abstract his thought can be, but he is ranked as one of America's greatest writers, for he not only produced a sizable body of excellent work himself but also encouraged younger writers, like Henry Thoreau and Walt Whitman, in their literary careers, which ironically surpassed Emerson's own.

Hamlet was shocked that his mother remarried so soon after his father's death, so he remains aloof from the life of the court, wondering to himself, what shall I do about my suspicions?

Take a lead off first base approximately the length of your body, and when the pitcher moves toward home plate, you should pivot on your left foot and dig toward second base, where you will slide toward the center field side.

6

The first sentence is overly long, shifts the point of view from **you** to **he,** and contains at least three separate main thoughts, each of which should have its own sentence, probably unrelated to the other two sentences. The second sentence is not necessarily too long, but it begins with the past tense, shifts to the present tense, and winds up ineptly asking a question. The various thoughts need a tighter unity. The third sentence begins with the imperative mood (giving of instructions) and then shifts to the indicative mood. It also shifts tenses rather confusingly, mixing the present with the future.

These two types of awkwardness—"upside-down subordination" and rambling sentences—emphasize the grammatical tangles that writers often get themselves into. Nearly all writers, in following out the complexities of their thought, at one time or another will need to revise these inexact and irritating expressions out of their work. In sum, we can say that awkwardness is simply the ineffective rhetorical use of perfectly grammatical structures, against which the writer must always be on guard.

6b10 inconsistent point of view

Another common error, touched on above, occurs when, within sentences, the subject (and references to it) or the verb form changes arbitrarily and probably confusingly. Consistency always makes for clarity and ease of reading; consequently, shifts should occur only when they are necessary to convey exact meaning. Note the following sentences, which demonstrate careless changes in the point of view:

In the movie, when the gang rode into town, the sheriff steps out of the saloon into the street, and began to fire both pistols. (tense changes needlessly from past tense to present tense and back to past tense)

Possible revision: In the movie, when the gang rides into town, the sheriff steps out of the saloon into the street, and begins to fire both pistols. (all verbs are in the present tense —the "living" or historical present—to recount the action as it occurs)

Students begin the enrollment procedure in Hoch Auditorium, and the procedure is completed in Carruth-O'Leary, where they pay their fees. (voice of verb changes needlessly from active to passive; subject changes needlessly from **students** to **procedure**)

Possible revision: Students begin the enrollment procedure in Hoch Auditorium and complete it in Carruth-O'Leary, where they pay their fees. (both verbs are in the active voice; subject remains **students**)

Everyone had to stand in line until their names were called, even if he had made an appointment with their counselor. (focus changes ungrammatically and illogically from **everyone,** which is singular, to **their,** which is plural, to **he,** which is singular, to **their,** which is plural)

Possible revision: Everyone had to stand in line until his name was called, even if he had made an appointment with his counselor. (**everyone, his, he,** and **his** are all singular and therefore consistent)

You will find Sunset Park on the west side of town, and Lincoln Park is ten miles north of here, near Indianola. (subject shifts needlessly from **you** to **Lincoln Park**)

Possible revision: You will find Sunset Park on the west side of town and Lincoln Park ten miles north of here, near Indianola. (subject remains **you**)

The contract was signed by both parties, and in it they agree to submit all disputes to an arbitration board. (subject changes needlessly from **contract** to **they;** voice changes needlessly from passive to active; tense changes needlessly from past to present)

Possible revision: The contract agreeing to submit all disputes to an arbitration board was signed by both parties. (deadwood and lack of subordination are corollary problems in the original, and by solving these problems we solve the problems of inconsistency in point of view as well)

Similar needless shifts in point of view from sentence to sentence within a paragraph cause similar problems for readers. Consistency in writing is always a virtue; and when meaning is at stake, of course, it is crucial. As a careful writer, you should always proofread your work to ensure as uniform a point of view as possible.

6b11 punctuation of restrictive and nonrestrictive modifiers

This final problem is a familiar one in writing of all kinds. A *restrictive modifier* identifies precisely what it modifies and is therefore not set off by commas. A *nonrestrictive modifier* is not essential to precise identification but simply describes or adds to what is modified, and is set off by commas. Consider the following sentence:

The student who was taking pictures saw the accident.

If the writer means that there was more than one student present when the accident occurred and that only the one taking pictures saw it happen, then the clause **who was taking pictures** is essential to the meaning of the sentence and should not be set off by commas:

The student who was taking pictures saw the accident. (no change necessary)

If, on the other hand, the writer means that there was only one student present when the accident occurred and that he happened to be taking pictures at the time, then the clause **who was taking pictures** is nonrestrictive and should be set off by commas:

The student, who was taking pictures, saw the accident.

The use or absence of commas shows the exact function of the clause and keeps the meaning clear. Here are two additional pairs of sentences employing restrictive and nonrestrictive modifiers and two final examples of restrictive clauses.

The letter which she wrote from Florida didn't arrive until last week. (the clause *which she wrote* identifies which letter it was and is therefore restrictive)

The letter, which she wrote from Florida, didn't arrive until last week. (the clause *which she wrote* simply denotes the origin of the letter but doesn't precisely identify the noun *letter* and is therefore nonrestrictive)

The girl who won the scholarship to Baker University is a friend of mine. (the clause *who won the scholarship* identifies which girl it was and is therefore restrictive)

The girl, who won the scholarship to Baker University, is a friend of mine. (the clause *who won the scholarship* simply denotes her accomplishment but doesn't precisely identify the noun *girl* and is therefore nonrestrictive)

The experience that I was telling you about last fall happened again to me yesterday. (the clause *that I was telling you about last fall,* introduced by the relative pronoun *that,* identifies which experience it was and is therefore restrictive)

The briefcase that he brought with him to the meeting was a present from the company for twenty years of service. (the clause *that he brought with him to the meeting,* introduced by the relative pronoun *that,* identifies which briefcase it was and is therefore restrictive)

Notice that both of the final two illustrative sentences contain restrictive clauses. **That** cannot be used to introduce a nonrestrictive clause; only **who** or **which** can be so used.

Fix this distinction between restrictive and nonrestrictive clauses and their proper punctuation in your mind. There is no reason that you should have to guess at what is correct or "punctuate by ear." And, as you can see from the examples above, whether or not you set the clause off by commas *does* make a significant difference in the meaning you convey. Make sure that it *is* the meaning that you intend.

mechanics 7

In this chapter we discuss all the important physical signs in writing—from punctuation to spelling—which you as a conscientious writer should remember as you prepare any sort of written material to be read by others. In this area, of course, the constant question of "correctness" arises all too often, for many students in composition courses fear that grades are based on the misuse of the comma or the number of misspelled words in a theme. Moreover, many people believe—erroneously, we assure you—that good writing is a simple matter of "correct grammar" and correct spelling and punctuation. Such notions are not only inaccurate but also deadly for good writing. On the other hand, however, we can confidently say that a modest amount of attention to modern standards for punctuation and a little common sense will bolster your writing performance.

7a punctuation

By using the various symbols that have been adopted for the punctuation of written English, we simply tell our readers how they are to read a sentence and to understand the relationships of parts of a sentence to the whole. If you like, we might call punctuation a system of visual signals by which writers try to help their readers in interpreting what has been written. In the nineteenth century, punctuation was both more rigid and more liberally used than it ordinarily is in our more informal day. But some basic necessities of punctuation for acceptable and respectable writing remain.

First, we can divide standard punctuation into two main classes—*external* and *internal* punctuation. That is, a mark of punctuation is found either *outside the sentence* or *within the sentence*.

7a1 external punctuation

Sentences must end with one of the external marks or signals, the means by which you indicate that a string of words is a unit and that you are making a statement, asking a question, or uttering an exclamation.

• *Period*   The period always follows any statement and indicates that the preceding string of words is to be interpreted *as* a statement. Even intentionally used sentence fragments that simply amplify or continue the statement of a preceding sentence are usually terminated by periods. Also, indirect questions (that is, questions contained within a statement) are punctuated by a period. Consider the following examples:

1. Ending a statement or declarative sentence.

The dean questioned the value of a course in surgery for psychiatrists.

2. Ending a fragment intentionally used for rhetorical effect.

The dean refused to meet with the leaders of the student strike. Absolutely and finally.

3. Ending a sentence containing an indirect question.

The dean asked what the strikers wanted.

4. In quoted statements, for ending *each* sentence.

"I'll never meet with the strikers," said the dean. "And I don't mean 'maybe.'"
"My office is closed to the strikers. Please remember that, Miss Terry," said the dean to his weeping secretary.

?   *Question Mark*   Direct questions, whether quoted or unquoted, must be ended with a question mark.

Does the dean still refuse to meet with the irate students?

"Will the dean continue to oppose the strikers?" asked the reporter from *The Campus Daily.*

!   *Exclamation Point*   A sentence or part of a sentence that expresses strong feeling should usually be ended with an exclamation point. On the other hand, the exclamation mark should be used with some restraint; too frequent use of it weakens its value and gives a composition a hysterical tone.

"Help! My office is burning!" cried the dean.

My composition teacher gives an "F" for any theme that contains a spelling error!

7a2 internal punctuation

Under this heading we will consider the various marks of punctuation that are generally found *within* sentences. They signal to readers how they should interpret internal relationships and the relationships of parts to the whole sentence.

'   *Comma*   The possible uses or misuses of the comma seem to cause undue grief to many student writers. Moreover, there are legitimate differences of opinion about the frequency and "correct" placement of commas. Some people prefer commas at every possible juncture; others advocate restraint. The difference arises between two "schools" of writers. There are those who prefer a high degree of formality to minimize the possibilities of misreading or misinterpretation and those who prefer a greater informality and thus greater dependence on the reader's judgment and sense of meaning and interrelationships within the sentence. In general, we recommend the use of the comma whenever the possibility of an ambiguity arises. A comma should be used:

1. To separate quoted words from the rest of the sentence.

The dean asked, "Who are you?"
"I'm nobody," replied the student.

2. To separate words, phrases, and clauses in a series.

He wore a muffler, a sweater, and a raincoat.
The large, hot, and heavy garments overwhelmed the runner.
Successful teachers try to make their classes interesting, to prepare thoroughly for each class, and to help their students.
Great opportunities for learning arise when good students and skillful teachers come together, when the campus is an intellectual forum, and when libraries and laboratories exceed mere adequacy.

We must point out, however, that today many writers and teachers omit the comma between the second and third parts of a series:

Each package contained red, gold and purple beads.

But because there is a possibility, no matter how slight, that such a sentence could be misread as a statement about two rather than three kinds of colored beads, we recommend that the comma be used to separate *all parts* of a series and thus to reinforce visually the parallelism of the unit:

Each package contained red, gold, and purple beads.

3. To separate interpolated or introductory words and phrases from the rest of the sentence.

Jim was, to be sure, a reasonably good student.
He was also, however, an outstanding runner.
Illinois, of course, has offered him a track scholarship.
In the absence of any other offers, Jim chose Kansas because of its famous relays.

4. To establish or follow a quotation.

Jim asked, "What can a runner do when he's forty?"
"He can be a track coach if he's lucky," said the old coach.
"I'm sure," said Jim, "that I can do something else."

5. To separate a dependent clause that precedes the main clause of the sentence — that is, to separate an introductory dependent clause from the rest of the sentence.

When the Prime Minister spoke, the nation listened.
After the ball was over, the dancers rushed to their cars.

But the comma is not generally used to separate a main clause and a dependent clause that *follows* it.

The dancers rushed to their cars after the ball was over.

6. To separate independent clauses when they are joined by a coordinating conjunction.

The Cadillac sped down the highway, and the Pinto followed right behind it.
The federal government must subsidize the railroads, or we must accept their disappearance.

7. To separate names of geographical locations, parts

of dates, titles and academic degrees, and appositives from the rest of the sentence.

Charles Arthur Fillmore, M.D., was the University's sixth president.

The delegates unanimously chose Bloomington, Indiana, as their meeting place on December 1, 1977, and Norman, Oklahoma, on December 17, 1984.

The period between meetings, seven years, will allow the host chapters to make elaborate plans.

My favorite poet, Robert Browning, married his favorite poet, Elizabeth Barrett.

But when the appositive is so restrictive that meaning would be lost or distorted by the presence of a comma, there should be no comma between the two names.

The poet Allen Ginsberg spent three weeks on our campus.

Since Ginsberg is not the only poet, the absence of commas shows his name to be restrictive and therefore essential to the meaning.

My sister Eileen often visited my dormitory.

The writer apparently has more than one sister, and therefore the name of Eileen is essential to the meaning of **sister.**

; *Semicolon* As its parts indicate, the semicolon has some characteristics of the period and the comma. It represents a stronger break than a comma and a weaker break than a period, but it is always found *within* the sentence. (If we view it from another perspective, however, it serves as a linking device, frequently substituting for a comma plus coordinating conjunction.) A semicolon is used:

1. To separate independent clauses not joined by a coordinating conjunction.

The dean announced his conditions for a conference with the striking students; his secretary had the dubious honor of reading them to the reporters.

Waiting for the news was boring; the news itself was exciting.

2. To separate independent clauses joined by conjunctive adverbs (**therefore, however, consequently, moreover,** and so on).

The reporters agreed to pool their notes; therefore, all their stories were similar.

The dean protested that the reporters had distorted his version of the conference; however, he liked the flattering photograph of himself on the front page.

3. To separate the parts of a series when commas are used internally within one or more of them.

One reporter brought to the press conference his cameras, a Nikon F2 and a Konica T3; a pouch with paper and pens; and four or five sandwiches.

Colon The colon is a strong indicator of something to follow or to be clarified. And in a few situations, it is interchangeable with commas, semicolons, and dashes. Use a colon:

1. To separate, more formally than a comma, quoted dialogue or information from the phrase or clause that introduces it.

The President solemnly announced: "America's part in the Viet Nam War is over."

Keats equated the intellect and the imagination in his famous words: "Beauty is truth, truth beauty."

2. To precede a formal listing, especially after words like **the following** or **as follows.**

The following characteristics of a poem must be considered: its rhythm, its language, and its theme.

He mentioned the most picturesque American rivers: the Mississippi, the Missouri, the Ohio, and the Hudson.

3. To introduce a clause in explanation or specification of what has gone before.

President Roosevelt announced to Congress what was already known: the Japanese had attacked Pearl Harbor on December 7.

The dean lay down an essential condition for his meeting the students: they would have to wear shirts, ties, and shoes.

— *Dash* Used sensibly and sparingly, dashes can add an attractive informality when they set off inserted phrases and clauses. Overused, they reveal a kind of breathless immaturity in writing. Use a dash or paired dashes:

1. To set off interpolated words or inserted explanations within or at the end of a sentence.

The Axis Powers—Germany, Italy, and Japan—expected much from their submarine fleets.

The leadership in photography—that is, the construction of fine cameras at relatively low cost—passed from Germany to Japan sometime in the 1950's.

The three Brontë sisters—along with their brother, Bramwell—constituted an isolated but intense literary society.

The Allies had counted heavily on one probability—America's entry into the war.

7

2. To indicate uncompleted sentences or trailing bits of dialogue.

The dean gasped, "The President is coming? Why did he — ?"

Marge wondered aloud, "If I write my theme before the party — but no, I won't have time."

"   *"*

Quotation Marks In the United States, double quotation marks (sometimes called "inverted commas") enclose direct speech, quoted material, some literary and musical titles, and words to which special attention is called, as in translations or definitions.

Randolph murmured, "I never miss a Big 8 Tournament."

"But why must it always be in Kansas City?" asked Pamela.

One famous photographer emphasizes the role of France in the development of photography: "Paris was probably the first city to be photographed, and even the French Government helped to promote the new medium. Besides, Daguerre and Niepce were both French."

The titles of short stories, magazine articles, chapters, short poems, and one-act plays — anything less than book-length or a performance of an hour or less — should be enclosed in quotation marks. Italics are required for titles of longer works (see page 265).

Almost every anthology of short fiction includes Fitzgerald's "Babylon Revisited."

Each Christmas we usually watch Menotti's one-act opera, "Amahl and the Night Visitors," on television.

One chapter in a recent book on writing is called "Tips for Increasing Your Readability."

Poe insisted that a long poem like Milton's *Paradise Lost* cannot hold a reader's interest very long; he preferred something more like his own "Israfel" or "The Raven."

If a quotation contains a quotation, use single quotation marks ('. . .') to set off the internal quotation or special word or phrase.

Neil Amdur recommends constant alertness during a game of tennis: "Don't let an opponent snap your concentration with small talk. If you allow a remark like 'Gee, you're serving so well today, I can't return a thing' to overinflate your confidence, it may take your mind off how well you're really doing."

"Courting Victory: Four Problems That Could Keep You from Winning," *Gentlemen's Quarterly*

Cell therapy has advanced in Great Britain too: "A fresh approach has been advanced in England at the London clinic of Dr. Peter Stephan who, at 31, is undoubtedly the youngest of the 'youth doctors.' "

Gentlemen's Quarterly

As one of my friends said, "On our campus 'dingbat' means 'clown.' "

( )   *Parentheses*   Parentheses are used as rather heavy punctuation for interpolated material, often instead of commas or dashes. If a parenthetical sentence occurs between two sentences, it should have its own terminal punctuation within the parentheses.

Jonathan Perry (the first settler in Willow Springs) was the great-grandfather of the present mayor of the town.

The reading public loved Twain (they never knew, of course, about his bawdy pieces).

When the single-lens reflex camera appeared, it largely replaced the best of the rangefinder models. (The close correlation between viewfinder and lens and the new cameras' adaptability to many lenses were probably the main attractions for buyers in the 1960's.) Today, however, used rangefinder cameras find a ready market.

7

[   ]   *Brackets*   Brackets enclose words inserted editorially within a quotation or words in matter already enclosed within parentheses.

Baker explains his kind of photography: "I use only one kind of camera [a Minolta SRT] and a normal lens [50 mm]."

Of course, if Baker, rather than the writer of the previous sentence, had made those explanatory insertions, he would have used parentheses.

If quoted material contains an error of fact, grammar, spelling, or even punctuation, the writer who is quoting the material indicates the error by placing the Latin word **sic** ("thus") in brackets after the error.

In his autobiography Baker claimed something of a record: "I have photographed every president since Rosevelt [*sic*]."

If your typewriter does not have bracket keys, you can either make them with slash marks and two underlining marks or simply draw them in by hand after you have finished typing the page.

• • •   *Ellipsis*   Three spaced periods form the punctuation device called the ellipsis, which indicates an omission or incomplete assertion in quoted material or dialogue. When the interruption comes before the end of a sentence, the three periods are enough to indicate the omission. But when the omission comes between the end of a sentence and the rest of the quotation, four periods—one in its proper place as the end punctuation of the statement and three to indicate the omission—are necessary.

Thoreau insisted: "Time is but the stream I go a-fishing in. . . . Its thin current slides away, but eternity remains. (An intervening sentence has been omitted, but because the

259

first quoted sentence is complete, its own period precedes the three-period ellipsis.)

Thoreau recommended reading the classics: "To read well, that is, to read true books in a true spirit, is a noble exercise . . . It requires a training such as the athletes underwent . . . ." (The first omission occurs before the end of a sentence and the beginning of a new sentence; hence, only three periods are needed there and a space is left between the last word and the first period. The second omission occurs before the completion of a sentence, too, but since no sentence follows and the quotation ends, three periods for ellipsis and a fourth period for end punctuation are needed.)

Mickey tried to guess the answer to the riddle, asking hopefully, "Was it . . . ?" (A dash could have been used instead of an ellipsis.)

In long quotations, the omission of a line or more of poetry or a paragraph or more of prose is indicated by a whole line of periods:

> When I see birches bend to left and right
> Across the lines of straighter darker trees,
> I like to think some boy's been swinging them.
> . . . .
> I should prefer to have some boy bend them
> As he went out and in to fetch the cows —
> Some boy too far from town to learn baseball,
> Whose only play was what he found himself,
> Summer or winter, and could play alone.
>
> Robert Frost, "Birches"

Avoid using an ellipsis to indicate a shift in thought or a wordless comment on what has gone before.

I don't go to many new movies; I like to wait and hear whether they're good before I buy a ticket. . . . Dad, when can you send me more money? (incorrect)

/ *Apostrophe* The apostrophe is used to indicate:

1. The possessive case of nouns and pronouns.

John's pen

the club's program

gentlemen's behavior

Henry James's novels (a one-syllable proper noun ending in **-s**)

William Carlos Williams' poetry (a proper noun of more than one syllable and ending in **-s**)

everyone's

one's

But no apostrophe is used for possessive forms of the so-called personal pronouns: **your, her, it, our, their** (modifying nouns) and **yours, hers, its, ours, theirs** (not modifying nouns).

Your book is valuable.

Yours is valuable.

2. Certain plural forms, like those of letters of the alphabet and numerals.

the ABC's

the 1970's (**1970s** is increasingly acceptable)

p's and q's

3. Contractions and omissions.

won't   can't   the winter of '76

don't   we'd (for **we would**)   o.k.'d

— *Hyphen* Hyphens are used between words that have become a unit or compound and between parts of words to show syllable divisions. In case of doubt, consult the dictionary.

   1. Compound nouns, verbs, and modifiers.

Nouns

secretary-treasurer (one person)
aide-de-camp
do-nothing
self-discipline

poet-critic (one person)
scholar-teacher (one person)
fade-out
mother-of-pearl

Verbs

air-dry
force-feed

cross-fertilize
cross-license

Modifiers

Indo-European region
seventeenth-century writer
fair-trade laws
fair-weather friend
play-by-play commentary

blow-by-blow account
push-button phone
cross-country race
cross-legged position
compound-complex sentence

Note: Some of these can also be used as nouns and then would not be hyphenated—for example:

The seventeenth century was marked by revolutions in England.
The Weather Bureau forecasts *fair weather* for tomorrow.

You can, of course, think of compound nouns, like **cross-stitch,** which are hyphenated when used as either adjective or noun.

You can name any number of compound words in all three of the above categories that are not hyphenated (for example, nouns like **Indo China, meal ticket, seventeenth century, book review, mountain range;** verbs like **backslide, uphold, upgrade;** modifiers like **crosstown, backslapping, upstate, handwritten**). The standard dictionary is usually a sound authority on such questions, though one dictionary's advice may differ from another's. Choose what seems the most persuasive and sensible advice and thereafter be consistent in using the form you have chosen.

2. Syllable divisions at the end of a line. If you reach the end of a line in handwriting or typing before you complete a word, divide the word at one of the syllable breaks and indicate the division by a hyphen. If you're at all uncertain about syllable divisions of a word, consult your dictionary.

7b capitalization

As you know, the first word of any sentence or intentional sentence fragment begins with a capital letter. But beyond that well-known fact, several aspects of capitalization can cause many writers some moments of uncertainty. Accordingly, we list below the most important cases in which capitalization is required.

7b1 sentences within sentences

Ordinarily, quoted sentences within sentences begin with a capital letter, unless the sentence is merged with your own phraseology.

The dean declared to his secretary, "I will never talk to the leader of a strike."

BUT

The dean declared to his secretary that he would "never talk to the leader of a strike."

7b2 names of people, titles and ranks, organizations, and places

All of these, when they are proper nouns or parts of nouns, are capitalized. Titles, ranks, and names of organizations are capitalized if they are associated with specific people or institutions; however, titles are usually not capitalized when they do not precede specific names, and generalized terms for organizations are not capitalized.

Franklin D. Roosevelt

President Roosevelt (but usually *the president*)

Professor Snarf (but *the professor*)

Iowa State University (usually *the University* when a specific institution is understood; otherwise, *the university* [as a type of institution], *universities*)

American Indian Movement (but *the movement, movements*)

Names of specific geographical or regional locations:

the South, the Middle West or the Midwest, the East (of the United States), but *I travel south* (the direction) *in the winter.*

the Middle East (the countries around the eastern Mediterranean Sea)

the Grand Canyon

the Continental Divide

the Mississippi Valley

the Caribbean Sea

the Indian Ocean

the Rocky Mountains

7

New York City
the Susquehanna River
Lake Erie

7b 3 titles of books, magazine articles, essays, poems, plays, operas, pamphlets, paintings, and names of magazines and newspapers

The first letters of all important words in such titles are capitalized, though prepositions, conjunctions, and articles that are not the first or last words of the title and that do not exceed four letters are not capitalized.

The History of Tom Jones (novel)
"Shooting Glassware" (magazine article)
"A Modest Proposal" (essay)
"Ode on a Grecian Urn" (poem)
The Iceman Cometh (long play)
"Riders to the Sea" (short play)
The Girl of the Golden West (long play and opera)
The MLA Style Sheet (pamphlet)
"Blue Boy" (painting)
Time (magazine)
Milwaukee Journal (newspaper)

7b 4 names of historical periods, political and artistic movements, and specific events

The important words of such labels and terms should be capitalized.

the Middle Ages
the Italian Renaissance

the Age of Reason
the Romantic Movement
Neo-Classicism
the New Deal
the Fourth of July
the Battle of the Bulge
the Great Depression
the First World War
the Bicentennial
the Douglas County Fair

7C italics (underlining)

Printing conventions require that the titles of many kinds
of literary, artistic, and musical works be set in italic type
and thus set apart from the more common roman type for
emphasis. On the typewriter or in longhand the equivalent
of italic type is achieved by underlining. Consider the
following examples:

1. Titles of books, long plays, long poems, operas, and
movies.

Gone With the Wind (novel and movie)
As You Like It (play)
Paradise Lost (long poem)
The Magic Flute (opera)
Butch Cassidy and the Sundance Kid (movie)

2. Names of newspapers and magazines.

The Kansas City Star (newspaper) (Some people prefer to
italicize or underline only the distinctive part of a news-

paper's or magazine's name—in this case, *Star;* but we recommend italicizing all parts of the title named in the masthead of a newspaper or on the cover of a magazine.)

Wall Street Journal (newspaper)

Playboy (magazine)

Ebony (magazine)

3. Foreign words and expressions. A good dictionary usually indicates a foreign word's degree of absorption and familiarity to speakers and writers of English. Thus, we underline or italicize:

joie de vivre	*Bildungsroman*
Zeitgeist	*roman à clef*
BUT NOT	
rodeo	espresso
café	mesa
autobahn	bel canto
tornado	per diem
esprit de corps	

4. Words considered as words. Italics are used to call attention to a word that is being used as a word. Quotation marks are also often used for this purpose.

My parents always refer to *speaking* as *elocution* or *declamation.* (The three italicized words might have been put within quotation marks.)

7d spelling

Even the best writer encounters questions about spelling now and then; and almost everyone has certain "trouble words." The English language, because of its mixture of Germanic and Latin roots and its casual adoption of variant forms throughout its development, does not lend itself to spelling rules. Nevertheless, all of us can make considerable headway toward good spelling by remembering and practicing the following guidelines for overcoming spelling problems.

1. **ei** and **ie** words.

Nearly always for the sound of long **–e** in English, **i** precedes **e** (**siege, believe, yield, piece**), except after **c,** when the **e** comes before the **i** (**conceive, ceiling, receive**). All other **ei** and **ie** sounds (long **–i,** long **–a,** short **–e,** for example) take **e** before **i** (**weigh, height, reign, freight, heifer**). A full list of the exceptions to either part of this "rule" would be lengthy, but offhand you can probably think of words like **leisure, seize, weird, either,** and **neither.**

2. Doubling a final consonant.

a. Words of one syllable or with a final accented syllable containing a vowel followed by a single and final consonant (examples: **sit, fit, pet, let, omit, permit, allot, recap, repot, occur, handicap**) usually double the final consonant to add a suffix beginning with a vowel (thus, **sitting, fitted, petted, letting, omitted, permitting, allotted, recapped, repotted, occurrence, handicapping**).

b. Words of more than one syllable whose accent falls on a syllable before the final one do not double a final consonant before a vowel suffix (thus, **benefit** becomes **benefited,** not **benefitted; travel** becomes **traveler,** not **traveller; hover** becomes **hovered** or **hovering**).

3. Final **–e.**

Drop a final silent **–e** before a suffix beginning with a vowel; retain a final silent **–e** before a suffix beginning with a consonant.

style	stylish
berate	berated, berating
promote	promoting, promoted, promoter
appreciate	appreciated, appreciative

7

hope	hoping (BUT hopeful)
wife	wifely
name	nameless, namely
polite	politely, politeness
use	useful

4. Final **–y.**

Words ending in **–y** that follows a consonant change **–y** to **–i** before suffixes except **–ing;** if final **–y** is preceded by a vowel, the **–y** remains.

ally	allies (BUT allying)
identify	identified (BUT identifying, identification)
worldly	worldliness
apply	applied (BUT applying, application) applicant
convey	conveyance
deploy	deployment deployed

5. Final **–al** and **–ly.**

Words ending in **–al** (many adjectives) retain the final **l** when **–ly** is added (for adverbial forms).

accidental	accidentally (NOT accidently)
typical	typically
practical	practically
theoretical	theoretically
theatrical	theatrically
usual	usually

Adjectives ending in **–ic** normally add **–ally** for the adverb forms.

chronic	chronically
ironic	ironically

sarcastic	sarcastically
caustic	caustically
democratic	democratically

6. Some general advice about spelling.

a. Try to identify the patterns of words with which you typically have problems. Master the simple group-rules outlined above, and try to remember the exceptions if there are any.

b. Try to observe the syllabic divisions of troublesome words. You might even try remembering to say the word to yourself by exaggerating syllabic divisions until you have the word fixed in your memory.

c. When you're at all uncertain about the spelling of a word (or its division into syllables), a quick check of the dictionary will set you straight.

d. Remember that the degree of accuracy of your spelling may well suggest to your readers the degree of your reliability as a writer, the degree to which they can take you seriously as an informed, literate person.

7e abbreviations

Abbreviations seem to have an irresistible attraction for twentieth-century Americans. The example of the federal government's shortened designations (**HEW** for Department of Health, Education, and Welfare; **TVA** for Tennessee Valley Authority; **FCC** for Federal Communications Commission; and so on for scores of similar substitutions of two or three letters for names) is a practice that dates back at least to the era of Franklin D. Roosevelt and accelerated during World War II, and it has conditioned all of us to speaking and writing in abbreviations. But what is acceptable in journalism or political talk is not always acceptable in formal writing.

1. Do *not* use abbreviations in formal prose for
a. Proper names:

Wm. C. Bryant, Edw. M. Kennedy, LBJ, JFK, J. Carter

b. Words designating locations or addresses:

W. Lafayette, S. Carolina or S.C., St., Ave., 5 mi. n., 1600 Pa. Ave., Wash., D.C.

c. **And** (**&**) unless the ampersand is part of the official title, as in **G. & C. Merriam Company.**
d. The words **chapter, volume, part, page** except in footnotes and bibliographies.

2. You may use abbreviations for
a. Titles that precede or follow the names of specific people, or that designate professional attainments and academic degrees:

Jr., Sr., Rev., Col. (Colonel), Prof., Ph.D., B.A., M.A., R.N., M.D., Ll.D.

b. Latin words frequently used in English, like **e.g.** (for example), **i.e.** (that is), **etc.** (and others, and so on), **p.m.** (afternoon), **a.m.** (forenoon), **A.D.** (in the year of Our Lord, *i.e.*, after Christ), and terms used in bibliographical citations (**viz., ibid., loc. cit.,** etc.; see pages 171–172).
c. National and governmental units such as **USSR, FBI, NASA, OPEC.** (Notice that no periods follow these abbreviations, but each letter of **U.S.** or **U.S.A.** is always followed by a period.)

3. When in doubt, write out the word or words instead of abbreviating. And again, don't forget the standard dictionaries as guides to preferred choices.

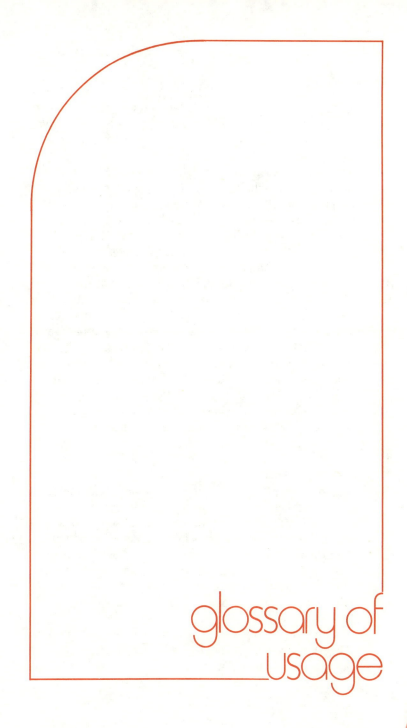

glossary of
usage

8

The glossary that follows lists a large number of words and phrases with which many writers, both experienced and inexperienced, have difficulty. It is primarily prescriptive, in that it states as exactly as possible just what usages are and are not acceptable in formal writing, the kind of writing required of students and people in the business and professional worlds. Although there is always disagreement about language and its use, a surprising consensus does in fact exist, and it is this consensus which, we hope, informs these advisory notes.

Essentially, three main levels of usage may be discriminated: informal spoken English, informal spoken and written English, and formal spoken and written English. What is appropriate to one level may not be appropriate to another. As a relatively trivial example, no one would think you uneducated if, in a conversation at a party, you said, "I sure am having a good time!" And very likely, your employer would not think you deficient in any way if you wrote in a memo, "I sure hope that the shipment arrives by Friday." But you might displease or even irritate the reader of a formal report if you stated, "Our Lawrence operation will sure fail unless we can increase our local advertising." Thus, to use language properly we must always consider the context and the audience and conform to their expectations.

Formal written English is the level to which this glossary is addressed. The notes have been compiled on the assumption that you are in doubt about some usage and want practical advice for solving specific writing problems rather than general discussion of various grammatical opinions. Thus, you will find myriad "do's" and "don't's" and illustrations, which, though they cannot pretend to absolute authority, should help you write more correctly and effectively.

We are indebted to many commentaries on American English usage, but particularly to *The American Heritage Dictionary of the English Language.*

a, an   Use the indefinite article **an** before words beginning with a vowel sound; use **a** before all other words that require an indefinite article.

a bicycle, *a* file, *a* joke; *an* apple, *an* idea, *an* honor.

accept, except   **Accept** means to receive; **except** means to exclude:

I *accept* the award.

You have been *excepted* from the list.

The preposition is always **except:**

Everyone *except* me had the measles.

affect, effect   **Affect** means to influence or have an influence on; **effect** means to cause or bring about.

How will this *affect* our vacation plans?

When will you *effect* your plans?

ain't   Avoid using this nonstandard contraction for **am not** in formal writing and speaking.

all, all of   The word **all** is always followed by the preposition **of** when it precedes a pronoun. Preceding a noun, however, **of** is not necessary and, for conciseness, may be omitted.

All of you have misbehaved.

All the boys wanted to go.

all ready, already   **All ready** is an adjective phrase indicating total readiness; **already** is an adverb signifying time.

We are *all ready* to leave.

They have *already* left.

all right, alright   **All right** is an adjective or adverb phrase meaning "acceptable" or "correct." It should not be spelled as one word, **alright.**

8

Is it **all right** to go?

He was **all right** after three days.

all together, altogether   The expression **all together** pertains to a gathering at one time or in one place; the word **altogether** means completely or totally.

The family was **all together** for the first time.

She visited us four times **altogether.**

allusion, illusion, delusion   These three nouns are often confused. **Allusion** means an indirect mention or reference. **Illusion** means a false perception or belief. **Delusion** means a false belief persisted in despite evidence to the contrary. **Delusion** implies a willful clinging to the false perception or belief; **illusion** implies only temporary mistakenness.

The **allusion** is to Shakespeare's *Hamlet.*

She has the **illusion** that she will become a movie star.

His basic symptom is a **delusion** of grandeur.

allusion, reference   These two words have slightly different meanings. A **reference** is a direct and specific mention of someone or something; an **allusion** is an indirect and nonspecific mention of someone or something.

Her **reference** to the plight of the poor in Houston was met with silence.

He cleverly slipped in a **reference** to his new novel.

I found only one **reference** in the entire report to curriculum changes.

His reply, "Nevermore!," was a humorous **allusion** to Poe's "The Raven."

Modern poetry frequently employs obscure **allusions** to earlier literature.

alot, a lot   Lot is a noun meaning a number of people or things and requires the indefinite article **a,** but the two words are never written together as one word—**alot.**

A lot of people will probably vote for Wilson.

A lot of things might happen.

already   See **all ready, already.**

alright   See **all right, alright.**

altar, alter   **Altar,** a noun, designates an elevated place or structure for religious ceremonies; **alter,** a verb, means to change, modify, or transform.

The priest approached the *altar.*

When you copy this poem, don't *alter* a word.

although, though   The alternate form of the conjunction **although** is **though,** meaning "in spite of the fact that," and they may be used virtually interchangeably. **Though** is the more commonly used form, but **although** most often begins sentences.

She loves him, *though* he treats her badly.

Although you failed the midterm exam, I am passing you in the course.

altogether   See **all together, altogether.**

alumnus, alumni; alumna, alumnae   An **alumnus** is a male graduate of a school, and an **alumna** is a female graduate; **alumni** and **alumnae** are their respective plurals. In practice, however, the word **alumni** is often used generally to refer to all the graduates of a school, male or female.

among, between   Use the preposition **between** when two objects are involved and the preposition **among** when three or more are involved.

It is difficult to choose *between* the two men for the job.

Among the team members Tom is the only bachelor.

Between may, however, be used even when more than two persons or things are involved if they are clearly individual and closely related:

8

The contract **between** the five companies expires at midnight.

If there is any question in your mind, observe the rule based on the number of parties involved.

amount, number   Both these words refer to quantity, but **number** applies when units, countable persons or things, are involved and **amount** when that is not the case.

The **number** of girls who have signed up for intramural sports far exceeds our estimate.

Count the **number** of automobiles that pass through this intersection in one hour.

We have decided to decrease the **number** of magazines we receive.

The **amount** of space allocated to us is 100 square feet.

Only a small **amount** of oil is needed to cool this engine.

No **amount** of effort can make up for a fundamental lack of talent.

an See **a, an.**

anywhere(s), nowhere(s), nowhere(s) near   Anywheres and nowheres are nonstandard forms of **anywhere** and **nowhere,** respectively, and should not be used in formal writing. **Nowhere(s) near** is an informal expression and should be replaced by **not nearly.**

I will go **anywhere** if necessary.

Anywhere I travel, I find kind and helpful people.

There is **nowhere** I would rather be than here.

They had **nowhere** to go.

A six-footer is **nowhere near** big enough to play center in basketball. (incorrect)

A six-footer is **not nearly** big enough to play center in basketball. (correct)

Your bid is **nowheres near** low enough. (incorrect)

Your bid is **not nearly** low enough. (correct)

as, as if (though), like   **Like,** a preposition, should generally not be used as a conjunction in formal writing except when the clause it introduces is omitted. The conjunctions **as, as if,** or **as though** are always acceptable.

This model works well, **as** you said it would.

It sounds **as if** you have changed your mind.

She looks **as though** she has not slept for days.

NOT: I mailed it to Peoria **like** you told me to.

BUT: Frank behaved **like** a clown. (That is, Frank behaved **as** a clown behaves.)

OR: The company attacked the enemy position **like** ants. (That is, the company attacked the enemy position **as** ants swarm about an anthill.)

assume, presume   The distinction between these two words is very fine. To **assume** means to take something for granted or to hypothesize, usually for some sound or plausible reason; to **presume** means to conclude something to be true, often without a sound or plausible reason.

We **assume** that most of the candidates will pass their examinations.

Let's **assume** that our plant will turn out 500 barrels per day.

You may **assume** that the Raiders will win the division title.

A person is **presumed** innocent until proven guilty.

You have **presumed,** quite unfairly I think, that she will not qualify for a scholarship.

We **presumed** that Copley and Associates would not want to bid on this job.

at this point in time, at this moment in time   These phrases have become popular, especially among politicians, but both are wordy and redundant. **At this time** or **now** is preferable.

average, mean, median   The **average** of a group of numbers is computed by dividing the sum of the numbers in the group by the number of numbers in the group.

8

The *average* of 10, 20, and 30 is 60 ÷ 3 = 20.

The **mean** between two numbers is the midpoint.

The *mean* of 20 and 60 is 40.

The **median** is a number in a group, above which are half of the remaining numbers and below which are the other half.

The *median* of the group 10, 20, 30, 40, 50, 60, 70 is 40.

The word **average** is also used to mean "typical" or "usual."

awful, awfully   **Awful** is an adjective; **awfully** is an adverb. Do not use the adjective for the adverb.

NOT: It was an *awful* nice party.

BUT: It was an *awfully* nice party.

NOT: He has an *awful* fast car.

BUT: He has an *awfully* fast car.

Awful as an adjective often means "extremely bad" or "terrible."

She baked an *awful* pie.

I played *awful* tennis today.

Although not necessarily incorrect, neither **awful** nor **awfully** belongs in formal prose.

awhile, a while   The adverb **awhile** means "for a short time." Consequently, using **for** with **awhile** is redundant. **For** may, however, be used with the indefinite article and noun, **a while.**

Why don't you stay *awhile* and talk?

He practiced *awhile* before going home.

She didn't know *for a while* what his name was.

The couple sat *for a while* and then, without speaking, parted.

bad, badly   **Bad** is an adjective; **badly** is an adverb. Be sure to use the part of speech called for by the context.

I feel *bad.*

This is a *bad* situation.

Can the boy be all *bad?*

He began the speech *badly* and finally stopped.

My brother drives *badly.*

I want to go *badly.*

> The most common error is to use the adverb with a verb of sense, like **feel, smell, taste,** and so forth.

NOT: He said that he feels *badly.*

BUT: He said that he feels *bad.*

NOT: The liquid smells *badly.*

BUT: The liquid smells *bad.*

because   See **due to the fact that, because.**

between   See **among, between.**

between you and I   **Between** is a preposition that takes an object; in this case both pronouns are the object and should be in the objective case. The objective case of **you** is **you** and the objective case of **I** is **me.** For some reason, many writers and speakers seem to think that **between you and I** sounds more elegant or more formal, but in fact the only correct form is **between you and me.**

burst, bust   The principal parts of **burst** are **burst, burst, burst;** the principal parts of **bust** are **bust, busted, busted.** Although **bust** is a variant or alternative to **burst,** most literate people prefer **burst.**

The new father is *bursting* with pride.

The dam *burst* last year.

He had *burst* a vessel in his leg.

can, may   **Can** denotes the ability to do something; **may** denotes permission to do something.

Roger knows that he *can* hit the ball.

You *can* do it.

8

This school year *can* be the most interesting we've ever had.

May I go this Thursday?

You *may* go if your room is cleaned up.

You *may* have three but no more.

See also **may, might.**

cannot, can not Use **cannot** unless you wish to emphasize **not.**

I *cannot* work this problem.

We *cannot* understand where the money has gone.

You most certainly *can not!*

capital, capitol **Capital** denotes the city or town in which government for a given political unit resides, and only **capitol** denotes the building in which the legislature for that unit meets.

The *capital* of Kansas is Topeka.

The *capital* of the United States is Washington, D.C.

The *capitol* in Topeka is modeled on the *Capitol* in Washington, D.C.

Any other meaning, such as **capital punishment** or **capital investment,** calls for **capital.**

censor, censure A **censor** is one who examines material and deletes what he or she finds objectionable. **Censure** is severe criticism or disapproval. The meanings of these two words used as verbs can easily be inferred.

We must not allow him to become a *censor* of the newspaper.

The legislature voted on *censure* of Representative Billings this afternoon.

Does the prison *censor* inmates' mail?

We should *censure* him for leaking grand jury information.

center around, center on By definition a center is a point; consequently, something must **center on** the point rather than **center around** it. The latter is simply illogical.

The controversy *centers on* federal aid to big cities.

The interpretations *center on* Huck Finn's treatment of Jim at the Phelps's farm.

His books all *center on* the effect of the small town on American life.

childish, childlike   **Childish** has a negative connotation, while **childlike** has a positive connotation. **Childish,** applied to adults, denotes the less desirable characteristics of the child, such as selfishness and irresponsibility. Applied to children, **childish** is merely description and connotatively neutral. **Childlike,** applied to either adults or children, connotes the more desirable characteristics of the child, such as innocence and trust.

Fred is the most *childish* man I have ever known.

Must you always act so *childish* when we celebrate New Year's Eve at the Martins'?

Even at sixty, she seemed *childlike.*

Childlike, he brought the picture to me for approval.

cite, sight, site   **Sight** may be either a noun or a verb; **cite** is always a verb; and **site** is always a noun. As a noun, **sight** means the faculty of vision or something seen; as a verb, **sight** means to see or to take aim.

The *sight* from Smoky Mountain is beautiful.

Did you *sight* the target?

To **cite** is to mention or to commend.

In my lecture I shall *cite* three speeches from *King Lear.*

This year we *cite* William Jefferson and James Holman for their contributions to Little League baseball.

A **site** is a specific place.

Nebraska is the *site* of next year's tournament.

The agency plans to sell that *site* north of town.

classic, classical   Often these two adjectives are interchangeable. **Classical** is often preferred to describe Greek and Roman cul-

8

ture, and **classic** is often preferred to describe the finest or highest of a group (an obvious exception is **classical music**).

This **classical** work still moves us after nearly 2,500 years.

The **classical** tradition should be required study for every college student.

An American Tragedy by Dreiser is a **classic** twentieth-century novel.

Her old Packard has **classic** lines.

compare, contrast   **Compare,** used generally, means to examine two or more things to show their similarities and differences. More specifically, **compare** means to show the similarities between two or more things; **contrast** means to show the differences.

The hitting of the New York Yankees **compares** favorably with that of the Kansas City Royals.

I would **compare** her acting with Katherine Hepburn's.

BUT: **Compare** the two specimens in terms of density and color. (used in general sense)

Different areas of Boston **contrast** strikingly.

Contrast her actions with his, and you will see what I mean.

compare to, compare with   **Compare with** is used when two or more essentially like things are examined for their similarities and differences. **Compare to** is used when the things compared are essentially unlike or only figuratively related.

Compared with Tom, I am a poor golfer.

Your score **compares** well **with** the top scores from other schools.

In the essay the man is **compared to** an elephant.

After her last date with him she **compared** him **to** an octopus.

compose, comprise, constitute   **Compose** means to make up the constituent parts of; **comprise** means to consist of, to be composed of; **constitute** means to make up the parts of and is therefore synonymous with **compose.** In short, smaller units **compose**

or **constitute** a larger unit; a larger unit **comprises** smaller units.

Two parts hydrogen and one part oxygen *compose* water.

Eight teams *compose* the league.

The essay *comprises* an introduction, a body, and a conclusion.

A baseball game *comprises* nine innings.

Three books *constitute* his entire library.

comprise See **compose, comprise, constitute.**

connote, connotate **Connote** means to suggest a meaning or consequence in addition to the literal meaning or obvious consequence. There is no such word as **connotate,** though it is proper to speak of a word's **connotation.**

The word *steed* **connotes** adventure and romance.

Their actions *connote* hostility and possible rebellion.

What are some of the *connotations* of the word *communism?*

connote, denote **Connote** means to suggest a meaning or consequence in addition to the literal meaning or obvious consequence. **Denote** means to signify the literal meaning or obvious consequence.

The word *mother* most often *connotes* warmth, security, and love.

Her tone of voice *connotes* anger.

The word *meadow* *denotes* a grassland.

Confidence in a crisis *denotes* training and experience.

consensus of opinion The word **consensus** means "collective opinion" or "agreement of opinion." Therefore, the expression **consensus of opinion** is redundant and should be avoided in formal writing.

The *consensus* is that we should buy the stocks at the current price.

Committee members, have you reached a *consensus?*

8

constitute   See **compose, comprise, constitute.**

consul, council, counsel   **Consul** denotes a government representative sent to a foreign country to promote trade and to protect the rights of fellow citizens. **Council** denotes a group meeting to conduct work of some kind. **Counsel** denotes advice or guidance.

Our new *consul* to England will be named next week.

What are the primary duties of the *consul* to West Germany?

The student *council* at North High School meets every Friday morning.

Four men and three women compose the city *council.*

The best *counsel* I can give you is to wait.

The *counsel* she received didn't satisfy her.

For the verb meaning to advise, the word is **counsel.**

The broker *counseled* me to sell my stock.

continue on   **Continue** means to go on; consequently, the expression **continue on** is redundant and should be avoided in formal writing.

Please *continue* what you were doing when I came into the room.

The new president will *continue* the plans set in operation last year.

contrast   See **compare, contrast.**

could of, could have (should of, should have; would of, would have)   The expression **could of** for **could have** has developed because of the sound of **could have** when pronounced rapidly — **could of. Could of,** however, is regarded as illiterate and should be avoided entirely.

The trip *could have* been fun if Harry hadn't gone.

I *could have* gotten the job if I had had a degree.

With additional drill the platoon *could have* won the trophy.

Similar illiteracies occur in **should of, would of, may of, might of, must of,** which should be **should have, would have, may have, might have, must have,** respectively.

council   See **consul, council, counsel.**

counsel   See **consul, council, counsel.**

criteria   The singular form of this word is **criterion. Criteria** is always plural and always requires a plural verb.

One *criterion* is not enough for the study we have in mind.

The feasibility report bases its conclusions on three *criteria:* manufacturing costs, efficiency of operation, and pollution control.

These *criteria* have been approved by the committee.

data   The word **data** is plural; the singular form of this word is **datum** (now seldom used). The use of a singular verb with **data** is increasingly acceptable, but formal writing still requires a plural verb. We advise you to maintain the traditional distinction between the singular and plural forms.

The *datum* we received does permit us to draw that conclusion.

Data for our experiment were gathered in North Carolina and Tennessee.

The *data* are incomplete.

delusion   See **allusion, illusion, delusion.**

denote   See **connote, denote.**

desert, dessert   Only the word denoting the last course of a meal, consisting of a sweet, is spelled with two **s**'s. The other word, **desert,** meaning a barren area, a deserved reward, or to abandon, is spelled with one **s.**

What are we having for *dessert?*

The *desert* lies just across the mountains.

8

He received his just *deserts.*

Please do not *desert* us as you did before.

different from, different than Both expressions are acceptable, but **different from** is preferable in formal writing, except when its use might result in wordiness.

Her opinion about the issue is *different from* mine.

This situation is *different from* any previous situation.

BUT: His answer was *different than* I expected. (preferable to the longer "His answer was *different from* the one I expected.")

discreet, discrete **Discreet** means "having propriety in behavior and speech"; **discrete** means "composed of individual entities."

You can count on her to be *discreet* in this matter.

You must be *discreet* to be a doctor, a lawyer, or a spy.

The book consists of *discrete* essays and sketches.

The result of the bombardment was three *discrete* particles which we have not yet identified.

disinterested, uninterested **Disinterested** means "unbiased" or "impartial"; **uninterested** means "not interested" or "indifferent."

Mr. Thompson would be a *disinterested* judge for the contest.

Let's submit this dispute to a *disinterested* third party for a decision.

I am *uninterested* in skeet shooting.

Uninterested students seldom finish the course in photography.

due to As part of an adjective phrase following a linking verb, **due to** is correct; as part of an adverbial phrase modifying a verb, it is not.

The decrease in sales is *due to* poorer merchandise.

His success in the Army was *due to* the R.O.T.C. training he received in college.

Their growing marital difficulties were *due to* their differences about religion.

NOT: He won the match *due to* his opponent's failure to rush the net.

NOT: The factory finally failed *due to* labor problems.

NOT: *Due to* new evidence, we have decided to reopen the case.

The substitution of **because of, on account of, as a result of,** or similar expressions for **due to** in the last three illustrations will correct them.

He won the match *because of* his opponent's failure to rush the net.

The factory finally failed *as a result of* labor problems.

On account of new evidence, we have decided to reopen the case.

due to the fact that, because The expression **due to the fact that** is always wordy and should always be replaced by **because.**

WORDY: *Due to the fact that* the brakes were bad, the car hit the curb and overturned.

Was the decision made *due to the fact that* we are overadministered?

He went home last weekend *due to the fact that* his sister was ill.

REVISED: *Because* the brakes were bad, the car hit the curb and overturned.

Was the decision made *because* we are overadministered?

He went home last weekend *because* his sister was ill.

effect See **affect, effect.**

e.g., i.e., viz. Because all three of these abbreviations of Latin words with similar meanings appear frequently in writing, it is important that you understand and use them correctly. **E.g.** stands for **exempli gratia,** which means "for the sake of example" or "for example." **I.e.** stands for **id est,** which means "that is." **Viz.** stands for **videlicet,** which means "it is easy to see" or "namely."

Many brilliant novels appeared in America in the 1920's— *e.g., An American Tragedy, The Sun Also Rises, The Sound and the Fury.*

Many of Hawthorne's novels and tales employ the theological doctrine of original sin—*i.e.,* the imperfection of human nature.

Three highways need additional repairs—*viz.,* 24, 40, 59.

egoism, egotism   The distinction between these two words is not always observed, but in general **egoism** denotes a philosophical concept having to do with the self, while **egotism** denotes excessive concern with one's self. Unless you intend to use the term somewhat technically, as in a discussion of ethics, for example, the proper word is probably **egotism.**

The philosophy of author Ayn Rand is a contemporary form of *egoism.*

Many actors, athletes, and other public figures are victims of *egotism.*

Her *egotism* has never bothered her friends.

element, factor   These are two of the most overworked and meaningless nouns in the English language. They are summoned as substitutes for **thing, attribute, part, cause, reason, detail,** and many other specific nouns when the writer refuses to think precisely and to give proper names to things.

There are many *factors* to consider in choosing a college. (weak)

There are social, economic, and intellectual questions to consider in choosing a college. (improved)

Name the various *elements* in staging a play. (weak)

Name the five basic theatrical requirements for staging a play. (improved)

elicit, illicit   **Elicit** is a verb meaning to draw out or evoke; **illicit** is an adjective meaning illegal.

What response did her speech before the assembly *elicit?*

This action could *elicit* further reprisals from the guerrillas.

He was arrested yesterday for the *illicit* sale of handguns.

From the moment he arrived in this country, his business dealings were *illicit.*

emigrate, immigrate   Probably no pair of verbs and their related nouns are more commonly confused than these two. **Emigrate** means to leave a country to live in another, and **immigrate** means to enter a country and settle in it. Thus, one could **emigrate from** Germany and at the same time **immigrate to** America.

Thousands of farmers *emigrated* from Germany in the nineteenth century.

The Jewish family will *emigrate* from Russia as soon as they receive permission.

These settlers *immigrated* to America for religious reasons.

Theodore's parents *immigrated* to this country twenty years before he was born.

eminence   See **immanence, imminence, eminence.**

end result, result   The word **result** means an event caused by another event and suggests an end of some kind. Consequently, the expression **end result** is redundant except when a series of causes and results is involved. Unless you actually wish to refer to the final result in a chain of results, the word you want is **result.**

The *end result* of the series of chemical reactions will prove or disprove Dr. Fitzgerald's hypothesis.

The flight of thousands of city dwellers to the suburbs has had several important *results.*

8

I am not sure what the *result* of using this new type of spark plug will be.

equally, equally as The adverb **as** means "equally"; consequently, the expression **equally as** is redundant and should never be used in formal expository prose.

This problem is *equally* difficult.

Her plan is *equally* good but costs too much.

The two governments are *equally* repressive.

eruption, irruption The two words are often confused, but they are clearly different, indeed opposed, in meaning. An **eruption** is a breaking or bursting *out,* whereas an **irruption** is a breaking or bursting *in.*

The *eruption* of lava from the volcano was the first in living memory.

Irruption of enemy troops into our country occurred completely without warning.

The *eruption* of water caused hundreds of deaths among the villagers.

The *irruption* of people into industrial cities has created severe social problems.

et al., etc. (et cetera) **Et al.** stands for the words **et alii,** which mean "and others," **others** referring to people rather than things. **Etc.** stands for the words **et cetera,** which mean **and other (things).** There seems to be no agreement on the occasions for use or omission of these terms, but generally, do not use them in formal writing. Both should be used sparingly and then mainly not in the text itself but rather in notes and references.

The Literary History of the United States was edited by Spiller *et al.*

The discovery of this specimen was made in 1936 by Tyler *et al.*

The garage sale we attended offered the biggest collection of junk I have ever seen: an old bedspring, a worn-out carburetor, a dilapidated card table, a scratched mirror, *etc.*

The course dealt with the full range of major issues of American history before 1900: the Puritan mind, the Enlightenment, Jacksonian Democracy, the Civil War, **et cetera.**

everyday, every day   The word **everyday** is an adjective meaning "ordinary," "typical," or "usual." The two-word expression **every day** means "each day."

Mother has decided to use the *everyday* dishes for dinner.

These are our *everyday* prices.

We go boating nearly *every day.*

A cardinal sings outside our window *every day.*

everyone, every one   **Everyone** denotes everybody or all persons generally. **Every one,** on the other hand, denotes each and every person involved.

Everyone found the movie dull.

Everyone enjoys driving through the Rocky Mountains in Colorado.

Every one of the persons interviewed had complaints about the high prices of gasoline.

He told *every one* of the counselors about the new rules.

everyplace, everywhere   The adverb **everywhere** is correct in formal writing, but **everyplace** as an adverb meaning everywhere is not correct. The two-word expression **every place,** however, meaning each place, is, of course, formally correct.

Everywhere in this town people are friendly and helpful.

We searched *everywhere* in the back yard, but we could not find it.

I want you to tell me about *every place* you visited on your vacation.

except   See **accept, except.**

factor   See **element, factor.**

8

farther, further A distinction in the formal use of these adverbs needs to be made. **Farther** is used to denote literal, physical distance, and **further** is used for all figurative senses of distance or remoteness. Some authorities think that **farther** will eventually disappear altogether.

How much *farther* is Hot Springs?

Farther down Main Street you will find the Gaslight Shopping Center.

We have just received some *further* details on the accident.

She will need *further* treatment at the hospital.

few, little **Few** denotes a small or limited number of persons or things that are countable. **Little** denotes a small or limited quantity of things that are not countable.

Few persons find such counseling sessions helpful.

From the thousands of applications, we selected only a *few* for further processing.

It will do *little* good to make the substitution now.

She has *little* talent for musical comedy.

fewer, less **Fewer** denotes a smaller quantity of persons or things that are countable. **Less** denotes a smaller quantity of things that are not countable, that are abstract, or that are considered collectively.

We need *fewer* critics and more creative artists.

Fewer people than ever are using South Park.

We hope to have *less* haggling over money this year.

Salina is *less* than forty miles from here. (*forty miles* is considered collectively)

He gave it *less* than his best effort.

first, firstly; second, secondly . . . It is generally best to use the common sequence of adverbs **first, second, third,** and so on, rather than the very formal **firstly, secondly, thirdly,** and so on. Do not mix sequences, such as **first, secondly, third.** You may even prefer to replace the words with the numerals **1, 2, 3** placed within parentheses or followed by a single parenthesis.

First, purchase regulation handball equipment at Francis' Sporting Goods; *second,* give the secretary in 308 Robinson Hall your name for entry into the tournament; and *third,* pick up a copy of the pairings by Friday of this week.

Follow these simple steps in writing your essay: *first,* make an outline; *second,* write a rough draft; *third,* lay the paper aside for a time; and *fourth,* revise and polish the rough draft.

The speaker made essentially three points: *(1)* city government is corrupt; *(2)* special-interest groups have too much influence on the city's decisions; and *(3)* the time is right for a sweeping change.

flammable, inflammable　These two words meaning "capable of burning easily and quickly" are virtually interchangeable. For speaking of a person's passionate temperament, however, only **inflammable** is correct. Then, too, in technical writing it is preferable to use **flammable** rather than **inflammable** because many people mistakenly believe that **inflammable** means "nonflammable," a misunderstanding that could be quite dangerous.

This cleaning liquid has the disadvantage of being highly *flammable.*

His *inflammable* nature has gotten him into trouble on job after job.

Shop workers must be reminded to use *inflammable* materials carefully.

flaunt, flout　These two verbs have distinctly different meanings which you should observe. **Flaunt** means to show off or display ostentatiously; **flout** means to show contempt or scorn for.

One of my professors last semester *flaunted* his learning shamelessly.

Parties at the country club give her a chance to *flaunt* her money and clothes.

You are making a mistake by *flouting* the church authorities in this matter.

Throughout the trial he *flouted* the judge's decrees and decisions.

8

flounder, founder These two verbs are commonly confused by many people, perhaps because they do seem to share a thin area of meaning. **Flounder** means to move or proceed clumsily, confusedly, ineffectually; **founder** means to fail, sink, break down, collapse.

I was *floundering* before I went to see Dr. Sheldon.

Without consistently good pitching and defense, the Red Sox *floundered* in the second division.

The ship finally *foundered* after three days of the storm.

Her plans for an education *foundered* when her father died.

flout See **flaunt, flout.**

fortuitous, fortunate These adjectives overlap slightly, though basically they have distinctly different meanings. **Fortuitous** means "by chance, unplanned, accidental," whereas **fortunate** means "lucky, occurring by good chance, characterized by an unexpected good." A **fortuitous** event could also be a **fortunate** one, but not necessarily.

The *fortuitous* meeting of Daniels and his chief competitor in Rome occurred last March.

His company assured us that the appearance of their salesman at just that time was *fortuitous.*

Fortuitous circumstances are often *fortunate.*

Fortunate people are seldom thankful.

Wasn't it *fortunate* that we were in Denver that particular weekend?

founder See **flounder, founder.**

further See **farther, further.**

get This verb has numerous meanings, as a look at any good dictionary will reveal. *The American Heritage Dictionary of the English Language* lists thirty different meanings for the verb used transitively and another six for the verb used intransitively. Clearly it has become a word used for a wide range of meanings. The best procedure to follow in using this word is to reflect for a moment on whether another word might be more exact. If so, use it rather than the all-purpose **get.** Consider the following examples:

I may ***get*** to go with you.

When do we ***get*** to Lawrence?

He ***gets*** more attention from Ms. Schneider than any other student in the class.

The children ***got*** colds last week.

You can ***get*** your prescription filled in our pharmacy.

These sentences illustrate just some of the many uses of this verb, and in all of them a more exact word could be used. Here are some possible revisions that suggest, at the very least, that the reviser has a larger and more functional vocabulary than the writer of the original sentences:

I may ***be allowed*** to go with you.

When do we ***arrive*** in Lawrence?

He ***receives*** more attention from Ms. Schneider than any other student in the class.

The children ***caught*** colds last week.

You can ***have*** your prescription filled in our pharmacy.

In short, if the word you need is **get,** use it; if another word is more precise or may impart needed variety to your writing, prefer it to **get.** See also **got, gotten.**

good, well You need to remember that **good** is an adjective and that **well** is generally an adverb. That distinction and a fundamental sense of grammar will enable you to use these two words properly. In particular, you need to recall that verbs of sense such as **feel, taste, smell,** and **sound,** and certain other verbs such as **seem,** are linking verbs, which are generally followed by predicate adjectives. Therefore, the expression **Mary feels good** is grammatically correct in indicating Mary's state of health. The expression **Mary feels well** would be grammatically correct only if the writer wished to indicate something about Mary's sense of touch—rather unlikely. Here are a num-

8

ber of examples which show **good** modifying nouns and pronouns and **well** modifying verbs, adjectives, and other adverbs, as grammatically required:

I feel *good* about the test I took this morning.

The pie that you baked tastes *good.*

Do you think that this smells *good?*

His idea sounds *good.*

His proposal seems *good* to me and to the other board members.

He thinks *well* on his feet.

She does *well* at bridge if she has a good partner.

I know *well* how eccentric he can be.

Mr. Johnson is *well* adjusted.

The house is *well* situated and inexpensive.

got, gotten Either of these words may be used in American English as the past participle of the verb **get.** The British use only **got,** and Americans tend to prefer **gotten.** You cannot go wrong here, though the sound of the sentence may help you decide which would be the better choice. In the following sentences **got** and **gotten** are interchangeable.

I have *got* three hits in the last two games.

They have *gotten* along well with their new neighbors.

Have you *got* a letter from him yet?

See also **get.**

graduate Current usage permits you to say either **Mary was graduated from college** or **Mary graduated from college.** Until recently the use of the passive voice was required, but now the usage is split between the active and the passive forms, with the active form being the more common. It is, however, unacceptable to say **Mary graduated college.** You must use the preposition **from** with both the active and the passive forms.

graffiti This is the plural form of the word **graffito,** meaning writing or drawing in public places, and it requires the use of a plural verb. The singular form is seldom used.

Graffiti were written in spray paint on buses.

Graffiti tell us a great deal about human nature.

Graffiti are often obscene.

hanged, hung These are alternative forms of the past tense and past participle of the verb **hang,** but there is a distinction to remember. **Hung** is used except when the verb refers to death from suspension by the neck.

The boys ***hung*** around the corner until midnight.

I have ***hung*** your clothes up to dry.

The territorial government ***hanged*** both outlaws in 1875.

The courts have ***hanged*** men for lesser offenses.

himself This pronoun, and its parallel forms (**herself, itself, myself,** and the like), should never be used as an ordinary direct object—for example: **The list includes Tim Brown and myself** (correct form—**me**). All are correctly used only when they are either reflexive or intensive. *Reflexive* denotes the grammatical condition when the subject acts on itself, and *intensive* when the subject is reiterated and stressed, as follows:

He hurt ***himself*** while diving into the pool. (reflexive)

We must blame ***ourselves*** for the mess we are in. (reflexive)

Sarah Evans removed ***herself*** from the election last night. (reflexive)

The pedestrians ***themselves*** admitted that they were not watching the traffic. (intensive)

I ***myself*** will do it if I have to. (intensive)

The magazine ***itself*** proved to be little more than a rehash of monthly events. (intensive)

hopefully This word means **with hope** or **in a hopeful manner,** but is increasingly used to mean **it is hoped that** or **let us hope that.** This second use, however, is unacceptable to a majority of authorities. Consequently, to be absolutely correct, avoid

8

using **hopefully** by substituting for it **it is hoped that, let us hope that, we hope that,** or some similar expression.

Hopefully, the new offices will be ready by February 1. (questionable)

The new procedure will *hopefully* double sales in the Midwest. (questionable)

Hopefully, you will be promoted soon. (questionable)

It is hoped that the new offices will be ready by February 1.

We hope that the new procedure will double sales in the Midwest.

Let us hope that you will be promoted soon.

i.e. See **e.g., i.e., viz.**

if, whether These words are used interchangeably to introduce noun clauses following the verbs **ask, doubt, know, remember, say, see, understand, wonder.** (When the statement contains an alternative, then the use of **whether** is preferable.)

She doubts *whether* she will have time to go. (The alternative is obviously that she may or may not have time to go. She isn't certain, but is leaning somewhat toward not having time to go.)

He asked *if* he could borrow my car for a few hours.

Let me see *whether* the repairman has arrived.

I wonder *if* you know how much time we have spent on this job.

He asked *whether* I had read the article or not.

Can you say *whether* this painting is his first? (*Or not* following *whether* may or may not be used.)

illicit See **elicit, illicit.**

illusion See **allusion, illusion, delusion.**

immanence, imminence, eminence These three words are unrelated but easily confused. **Immanence** means "presence in the world"; **imminence** means "a state in which something is about to happen''; **eminence** means ''a position of achievement or rank.''

The Transcendentalists affirmed the ***immanence*** of God as a fundamental principle.

The ***imminence*** of World War II made them delay their plans for marriage.

The ***eminence*** of the speakers undoubtedly accounts for the large crowds.

immigrate See **emigrate, immigrate.**

imply, infer These two verbs are not interchangeable. **Imply** means to suggest indirectly, and **infer** means to conclude from evidence. In other words, a speaker or writer **implies,** whereas a listener or reader **infers.**

The letter ***implied*** that it would do little good for me to apply for admission to law school.

Are you ***implying*** that he was the cause of the accident?

We ***infer*** from your statement that Tyler has been a poor worker.

The officers ***inferred*** from his statement that he was not the cause of the accident.

impracticable, impractical Very similar in appearance, these adjectives have slightly different meanings. **Impracticable** means ''not feasible'' or ''not capable of being done''; **impractical** means ''not useful or desirable.'' For example, using orange baseballs in major league games is certainly not **impracticable,** but it may very well be **impractical.**

At the present time powering the automobile with a solar battery is ***impracticable.***

Teaching writing to students by means of large lecture sections is ***impractical.***

She thinks that taking the bus from Seattle to Miami is ***impractical.***

See also **practicable, practical.**

8

individual(s), people, persons Use **people** when you are referring to a large group, the members of which are thought of collectively rather than individually. Conversely, use **persons** when you are referring to a rather small number of individual human beings. Use **individual** or **individuals** to mean a person(s) only when you want to contrast person(s) with the group.

Individuals as well as groups may apply for grants.

Most *people* watch less television in the summer than in the winter.

People in this town have been protesting the mayor's decision.

In a crisis *people* will often cooperate incredibly well.

Four *persons* were killed this morning on Highway 35.

Those *persons* interested in the needlepoint course should sign up in the room next door.

How many *persons* have donated their time thus far?

His constant theme is that we must remain *individuals* in our mass society.

The *individual* must have certain rights apart from the group.

infer See **imply, infer.**

inflammable See **flammable, inflammable.**

ingenious, ingenuous **Ingenious** means clever or cunning; **ingenuous** means naive, innocent, honest, without guile.

Your solution to that problem was *ingenious.*

He is *ingenious* but dishonest.

Although he failed as a businessman, he developed several *ingenious* sales techniques.

The *ingenuous* child led the thieves to the wall safe.

Despite being well read and widely traveled, my Aunt Maude always seemed *ingenuous* to me.

The story is about an *ingenuous* country girl learning to cope with big-city ways.

inside, inside of; outside, outside of When used as nouns, **inside** and **outside** must be followed by the preposition **of.**

The *inside of* the house was much nicer than we expected.

The *outside of* the cabinet had recently been painted.

Be sure that you inspect both the *inside* and the *outside of* each carton.

> When either of these two words is used as part of a prepositional phrase, however, **of** should be omitted.

Have you looked *inside* the car?

We played *outside* the school until the bell rang.

Look *inside* and *outside* the toolshed for the wrench I lost.

irregardless, regardless Never use **irregardless** for **regardless,** which means "despite everything." **Irregardless** is a double negative considered nonstandard by nearly all literate persons. Also, **regardless** should always be followed by the preposition **of.**

Regardless of the weather, we shall leave for home tomorrow.

He plans to carry out the experiment, *regardless of* the consequences.

Regardless of the price, we should buy a new car now.

irruption See **eruption, irruption.**

is when, is where **When** and **where** may be used as subordinating conjunctions to introduce clauses after the linking verb **is** in informal but not formal writing. They should never be so used in definitions.

Thursday *is when* I usually play handball with Tom. (correct, informal)

Montreal *is where* the next All-Star game will be played. (correct, informal)

A riot *is when* a wild disturbance is caused by a large number of people. (unacceptable)

8

A hootenanny *is where* folk singers gather, with participation by the audience. (unacceptable)

Thursday is the day I usually play handball with Tom. (correct, formal)

Montreal is the site of the next All-Star game. (correct, formal)

A riot is a wild disturbance caused by a large number of people. (correct, formal)

A hootenanny is a gathering of folk singers, with participation by the audience. (correct, formal)

it is, there is (are) These phrases are useful, but often result in wordiness and deadwood. For example, consider the following statement:

There are twenty teachers who have applied for this position.

As you can see, **there are** and **who** are merely padding, and the sentence can be made leaner, as follows:

Twenty teachers have applied for this position.

Thus, use **it is, there is,** and **there are** only when they are necessary and when they do not bloat the sentence of which they are a part.

It is the feeling of many students that the advising system is a failure. (weak)

Many students feel that the advising system is a failure. (improved)

There is a reference book entitled *Facts You Need to Know* that answers that question. (weak)

A reference book entitled *Facts You Need to Know* answers that question. (improved)

There are few things more troublesome than an unreliable automobile. (weak)

Few things are more troublesome than an unreliable automobile. (improved)

It is time to leave. (acceptable)

There is safety in numbers. (acceptable)

There are four time zones in the United States. (acceptable)

it is I, it's me Grammatically, the subjective forms of the pronouns **I, he, we, they,** and the like, are required following the linking verb **is** or its various forms like **was, will be,** and so on.

It is I who chose the date and time for the meeting.

It was he whom the students chose to represent them.

It will be they who are responsible for making the final decision.

But notice that although these statements are correct, they sound overly formal and somewhat stilted. Consequently, in speech and in writing that does not require a formal tone, you may use a contraction and the objective form of the pronoun, **it's me,** without being thought uneducated:

It's me who usually has to clean up.

Expressions like **it's him, it's us,** and **it's them,** however, while perfectly acceptable in speech, are perhaps less acceptable in writing than **it's me.**

It's him who's been wrong from the beginning.

It's us who have been treated unfairly.

It's them who are to blame.

But notice that in these cases, although these statements are familiar to the ear, they sound somewhat uneducated. If you feel unsure about your choice, therefore, you should probably use the grammatically correct subjective forms of these pronouns.

its, it's **Its** is the possessive form of the pronoun **it; it's** is the contraction of **it is** or **it has.** Many people mistakenly think that the use of the apostrophe in **it's** indicates possession; it indicates, rather, the omission of letters.

New York City has never lost *its* appeal for me.

The cat appeared in the morning for *its* food.

The book has little new to say about the Civil War, but *its* photographs are splendid.

It's time for the meeting to begin.

It's been the most prosperous county in the state for many years.

He says that *it's* his typewriter.

–ize, –wise Added to certain words, these suffixes perform invaluable service to the language: **bowdlerize, criticize, jeopardize, minimize, sterilize,** and **clockwise, lengthwise, likewise, otherwise, sidewise.** But many writers form new words unacceptable in formal writing: **finalize, horizontalize, radicalize, randomize, regularize,** and **newswise, powerwise, servicewise, moneywise, talentwise.** Most of these coined words never make their way permanently into the language and are therefore generally to be avoided. Good rules to remember are the following: (1) always consult the dictionary about a questionable word, and (2) use a coined word only if no other word or brief expression is available. Thus the sentence, **The engineers finalized the report,** would be much improved if it read, **The engineers finished the report.**

join, join together The verb **join** means to put or bring together; consequently, the phrase **join together** is redundant and should be avoided.

Let us *join* in singing the third verse.

They *joined* the railroad tracks at Promontory Point, Utah.

Join the pieces as illustrated.

kind of, sort of Unless the sense of the statement requires the discrimination that **kind of** and **sort of** provide, do not use them. The following examples do require such discrimination and are correct:

This *kind of* humor [the tall tale] has had an important place in American literature.

Most buyers prefer that *sort of* wrapping [cellophane].

That *kind of* engine [rotary] provides the automobile with excellent acceleration.

Americans have always been fascinated with this *sort of* ship [the clipper].

The following examples, however, do not require division and are merely wordy and inexact:

She is the *kind of* girl I would like to date.

This is the *sort of* record jacket that catches the eye.

This *kind of* opportunity is hard to pass up.

That *sort of* vacation has never appealed to me.

In formal writing, you must also match plural demonstrative pronouns with the plural forms of **kind of** and **sort of: these kinds** of, **these sorts** of, **those kinds** of, **those sorts** of. But the category in each of the following expressions may be either singular or plural.

These kinds of test (tests) are machine-graded.

Those sorts of religions (religion) have seldom been popular in the Western world.

Although **sort of** and **kind of** are used colloquially to mean "rather" or "somewhat," they are not acceptable in formal writing:

I feel *sort of* sick. (incorrect)

I feel *somewhat* sick. (correct)

I feel *kind of* weary. (incorrect)

I feel *rather* weary. (correct)

lay, lie These are two different verbs, and you must know and use correctly their various forms. **Lay,** meaning to place, is a transitive verb (takes a direct object), whose principal parts are **lay** (present tense), **laid** (past tense), **laid** (past participle). **Lie,** meaning to recline, is an intransitive verb (does not take a direct object), whose principal parts are **lie** (present tense), **lay** (past tense), **lain** (past participle).

Present tense: He *lay* the book on the table.

8

Past tense: He *laid* the book on the table.

Perfect tense: He *had laid* the book on the table.

Present tense: She *lies* on the beach all day.

Past tense: She *lay* on the beach all day.

Perfect tense: She *has lain* on the beach all day.

Memorizing the conjugations of the two verbs is the easiest way to deal with the problem.

lead, led The principal parts of the verb **lead,** meaning to guide or direct, are **led** (past tense) and **led** (past participle). Many persons mistakenly use **lead** for **led,** perhaps because **led** and the word for the metal Pb (**lead**) are pronounced the same way.

Present tense: I *lead* an interesting life in England.

Past tense: I *led* an interesting life in England.

Perfect tense: I *have led* an interesting life in England.

leave, let These verbs have the same meaning only in the expressions **leave alone** and **let alone:**

Please *leave* Mary Jane *alone.*

Please *let* Mary Jane *alone.*

I just can't *leave* candy *alone.*

I just can't *let* candy *alone.*

The expression **leave alone,** however, can also mean to depart and leave in solitude:

The couple seldom *leave* the children *alone* when they go out.

Don't *leave* us *alone* on this island!

We cannot *leave* you *alone* in a city this big.

Do not use **leave** to mean allow or permit, one of the fundamental meanings of **let:**

Let her be. (NOT *Leave* her be.)

Let us recite the pledge. (NOT *Leave* us recite the pledge.)

Let it go. (NOT *Leave* it go.)

led See **lead, led.**

lend, loan Many people use **loan** as a transitive verb (takes a direct object), especially in business contexts. You will satisfy everyone, however, if you prefer **lend** to **loan** and use the latter only as a noun.

He asked me to *lend* him $100.

Will you *lend* me your copy of *Mourning Becomes Electra* for a few days?

Mr. Hanson plans to *lend* his Picasso painting to the Metropolitan Museum of Art.

I appreciate the *loan.*

We applied for a *loan* from the Credit Union.

This is his third *loan* in ten months.

less See **fewer, less.**

let See **leave, let.**

let's **Let's** is the contraction of **let us;** consequently, it is redundant to follow it with **us.**

Let's us go swimming this afternoon. (incorrect)

Let's go swimming this afternoon. (correct)

Let's us paint the porch this weekend. (incorrect)

Let's paint the porch this weekend. (correct)

Let's us visit the Nelsons sometime soon. (incorrect)

Let's visit the Nelsons sometime soon. (correct)

lie See **lay, lie.**

like See **as, as if (though), like.**

literally The word **literally** means "in a strict, real, or actual rather than a figurative sense." It is mistakenly used by many writers to emphasize or underscore their statements, often with hilarious or absurd results:

8

As a thinker and writer, she *literally* burst with ideas.

He was *literally* the father of his country.

The manager *literally* treated the team with kid gloves.

In each of these examples, **literally** means "figuratively" — just the opposite of its actual meaning! In the following examples the word is correctly used to mean **actually:**

Many high school students in large metropolitan schools *literally* cannot read even nursery rhymes.

When the wind shifted abruptly, Mark *literally* flew from one side of the boat to the other.

According to researchers, the noise of the factory is *literally* deafening.

little See **few, little.**

loan See **lend, loan.**

loose, lose Often confused, these two verbs have completely different meanings. As an adjective, **loose** means unbound or slack, and as a verb it means to set free or release. The verb **lose** means to be deprived of, to fail to win, to fail to maintain, and so forth. Many times a writer's confusion about these two verbs is apparent; the actual mistake is just careless spelling.

The arrangement was too *loose* to suit me.

His *loose* play around second base cost them the game.

The book has several *loose* pages.

She *loosed* the horse from his tether and let him go free.

You must first *loose* the three knots on the left.

They will *loose* this weapon on the world within six months.

Whenever I play Curt, I *lose.*

We may *lose* the contract to Gordon Paving.

How much weight do you plan to *lose?*

many, much **Many** denotes a large, indefinite number of persons or things; **much** denotes a large quantity or amount. The distinction between them is that **many** is used when the quantity is countable (that is, the persons or things are essentially discrete) and **much** when it is not.

They had not caught *many* fish by late afternoon.

Many months passed before he heard from them again.

How *many* roads does the county plan to build?

Leonardo da Vinci made *many* important scientific discoveries.

This faulty switch has caused my company *much* trouble.

How *much* pride did he show?

My family has given me *much* joy.

I can see that you have put *much* effort into your project.

may See **can, may.** See **may, might.**

may, might   **Might** is actually the past tense of **may,** but in the present and the future tenses, both words denote possibility or permission. They differ essentially in the degree of possibility or permission conveyed, **may** being the stronger of the two: **They may buy the house** conveys greater possibility than **They might buy the house. It may rain this afternoon** conveys greater possibility than **It might rain this afternoon. He said that I may have tomorrow off** conveys stronger permission than **He said that I might have tomorrow off. May I interrupt for a moment?** conveys stronger permission than **Might I interrupt for a moment?** For hypothetical conditional statements, **might** is correct:

If I had known that you planned to be there, I *might* have come.

If there had been some response to our letter, we *might* not have brought this legal action.

If I had joined the army when I graduated from high school, I *might* have matured more rapidly.

See also **can, may.**

mean See **average, mean, median.**

8

media This noun, meaning **mediums** of mass communications, is plural and requires a plural verb.

The *media perform* a great public service.

The *media are* more sensitive to the issue of fairness than ever before.

The *media have been criticized* recently by some prominent legislators.

median See **average, mean, median.**

might See **may, might.**

myself See **himself.**

nauseated, nauseous (nauseating) These two adjectives have opposing meanings. **Nauseated** means "suffering from nausea"; **nauseous** or **nauseating** means "causing nausea."

She was *nauseated* from the strenuous exercise.

The nurse called the doctor to attend to the *nauseated* patient in Room 305.

Was he *nauseated* when you arrived at the scene of the accident?

Much of his night-club routine is *nauseous (nauseating).*

The *nauseous (nauseating)* sport of cockfighting is illegal in this state.

The living conditions among these migrant workers are *nauseous (nauseating).*

none This word may take either a singular or a plural verb, depending upon the context. It is, surprisingly, more often plural than singular. A good general rule is the following: use a plural verb unless the idea of singularity is stressed or unless **none** is followed by a singular noun in a prepositional phrase.

None of us *is* willing to make the decision.

None of us *thinks* the defendant is guilty.

None of the repair work *is* finished.

None of the conversation *was* interesting.

None of the players *have* arrived.

nowhere(s), nowhere(s) near See **anywhere(s), nowhere(s), nowhere(s) near.**

number See **amount, number.**

obligated, obliged Both of these words mean "bound" or "constrained," but **obliged** is the more general, the broader of the two. **Obliged** is used when the constraint stems from circumstance, legal or moral demand, or debt by favor or service. **Obligated,** on the other hand, applies only in the case of legal or moral duty. You may, therefore, use **obliged** for **obligated,** but not the reverse. Also, **obliged** often involves an inner sense of obligation, whereas **obligated** does not necessarily.

I am *obligated* to pay back the loan by July 1 of next year.

You are *obligated* to serve in Germany for three years.

Are they *obligated* to report their progress every month?

We are *obliged* to you for helping in the United Fund drive.

When he lost his job, I felt *obliged* to hire him temporarily.

They were *obliged* to fly to Detroit when their car broke down.

But notice:

According to this contract you are *obliged* (or *obligated*) to make one payment each month.

As was said above, **obliged** includes **obligated** as one of its meanings.

off of, off from In written prose do not follow **off** with the prepositions **of** or **from.**

The worker fell *off of* the tower. (incorrect)

The worker fell *off* the tower. (correct)

The boy jumped *off from* the roof. (incorrect)

8

The boy jumped *off* the roof. (correct)

The driver turned *off of* the road. (incorrect)
The driver turned *off* the road. (correct)

In addition, you should substitute **from** for **off** in a statement such as the following:

How much money were you able to get *off* him? (incorrect)
How much money were you able to get *from* him? (correct)

on account of In formal prose always prefer **because** or **because of** to the colloquial and wordy expression **on account of.**

On account of our entries in the county fair, we won't take a vacation this summer. (incorrect)

Because of our entries in the county fair, we won't take a vacation this summer. (correct)

Helen turned down his proposal of marriage *on account of* his drinking problem. (incorrect)

Helen turned down his proposal of marriage *because of* his drinking problem. (correct)

Energy costs are rising *on account of* international politics. (incorrect)

Energy costs are rising *because of* international politics. (correct)

Bill Hunter quit his job *on account of* his supervisor continually interfered with his work. (incorrect)

Bill Hunter quit his job *because* his supervisor continually interfered with his work. (correct)

On account of the sewing machine malfunctioned, my wife has not finished the dress. (incorrect)

Because the sewing machine malfunctioned, my wife has not finished the dress. (correct)

one, you Overuse of the impersonal pronoun **one** results in an overly formal effect, and overuse of the indefinite pronoun **you** (not the personal pronoun **you**) results in an overly informal effect, as in the following examples:

One sometimes concludes that *one* must simply make the best of *one's* circumstances.

How is *one* to know how to change the oil when *one* has never done it before?

Professor Green feels that *one* should write from *one's* experience.

As *you* grow older, *you* find that *you* are less able to respond fully to *your* environment.

You never know what *you* will do in a crisis until *you* find *yourself* in it.

You need to study history so that *you* will better understand the present and better plan the future.

These sentences could be revised as follows:

A *person* sometimes concludes that *he* must simply make the best of *his* circumstances.

How am *I* to know how to change the oil when *I* have never done it before?

Professor Green feels that *one* should write from *his* experience.

As *I* grow older, *I* find that *I* am less able to respond fully to *my* environment.

A *person* never knows what *he* will do in a crisis until *he* finds *himself* in it.

We need to study history so that *we* shall better understand the present and better plan the future.

Notice that the tone of the revised sentences is neither too formal nor too informal and that, moreover, the sentences are less sweeping than before, though still perhaps too general. No hard and fast rule can be given for the use of these words, but by simply being aware of their use and misuse, you can guard against their undesirable effects. One final caution: do not mix **one** and **you** as in the following statements:

If *one* is truly serious about an education, *you* can usually get one.

One can drive through that part of the city, but *you* don't dare stop and look around.

8

Although *you* are permitted three attempts, *one* usually finds that they are not enough.

These sentences can be improved as follows:

If *you* are truly serious about an education, *you* can usually get one.

One can drive through that part of the city, but *one* doesn't dare stop and look around.

Although *you* are permitted three attempts, *you* usually find that they are not enough.

But it is possible to improve them even more by altering their tone, as was shown above.

orient, orientate There is no such word as **orientate,** though one hears it occasionally in conversation. Evidently, some people mistakenly think that the verb related to the noun **orientation** must be **orientate,** but no dictionary lists it. Use only **orient** when you mean to locate or place or cause to become familiar with.

The scouts *oriented* themselves by means of the compass.

The personnel department will *orient* new employees about the general regulations of the company.

Orient the first section at 90° to the second section.

outside, outside of See **inside, inside of; outside, outside of.**

para–, pseudo–, quasi– These three prefixes are quite close in meaning but can be distinguished. **Para-** is neutral and in the context in question means resembling or similar to, as in **para-professional,** one who though not a professional performs many professional functions. **Pseudo–** and **quasi–** both have a negative character, **pseudo-** being by far the more negative of the two. **Quasi-** means resembling but not being the thing involved, as in **quasi-judicial** – that is, judicial in character but not having the full legal power of the judicial. **Pseudo–** means deceptively similar but false, as in **pseudo-classic** – that is, erroneously regarded by some as being a classic.

The underground movement is conducted along **paramilitary** lines.

The doctor diagnosed the illness as **paratyphoid.**

I would call their performance this afternoon a **quasi-concert.**

This handbook has a **quasi-technical** character.

During the '60's she was a **pseudo-liberal.**

Despite his pretensions, he is at best a **pseudo-intellectual.**

people See **individual(s), people, persons.**

persons See **individual(s), people, persons.**

phenomenon This word is singular and requires a singular verb. The plural is usually **phenomena,** though **phenomenons** is correct when the word means extraordinary or remarkable persons or things. Also, **phenomenon** is used to suggest particularity of remarkable entities within a class.

The Smithsonian Institution displayed five **phenomenons** of ivory carving.

Both **phenomena** and **phenomenons** require a plural verb.

This **phenomenon was observed** some ten years ago in Arkansas.

That **phenomenon is called** Halley's comet.

These **phenomena are** under investigation.

These musical **phenomenons have signed** a contract to do a television series.

Those **phenomenons** called the U.C.L.A. Bruins **play** their best when the championship is at stake.

poorly Although the dictionary permits the use of the adverb **poorly** as an adjective meaning sick or ill — **I have been feeling poorly** — it belongs to regional dialect and should not be so used in formal writing. Replace it not with the adjective **poor,** which does not mean sick or ill, but rather with some other adjective such as **sick** or **ill.** In other words, you are well advised to use **poorly** always as an adverb meaning **in a poor manner.**

I have been feeling *ill* the past week or so.

Martha has been feeling *indisposed* since the weekend.

Jeff pole-vaulted *poorly* at the meet in California.

All the students in the class did *poorly* on the test.

The secretary in our office types *poorly.*

practicable, practical Very similar in appearance, these adjectives have slightly different meanings. **Practicable** means feasible or capable of being done; **practical** means useful or desirable. For example, using orange baseballs in major league games is **practicable,** but it may not be **practical.**

The calculations he is working on should reveal whether or not the design for the cooling tower is *practicable.*

I found his outline for a paper on the poetry of Hart Crane *practicable.*

My wife and I have decided that living in the country is *practical* after all.

The *practical* solution to this problem is to hire three more sales representatives.

See also **impracticable, impractical.**

precede, proceed **Precede** means to come before in time, rank, importance, or the like. **Proceed** means to go forward, carry on, continue, and so forth.

The War of 1812 *preceded* the Civil War by nearly half a century.

As a colonel, he *precedes* the rest of the officers in the detachment.

Plan C *precedes* the other two plans because it provides a complete cost analysis.

Turn left at the next intersection and *proceed* three miles.

Please *proceed* with your work.

If there are no questions, let's *proceed* with the meeting.

predominant, predominate The distinction between these two words is simple: **predominate** is a verb and **predominant** is an adjective.

In the world of fashion he clearly *predominates.*

She *predominates* over the other children on the playground.

Hofstader's position is that anti-intellectualism has *predominated* in American Life.

The *predominant* opinion of the committee members is to limit debate on this issue.

In this part of the world democracy has been *predominant* since World War II.

The *predominant* summer activities among teen-agers in Culver City take place at the beach.

prescribe, proscribe These similar verbs are very different in meaning. **Prescribe** means to recommend, order, ordain, or to lay down a rule or guide. **Proscribe** means to prohibit, condemn, or forbid.

Dr. Nelson *prescribed* this medicine for my eyes.

The manager's memorandum *prescribes* new regulations for shipping.

Can you *prescribe* a policy for dealing with customer complaints?

Our school system *proscribes* teachers tutoring their own students for money.

Regulation 110 *proscribes* use of company equipment for personal or private work.

Nearly all high school and college coaches *proscribe* smoking and drinking by team members during the season.

presume See **assume, presume.**

pretty As an adverb, **pretty** most often means "moderately," but it can also mean "in some degree." Used in this latter sense, however, it is colloquial, but more importantly, it is vague.

8

What, for example, does the writer mean in the sentence **He owns a pretty modern car**? Does he mean a *somewhat* modern car, like a 1969 Chevrolet, or does he mean a *very* modern car, like a 1977 Ford? If you do choose to use **pretty** in this way in formal writing, be sure that the meaning conveyed is clear.

We have had a *pretty* mild winter this year.

A recent review said that the movie was *pretty* bad.

They made a *pretty* good effort to find out the truth.

The map was *pretty* useful to us in the mountains.

preventative, preventive These words, which may function as either nouns or adjectives, are interchangeable. Because it is the shorter of the two, however, **preventive** is preferable.

Our mechanic has had a course in *preventive* maintenance.

What *preventive* do you plan to adopt?

We must take some *preventive* action before it is too late.

This *preventive* is both effective and economical.

principal, principle These two words are frequently confused, but in fact have completely different meanings. **Principal** as a noun means the leader or head of a school, the leading or main figure, or (in finance) the capital worth of an estate or holding, and as an adjective means the most important, the highest-ranking, or the main. **Principle,** however, functions only as a noun meaning a truth, law, rule, or theory.

The *principal* of Westwood High is Ronald Norton.

The *principal* witness for the prosecution became seriously ill.

What interest would accumulate on this *principal* in six months?

The *principals* in *A Moon for the Misbegotten* are Jason Robards, Jr., Colleen Dewhurst, and Ed Flanders.

Philosophy tries to establish first *principles.*

Several of the most important *principles* of electricity were formulated by Ben Franklin.

Her *principle* of conduct is the golden rule.

proceed See **precede, proceed.**

proscribe See **prescribe, proscribe.**

pseudo– See **para-, pseudo-, quasi-.**

quasi– See **para-, pseudo-, quasi-.**

raise, rise These words function both as nouns and verbs. **Raise** is a transitive verb (takes a direct object) meaning to lift, elevate, move upward, and rear (as in **to rear children**), among other things. Its principal parts are **raise, raised, raised.** As a noun it means essentially an increase in wages, salary, or pay. Some authorities continue to insist that we **rear** children and **raise** livestock, but in fact the expression **raise children** is perfectly acceptable in formal prose. Do not, however, use the expression **pay raise,** in which **pay** is redundant. **Rise** is an intransitive verb (does not take a direct object) meaning to move upward, to get up, and to increase in height or intensity, among other things. Its principal parts are **rise, rose, risen.** As a noun it means an ascent, an increase (as of prices or the like), and an origin or beginning, among other things.

Please *raise* the windows before you leave the room.

My parents *raised* seven children on a farm.

I plan to ask my employer for a *raise.*

The balloon *rose* slowly and finally disappeared.

At camp we *rise* at 6:00 a.m. for calisthenics.

He lectured on the *rise* of civilization in North America.

People are angry about the recent *rises* in the prices of consumer goods.

real, really **Real** is an adjective meaning true, actual, or genuine; **really** is an adverb meaning truly, in reality, or indeed. Do not use **real** as an adverb, as in the following examples:

She is a *real* pretty girl.

She told a *real* interesting story.

He has *real* fine credentials.

8

Also, avoid overusing **really** as an intensifier. For example, even if we were to revise the examples above to make them grammatical — **really pretty girl, really interesting story, really fine credentials** — we could still improve each of them by substituting a more exact word for the intensifier and adjective:

She is a *beautiful* girl.

She told an *engrossing* story.

He has *superb* credentials.

In other words, be sure to use **real** and **really** grammatically, and **really** judiciously.

They found the *real* Barbara Thomas living in Memphis.

The *real* reason for going to New York is to see a Broadway play.

Let's talk about the *real* world for a change.

In the mountains a person can be *really* free.

He has *really* modern ideas about architecture.

What we need in our writing courses is a *really* practical textbook.

In the first group of sentences, **real** and **really** are being used by a lazy writer, who could have used, as we have shown, many more exact words. In this last group, there are no superior substitutes for **real** or **really,** so their use is legitimate in these instances.

reason . . . is because   **Because** means "for the reason that." Consequently, the expression **reason . . . is because** is redundant, and should be revised using either **reason** or **because.**

The *reason* for the delay *is because* Company C has not arrived. (incorrect)

The *reason* for the delay *is that* Company C has not arrived. (correct)

The *reason* that contemporary poetry is so difficult *is because* poets do not feel they are writing to a wide audience. (incorrect)

Contemporary poetry is so difficult *because* poets do not feel they are writing to a wide audience. (correct)

The *reason* he lost the race *is because* he got a poor start. (incorrect)

The *reason* he lost the race *is that* he got a poor start. (correct)

The *reason* that many settlers came to America *was because* they were seeking religious freedom. (incorrect)

Many settlers came to America *because* they were seeking religious freedom. (correct)

Similar redundant and ungrammatical expressions, like **the reason why is that, the reason why is because,** and **the reason is, is that,** should be avoided.

reference See **allusion, reference.**

regardless See **irregardless, regardless.**

relevant This badly overused and often misused word means "related to or bearing on the matter at hand," and to use it properly, you must state what "the matter at hand" is. That is, something is or is not **relevant to** something else; it is never simply **relevant** or **not relevant.**

Marriage is no longer *relevant.* (incorrect)

Let's try to make our political platform *relevant.* (incorrect)

Your comment is the only *relevant* one I've heard. (incorrect)

Old Man Thompson just isn't *relevant* anymore. (incorrect)

These facts are *relevant to* our decision. (correct)

His lectures were seldom *relevant to* the needs of his students. (correct)

A consideration of this event in Franklin's life is *relevant to* our understanding of his achievement. (correct)

result See **end result, result.**

rise See **raise, rise.**

second, secondly See **first, firstly; second, secondly . . . .**

8

–self See **himself.**

sensual, sensuous Both of these words mean "pertaining to, affecting, or satisfying the senses," but to use them accurately and perhaps avoid embarrassment, you need to distinguish between them. **Sensuous** is the broader of the two, since it can refer to any of the senses. In general, however, it refers to the sensory experience of poetry, painting, music, nature, and so forth. **Sensual,** on the other hand, refers to the sensory experience of sex and other satisfaction of physical appetites.

He is portrayed in the movie as a boisterous and *sensual* man.

Suppression of the *sensual* dimension of life often causes psychological problems.

Life in America has become increasingly *sensual.*

The imagery of Keats's poetry is particularly *sensuous.*

A walk through the woods in autumn is a *sensuous* experience.

Sensuous church music stimulates thoughts about God.

set, sit **Set** is primarily a transitive verb (takes a direct object) meaning to place, whereas **sit** is primarily an intransitive verb (does not take a direct object) meaning to rest on the buttocks. The principal parts of the two verbs are **set, set, set** and **sit, sat, sat,** respectively.

Set the typewriter on the desk.

He *set* the box in the living room.

Mother has *set* the pies on the table to cool.

Sit down and talk for a while.

The boy *sat* alone on the porch.

They *sat* there for several hours.

But keep in mind that there are important exceptions to these general patterns, as in the following examples:

The sun *sets* in the west. (intransitive)

The hen *sets.* (intransitive)

He *sits* a horse well. (transitive)

She *sat* the child in the chair. (transitive)

shall, will Traditionally, to express futurity, **shall** was used in the first person, singular and plural, and **will** was used in the second and third persons, singular and plural; and to express determination, these usages were simply reversed, **will** being used in the first person and **shall** in the second and third persons. This practice has, however, largely faded away, even among excellent writers. Consequently, you may use **will** for futurity and determination in all three persons, both singular and plural, and avoid using **shall** altogether. If you do choose to honor the **shall-will** distinction, be sure that you use it correctly and consistently.

Traditional usage		*Contemporary usage*	
Futurity		*Futurity*	
Singular	Plural	Singular	Plural
I shall work.	We shall work.	I will work.	We will work.
You will work.	You will work.	You will work.	You will work.
He, she, it will work.	They will work.	He, she, it will work.	They will work.
Determination		*Determination*	
Singular	*Plural*	*Singular*	*Plural*
I will work.	We will work.	I will work.	We will work.
You shall work.	You shall work.	You will work.	You will work.
He, she, it shall work.	They shall work.	He, she, it will work.	They will work.

Of course, **shall** is still much used in questions in which it has the meaning of **should:**

Shall I take the car in to be repaired?

Shall we go tomorrow?

Shall they be held accountable for their actions?

See also **should, would.**

8

should, would Traditionally, **should** and **would** as auxiliary verbs are analogous to **shall** and **will, should** being used in the first person, singular and plural, and **would** being used in the second and third persons, singular and plural.

Singular	*Plural*
I should like to eat.	We should like to eat.
You would like to eat.	You would like to eat.
He, she, it would like to eat.	They would like to eat.

As with the **shall-will** distinction, however, the **should-would** distinction has largely disappeared, and **would** is generally used in all three persons: **I would like to eat, we would like to eat, you would like to eat, she would like to eat, they would like to eat,** and so forth. You may, of course, preserve the use of **should** in the first person; if you do, be sure that you are consistent and that you maintain a parallel use with **shall.**

I *would* (*should*) not have behaved that way if Mary had been there.

We *would* (*should*) be glad to do what we can for you.

I *would* (*should*) like you to understand how I feel.

Had you let us know, we *would* (*should*) have been able to repair the car Monday.

I *would* (*should*) have preferred to hear Mozart.

We *would* (*should*) like to have seen you in Italy.

should of, should have See **could of, could have.** See also **shall, will.**

sic This word is Latin for **thus** or **so** — i.e., "thus it is" — and is used within brackets and underscored to indicate that what is quoted or referred to is exactly as its original author spoke it or wrote it. Use it only when there may be doubt in your reader's mind that you have accurately cited the quotation or reference, such as when it contains an error of some kind, not when you merely want to poke fun at it. Also, you need not use an exclamation mark after **sic.**

The paper quoted him as saying: "Yogi Beara [*sic*] is the best catcher I ever saw."

The reference book states: "Thoreau published *Walden* in 1954" [*sic*].

Mrs. Johnson said: "Are you inferring [*sic*] by your remark that I have no taste in art?"

The *New York Times* reported that he said: "Planning the experiment and interpreting the data is [*sic*] the most diffi-cult part of our research."

sight See **cite, sight, site.**

since You may use **since** for **because** only when its connotation of time does not make the statement ambiguous. For example, in the sentence **He is running on the cross-country team, since he didn't make the football squad,** the reader is not certain whether the cause-and-effect relationship or the time sequence is in-tended. Is he running *because* he didn't make the football squad, or is he running now that he is *no longer* trying out for the foot-ball squad? The precise meaning is hazy. In the following ex-amples, the use of **since** makes it clear which of the meanings— cause-and-effect or time—is meant:

Since she has a Southern accent, she should be perfect for the role of Blanche Dubois in *Streetcar Named Desire.* (cause-and-effect)

Since they have been married, they have lived in five coun-tries. (time)

He will be permitted to enroll late *since* he has been ill. (cause-and-effect)

At least three interesting books on tennis have appeared *since* I began playing in 1970. (time)

sit See **set, sit.**

site See **cite, sight, site.**

so, so that The conjunction **so that** may introduce a clause giving the reason for an action expressed in another clause:

8

They planned a detailed itinerary **so *that*** they would not miss any of the important landmarks.

He studied physics in high school **so *that*** he would be better prepared for the engineering curriculum in college.

Father took us to the museum **so *that*** we would develop an interest in art.

So should not be used for this purpose. So may, however, introduce a clause giving the result of an action expressed in another clause.

He had grown up poor, **so** as an adult he was very careful with his money.

The wind was blowing hard, **so** the water was extremely rough.

The car broke down last week, **so** they left only yesterday.

Even though these usages are acceptable, it is sometimes preferable to use different conjunctions or constructions for these purposes because (1) so and so that are generally overused and (2) more exact words or expressions are often available. Thus, we could improve each of the examples above by revising them as follows:

They planned a detailed itinerary in order not to miss any of the important landmarks.

He studied physics in high school, to be better prepared for the engineering curriculum in college.

Father took us to the museum to develop our interest in art.

Because he had grown up poor, as an adult he was very careful with his money.

Since the wind was blowing hard, the water was extremely rough.

Because the car broke down last week, they left only yesterday.

The last three sentences, especially, are much improved, since the exact relationship between the clauses in each case is more sharply expressed.

sort of See **kind of, sort of.**

stationary, stationery These words are often confused, but they have nothing in common. **Stationary** is generally an adjective meaning "fixed, not moving"; **stationery** is a noun meaning "writing paper and other writing materials."

The cloud seemed to remain *stationary.*

The forecast calls for *stationary* weather conditions for the next week.

This particular engine is *stationary.*

Tom bought her *stationery* for her birthday.

Please conserve company *stationery.*

You can buy *stationery* in a great variety of sizes, colors, and designs.

sure, surely **Sure** is an adjective and **surely** is an adverb; formal writing requires that you use them correctly. If **surely** seems particularly stilted or stuffy in a certain context, you may be able to replace it with another word, such as **certainly** or **really.** In this instance, however, correctness probably outweighs real or imagined stiltedness.

Mason is very *sure* of himself.

He is a *sure* bet to win the talent contest.

Before you start down, get a *sure* grip on the rope.

You have *surely* (*certainly*) heard of the Louisiana Purchase!

My neighbor *surely* (*really*) knows a lot about gardening.

I *surely* (*certainly*) wish that I could see Europe.

temerity, timorousness Although sometimes confused, these two nouns have opposed meanings. **Temerity** means reckless boldness, and **timorousness** means timidity.

Temerity is seldom an unmixed virtue.

Both armies attacked with a certain *temerity.*

8

I have always felt that *temerity* is more characteristic of men than of women.

The club members made fun of his *timorousness.*

Overcoming *timorousness* is a complicated psychological process.

Timorousness has prevented him from achieving much success as an interviewer.

that, which, who (whom) The several traditions governing the use of these three relative pronouns used to introduce subordinate clauses are not difficult to understand. **That** refers to both persons and things (including animals); **which** refers only to things (including animals); and **who (whom)** refers only to persons. Thus:

The accountants *that* audited the books have not been paid.

The bread *that* Sarah brought home is stale.

The bread *which* Sarah brought home is stale.

The accountants *who* audited the books have not been paid.

The hikers *whom* we saw south of town were picked up by the highway patrol.

In addition, **that** introduces only restrictive clauses (clauses which, because they significantly limit independent clauses, are not set off by commas), whereas **which** and **who (whom)** introduce both restrictive and nonrestrictive clauses (clauses which, because they do not significantly limit independent clauses, are set off by commas). Thus:

The woman *that* I marry must love nature as much as I do.

The parts *which* you ordered last month have arrived.

The handbook, *which* contained a section on usage, helped him in freshman English.

Students *who* finish before the end of the period should proofread their work.

Faulkner, *who* wrote mostly about his native South, received the Nobel Prize for Literature in 1950.

The agent *whom* the farmers in this area trust most is Douglas Norton.

The two workers, *whom* we hired to help in the wheat harvest, had never been west of the Mississippi River before.

Some authorities suggest that since **that** is used only for restrictive clauses, **which** and **who (whom)** should be used only for nonrestrictive clauses, but you may do as you please.

A final point or two about **that.** Often **that** may be omitted from the clause it introduces without loss of sense:

The music (*that*) I played is from *Oklahoma.*

The promise (*that*) she made turned out to be worthless.

The towns (*that*) I visited in England were picturesque and interesting.

Never omit it, however, if any misreading whatsoever is possible. For example:

He reported the boy passed his lifesaving test.

The officer signaled the men were in trouble.

Notice that in either sentence readers may perhaps understand one meaning through **boy** and **men,** respectively, but quite another one when they reach the end of the sentence. In the first, he didn't report **the boy,** he reported **that the boy . . . .** In the second, he didn't signal **the men,** he signaled **that the men . . . .** In other words, the omission of **that** forces readers to go back and reread the sentence, mentally supplying the omitted **that.** Then, too, you should avoid the awkward repetition caused by successive uses or overuse of **that:**

That is a fact *that* you need to keep in mind.

He said *that* the contract *that* they signed was void.

The researchers found *that* the samples *that* they had been using were contaminated.

These awkwardnesses are easily eliminated as follows:

That is a fact *which* you need to keep in mind.

8

He said *that* the contract they signed was void.

The researchers found *that* the samples they had been using were contaminated.

See also **whose (of which), who's.**

that much, that well . . . Do not use the demonstrative adjective **that** for an adverb intensifier like **very,** as in the following examples:

Harper hasn't played *that much.*

She doesn't sing *that well.*

The house isn't *that large.*

The novel isn't *that good.*

Accuracy isn't *that important.*

In addition to being marred by the grammatical error (an adjective is used to modify an adverb or adjective), such statements as these are sometimes ambiguous. For instance, in the second example sentence, does the writer mean that she doesn't sing **that** particular song well, or that she doesn't sing **very well** in general? Thus we have another illustration of how faulty grammar can lead to ambiguous writing. The faulty sentences above can be revised as follows:

Harper hasn't played *very much.*

She doesn't sing *very well.*

The house isn't *very large.*

The novel isn't *very good.*

Accuracy isn't *very important.*

In revising, however, you should remember (1) that **very** should be used sparingly as an intensifier and (2) that a word more precise than the expression **very . . .** is frequently available. See also **very.**

there is (are) See **it is, there is (are).**

though See **although, though.**

through, thru Dictionaries list **thru** as a variant, an informal spelling, of **through,** but do not use it in formal writing.

I am *through* with my work.

One can see *through* this fabric.

We walked *through* the woods.

till, until   **Till** and **until** may be used interchangeably in formal writing, though **until** is preferable for beginning sentences. Do not, however, use such variants as **'til** and **'till.**

Mary and I stayed *till* the band went home.

Can you wait *until* the secretary returns?

Until we stop bickering among ourselves, we shall not solve this problem.

timorousness See **temerity, timorousness.**

to, too   **To** is primarily a preposition meaning, among other things, "in the direction of," and **too** is an adverb meaning primarily "also" or "excessively." But in this case it is not grammar which causes writing errors but rather just careless spelling habits. Always check to see that you have spelled the word correctly.

They *too* are planning a trip *to* Miami.

He drove over *to* Trenton, *too.*

The candidate's speech was *too* long.

I want *to* go, *too.*

The police were *too* late *to* catch the thief.

In the case of **too,** do not use the expression **not too** to mean **not very.**

I am *not too* happy with my progress. (weak)

I am *not very* happy with my progress. (improved)

Management has *not* been *too* sympathetic with union members. (weak)

8

Management has **not** been **very** sympathetic with union members. (improved)

This text has **not** been **too** helpful. (weak)

This text has **not** been **very** helpful. (improved)

toward, towards These forms are interchangeable, with **toward** being predominant in the United States and **towards** in Great Britain. Having made your choice between the two words, use it consistently.

John ran **toward** the cabin.

The boat is headed **toward** Catalina.

How would you describe his attitude **toward** his employer?

The Carsons left for home **toward** evening.

transpire Formally, this verb means to give off waste products, as from the surface of the body, or to become known. Informally, it means to happen or to occur. Although many fine writers use **transpire** in this latter sense, some authorities object, maintaining that such use is further debasement of the language. Why, they say, is it necessary to wrench the meaning of **transpire** when perfectly good words like **happen** and **occur** are available to the writer? Consequently, if you follow their advice, you are assured of being correct. Note the correct usage of terms in the following examples:

And while thy willing soul **transpires**
At every pore with instant fires . . .
                          Andrew Marvell, "To His Coy Mistress"

Does any mammal **transpire** carbon dioxide constantly?

Rose's debut **occurred** during the last war.

Accidents seem to **happen** to Tom all too regularly.

trivia This noun is plural and requires a plural verb.

Trivia about movies **were scattered** throughout her paper on popular culture.

The *trivia* you have collected *are* of interest to all sports fans.

These *trivia have taken* enough of our time.

try and, try to   **Try and,** though a common expression in speech, is almost never acceptable in formal writing. The correct expression is, of course, **try to,** which you would do well to use in both speech and writing.

Try to remember which flower she prefers.

I will *try to* find the information you requested.

Will you *try to* repair the bicycle this afternoon?

Try to read this book within a week.

type   Do not use the word **type** when the expression **type of** is clearly called for, as in the following faulty examples:

What *type* engine is it?

This *type* coin is quite rare.

The *type* shirt I have in mind is collarless.

These sentences should, of course, be revised as follows:

What *type of* engine is it?

This *type of* coin is quite rare.

The *type of* shirt I have in mind is collarless.

In addition, do not use **type** when you actually mean **kind** or **sort. Type** implies that all members of its class closely resemble one another, whereas **kind** and **sort** imply less resemblance among the members of the class. Thus, **type of coin, type of shirt, type of engine** are all correct, but **type of man, type of poet, type of homemaker** are not. These latter expressions should be revised as follows: **kind (sort) of man, kind (sort) of poet, kind (sort) of homemaker.**

Finally, form compound adjectives using **type** only when they are technically or scientifically necessary, as a **monolithic-type concrete floor, cartridge-type fountain pen, jacket-type life preserver.** Notice that even these legitimate expressions

8

could be improved by deleting **–type: monolithic concrete floor, cartridge fountain pen, jacket life preserver.** And never form compounds like the following, which are both unnecessary and inept.

She bought a *kitchen-type appliance* at the store.

They were involved in a *guerilla-type action* in Latin America.

Ahab was the captain of a *whaling-type ship* called the *Pequod.*

This new book on Dickens takes a *psychological-type approach* to his life and works.

Each of these sentences can be improved simply by omitting **-type.**

uninterested See **disinterested, uninterested.**

unique   **Unique** means "the only one of its kind." As an absolute, it has no degree of comparison, such as the incorrect **less unique, more unique, most unique, rather unique, very unique, somewhat unique,** and the like. Either someone or something is **unique** or he, she, or it isn't.

His style of pitching is *unique.*

So far as I know, Janice's hobby of collecting colored shoestrings is *unique.*

This *unique* anthology should sell very well.

We must recognize that every human being is *unique.*

(*Ideal* and *perfect* are other such absolutes.)

until See **till, until.**

usage, use   **Use** denotes the act or manner of using or the state of being used, whereas **usage** denotes customary, habitual, or traditional use or practice.

My religion forbids the *use* of alcohol.

What *use* can we make of this lumber?

The *use* of *use* in this sentence is correct.

American English *usage* calls for *usage* in this sentence.

Is this kind of worship service consistent with Christian *usage*?

Following baseball *usage,* we should bunt in this situation.

use, utilize The verb **use** means to put into service or employ, and may be used in all contexts. The verb **utilize** is much narrower, meaning to use for some particular practical or productive purpose.

Let's *use* wallpaper rather than paint.

We shall *use* approximately four boxes of stationery this week.

The car *uses* a quart of oil every thousand miles.

The troops can *utilize* the natural camouflage in the area.

The town will *utilize* waste products to produce energy.

The hospital must *utilize* its work force more effectively.

Keep in mind, however, that in almost every case **use** could be substituted for **utilize,** and probably should be, since **utilize** has an artificial ring.

use to, used to The verb **use** is used intransitively (does not take a direct object) in the past tense with **to** to indicate a former condition or circumstance:

I *used to* like her.

The house *used to* be white.

The garden *used to* be much larger.

Do not unknowingly or carelessly omit the **d** from **use,** as some writers do:

I *use to* like her.

The house *use to* be white.

The garden *use to* be much larger.

This error makes the writer seem uneducated, even ignorant.

8

When the auxiliary verb **did** is used with **use,** however, the proper form is **use,** without the **d:**

I *did use* to like her.

The house *did use* to be white.

The garden *did use* to be much larger.

The negative and interrogative constructions are consistent with these usages:

I *used not to* like her.

I *did not use to* like her.

Did I *use to* like her?

Did I *not use to* like her?

utilize See **use, utilize.**

very Traditional usage permits the adverb **very** to modify an adjective, but not a past participle. Thus, you may write **very happy, very fast, very hot,** but not **very praised, very loved, very shared.** For the last three, of course, we would say **very much praised, very much loved, very much shared,** in which the adverb **much** modifies the past participle and **very** in turn modifies **much.** But often the participle will seem to be as much an adjective as a verb, and when this is the case, it is permissible to modify it with **very,** as in the following instances: **very simplified, very spoiled, very inspired.** Do not, however, make the mistake of overusing **very** as an intensifier: **very pretty, very interesting, very bad,** and the like. Such overuse tends to drain your writing of its force: when everything is intensified in this way, nothing is intense. Consequently, use **very** as an intensifier sparingly—only when you need it. And keep in mind that often you can replace **very . . .** with a more exact word. For example, the last three expressions above may profitably be replaced by **beautiful, fascinating, egregious,** respectively. See also **that much, that well. . . .**

viz. See **e.g., i.e., viz.**

we In the past, writers have commonly used **we** when they meant **I** in order to maintain as objective and impersonal a tone as possible. Other strategies for this purpose were to use **one** and the passive voice. At present, however, authorities generally agree that it is better to use **I** when it is called for, both because it is more honest and because it eliminates possible ambiguity.

We have found Antonioni's previous movies interesting. (stilted)

I have found Antonioni's previous movies interesting. (improved)

Throughout this essay **we** have stressed the importance of exercise. (stilted)

Throughout this essay **I** have stressed the importance of exercise. (improved)

In **our** argument **we** shall demonstrate that team sports build character. (stilted)

In **my** argument **I** shall demonstrate that team sports build character. (improved)

One thinks that Mr. Elliot was lying about his part in the plot. (stilted)

I think that Mr. Elliot was lying about his part in the plot. (improved)

It is believed that we must purchase this stock immediately. (stilted)

I believe that we must purchase this stock immediately. (improved)

well See **good, well.**

when See **is when, is where.**

where See **is when, is where.**

whether See **if, whether.**

which See **that, which, who (whom).**

while As a conjunction **while** means principally "during the time that"—that is, it has a temporal meaning.

While our son and I played tennis, my husband went shopping.

He worked part-time as a janitor *while* he attended medical school.

While the group auditioned, the producer whispered comments to his assistant.

While can also mean **although, whereas, but,** or **and,** but these uses can be ambiguous and are not acceptable to many authorities. For example: **While the policeman was trained in riot control, he fired wildly at the mob.** Does the writer mean **Although the policeman . . . .** or **During the time that the policeman . . . . ?** The reader would probably eventually conclude that the writer meant the former, but the sentence would still be a bad one. Consequently, you are well advised to use **while** only in its temporal sense and to make certain that no ambiguity is involved.

who, whom   **Who** is the subject form of the pronoun, **whom** the object form. In speech **who** is often used as an object as well:

Who did he find to work for him?

I recommend Benson and Shaw, *who* I have done business with for years.

Who I chose must remain a secret.

Who were you looking for?

Thompson, *who* I spoke of, will call you this afternoon.

Who can I turn to?

In formal writing, however, correct subject and object forms must be used.

Who is going on the camping trip?

The commissioner honored employees *who* have served twenty or more years in the Fire Department.

I bought a book of poems by Robert Frost, *who* I think is the finest modern poet. (The phrase *I think* is parenthetical.)

Do you know *who* will be fired? (The subject and verb of the main clause are *you* and *do know,* respectively. **Who** is the subject of the subordinate clause—*who will be fired*—which serves as the direct object of *do know.*)

Whom did he nominate for secretary?

Find a person with *whom* we can all work.

The doctor, *whom* the hospital had difficulty reaching, finally arrived around 10:00 p.m.

From *whom* have you learned the most this semester?

Whom should we invite to the party?

Whoever and *whomever* are parallel with *who* and *whom.*

See also **that, which, who (whom).**

whose (of which), who's   **Whose** is the possessive form of the relative pronoun **who; who's** is the contraction of **who is** or **who has.** Some writers confuse them, thinking perhaps that somehow the apostrophe denotes possessive case, which of course it does not in this instance.

Whose pasture is this?

The person *whose* number is called will win a prize.

This table was made by Mr. Rogers, *whose* work I have always admired.

He is the only applicant *whose* dossier is complete.

Who's the girl by the piano?

Who's visited Canada?

Who's going to drive the blue car?

We shall soon know *who's* responsible for this prank.

Whose may also be correctly used as the possessive form of the relative pronoun **which,** since the latter does not have its own form, except for the phrase **of which.** Thus, even though **who** refers only to persons and **which** refers only to things (including animals), **whose** can refer to both. Moreover, because constructions involving **of which** are often wordy and cumbersome, replacing the phrase with **whose** is highly desirable.

The pamphlet, the authors *of which* are socialists, is badly written. (weak)

8

The pamphlet, *whose* authors are socialists, is badly written. (improved)

The dog, the owner *of which* lives in Texas, has been in three television shows. (weak)

The dog, *whose* owner lives in Texas, has been in three television shows. (improved)

American Indian legends, the similarity *of which* to myths from other parts of the world is striking, embody sophisticated values and ideals. (weak)

American Indian legends, *whose* similarity to myths from other parts of the world is striking, embody sophisticated values and ideals. (improved)

See also **that, which, who (whom)**.

will, shall See **shall, will**.

–wise See **–ize, –wise**.

would of, would have See **could of, could have**.

you See **one, you**.

your, you're   **Your** is the possessive of the pronoun **you; you're** is the contraction of **you are**.

Your answer is correct.

I like *your* jokes.

Is this *your* locker?

You're too conservative.

The coach thinks *you're* loafing.

You're my choice for captain of the team.

Index

The Index should be used in conjunction with the Glossary of Usage (pp. 271–340). Together they provide a guide for solving specific writing problems and a key to locating general discussions of grammatical and rhetorical questions.

A 7
B 8
C 9
D 0
E 1
F 2
G 3
H 4
I 5
J 6

chapter 5   the research paper

part two   handbook

chapter 6   grammar